CHILDREN AND SOCIAL SECURITY

International Studies on Social Security

Volume 8

Children and Social Security

Edited by

JONATHAN BRADSHAW
University of York, UK

ASHGATE

Published by
Ashgate Publishing Limited
Gower House
Croft Road
Aldershot
Hampshire GU11 3HR
England

Ashgate Publishing Company
Suite 420
101 Cherry Street
Burlington, VT 05401-4405
USA

Ashgate website: http://www.ashgate.com

British Library Cataloguing in Publication Data
Children and social security. - (International studies on
    social security ; v. 8)
    1. Poor children - Developed countries 2. Social security -
    Developed countries
    I. Bradshaw, Jonathan, 1944-
    362.7'086942'091722

Library of Congress Cataloging-in-Publication Data
Children and social security / edited by Jonathan Bradshaw.
    p. cm -- (International studies in social security ; v. 8)
    Includes bibliographical references.
    ISBN 0-7546-3164-8
    1. Child welfare--Cross-cultural studies. I. Bradshaw, Jonathan. II. Series.

HV713 .C3958 2002
362.7--dc21

2002018641

ISBN 0 7546 3164 8

Printed and bound in Great Britain by MPG Books Ltd, Bodmin, Cornwall

Contents

List of Figures

List of Tables

List of Contributors

Laura Adelman
Loughborough University, UK

James Banks
Institute for Fiscal Studies, UK

Tobias Bauer
Bureau for Studies in Labour and Social Policy, Switzerland

Steen Bengtsson
University of Roskilde, Denmark

Anne Benson
US Office of Child Support Enforcement, USA

Jonathan Bradshaw
University of York, UK

Mike Brewer
Institute for Fiscal Studies, UK

Bea Cantillon
University of Antwerp and Centre for Social Policy, Belgium

Sheldon Danziger
University of Michigan, USA

Björn Gustafsson
University of Göteborg and Swedish Council for Working Life and Social
Research, Sweden

Mats Johansson
Institute for Future Studies, Stockholm, Sweden

Michael Mendelson
Caledon Institute of Social Policy, Ottawa, Canada

Nina Middelboe
University of Odense, Denmark

Sue Middleton
Loughborough University, UK

Karin Müller Kucera
Service de Recherche en Education, Switzerland

Edward Palmer
University of Uppsla and National Insurance Board, Stockholm, Sweden

Hester Rossouw
University of Stellenbosch, South Africa

Peter Scherer
OECD

Robert Stephens
Victoria University of Wellington, New Zealand

Rudi Van Dam
University of Antwerp, Belgium

Karel Van Den Bosch
University of Antwerp, Belgium

Bart Van Hoorebeeck
University of Antwerp, Belgium

Jan Vorster
University of Stellenbosch, South Africa

Martin Werding
Ifo Institute of Economic Research, Germany

Preface

Jonathan Bradshaw

In recent years there has been growing anxiety from national governments, but more especially from some international bodies, about the consequences of social and economic change for children in industrial countries.

It was in this context that the Foundation for International Studies in Social Security chose Children and Social Security as the theme of its conference held in June 2001.

The proceedings of previous FISS conferences have been published as follows:

- *Curing the Dutch Disease: An International Perspective on Disability Policy Reform* (1996) (ed.) Leo J.M. Aarts, Richard V. Burkhauser and Philip R. De Jong.
- *Social Policy and the Labour Market* (1997) (ed.) Philip R. De Jong and Theodore R. Marmor.
- *Ageing, Social Security and Affordability* (1998) (ed.) Peter Flora, Philip R. De Jong, Julian Le Grand and Jun-Young Kim.
- *Fighting Poverty: Caring for Children, Parents, the Elderly and Health,* (1999) (ed.) Stein Ringen and Philip R. De Jong.
- *Domain Linkages and Privatisation in Social Security* (2000) (ed.) Jun-Young Kim and Per-Gunnar Svensson.
- *Ethics and Social Security Reform* (2001) (ed.) Erik Schokkaert.

The first volume was based on papers presented at a FISS conference in Rotterdam in 1992. All the other volumes are based on a selection of papers presented at the small annual international conference in Sigtuna - the Sigtuna seminars. They bring together scholars from all over the world, though predominantly from Europe, Asia and North America to present and discuss findings on economic, legal and social aspects of social security and its relationships with other aspects of society.

Acknowledgements

FISS would like to thank the members of the Editorial Board; Jennifer Shervington in Birmingham for her work in administering the seminar; Åsa Almerud, Emese Pallagi Mayhew at the University of York for proof reading the chapters for this collection; and Sally Pulleyn in the Social Policy Research Unit at the University of York for preparing the manuscript for printing.

The 2001 Sigtuna seminar was the last to be organised by our joint General Secretary and founder, Han Emanuel, and we all owe him a terrific debt of gratitude for the work he has undertaken in establishing FISS and organising these occasions.

Introduction and overview

Jonathan Bradshaw

A review of comparative research on child poverty

Concerned about the impact of social and economic change on children in richer countries UNICEF, for the first time in its history, launched a study of the well-being of children in industrialised countries (Cornia and Danziger, 1996). It has since begun to publish a *Report Card* series, the first devoted to *Child Poverty in Rich Nations* (UNICEF 2000), based largely on the analysis of the Luxembourg Income Survey by Bradbury and Jantti (1999). In the European Union the European Community Household Panel Survey has been used to monitor the well-being of children (Eurostat, 1999) and this effort has been redoubled since the Lisbon Summit, and continuing with the Nice Summit, Member States are now required to develop priorities for the combating of poverty and social exclusion. Under the Belgian Presidency Atkinson *et al.* (2001) have established a set of Indicators of Social Inclusion which will be used in future within the EU. Even OECD have recently applied their minds to comparisons of child poverty in a selection of member countries (Oxley, 2001). From this interest and activity has emerged a body of good international comparative research on child poverty (see for example Gordon and Townsend, 2000; Bradbury, Jenkins and Micklewright, 2001; Vleminckz and Smeeding, 2001).

In this introduction I will review this research and then introduce the papers that have been included in the collection.

In the last decade our capacity to analyse child poverty comparatively has been greatly enhanced by the availability of new data. Thus, the Luxembourg Income Study has included more countries, more sweeps and become the vehicle for very detailed analysis of child poverty (Bradbury and Jantti, 1999; Bradshaw, 1999). OECD (Oxley *et al.*, 2001) have obtained data on from national sources on child poverty in 16 countries and undertaken a detailed analysis of child poverty rates and trends over time. At last, the results of the European Community Household Panel Survey (ECHP) (Eurostat, 2001) are emerging more quickly, and the survey is becoming a rich source of comparative analysis within the European Union.

xvii

But there are limitations. With the exception of the ECHP, poverty and child poverty in these data sets is defined as an arbitrary point on the general distribution of income (albeit equivalised). Thus, LIS analysis generally employs a 50 per cent of median equivalent income threshold as does the OECD. Eurostat has recently adopted a threshold of 60 per cent of equivalent median income. Most analysis has settled for the modified OECD equivalence scale, despite the fact that research based on budget standards suggests that it (and most other scales) underestimates the real costs of children (Bradshaw, 1993).

These measures of a relative lack of income are not by themselves particularly good indicators of poverty.

- Poverty rates (and the composition of the poor) vary with different definitions of income especially whether it is before or after housing costs.
- The results are sensitive to the general shape of the income distribution.
- Income tends to misrepresent the real living standards of farmers, the self-employed and students.
- Income 'lumping' at points of the distribution where large numbers of households are receiving the (same) minimum income creates big variations in the poverty rate for small changes in the threshold.
- A household income measure fails to take account of the distribution of income within families - especially problematic for those (southern EU) countries with significant minorities of children living in multi-unit households.
- Most analyses report poverty rates, not poverty gaps - how far below the poverty line children are.
- The cross sectional data sets do not allow an analysis of how often or how long children are in poverty (though see below).
- Finally because they are based on survey data these estimates take time to emerge - currently researchers are working on the LIS data for circa 1995 (LIS website), the OECD data is 1993-1995 and the latest published ECHP analysis of poverty is for the fourth 1998 sweep (1997 income data).

Nevertheless we know from this work that:

- Child poverty varies considerably between countries. LIS data produces a ranking of 25 countries and shows that the UK, the USA and Russia were top of the child poverty league table in the mid 1990s (UNICEF, 2000). The most recent data on child poverty is from the 1998 ECHP (income data for 1997) and this finds the UK with the highest child poverty rate in the EU by some margin (Table 1, column 1).

Table 1   Relative poverty rates (60 per cent median equivalised income) for children and families with children 1997

	Children 0-15	Single parent with at least one child	2 adults, 1 child	2 adults, 2 children	2 adults, 3+ children
Belgium	15	30	7	12	18
Denmark	3	9	0	3	6
Germany	24	48	8	12	38 (1996)
Greece	21	24	13	14	26
Spain	25	30	14	21	33
France	24	31 (1996)	7	8	30
Ireland	28	40	14	12	38
Italy	24	25	15	21	34
Luxembourg	17 (1996)	27 (1996)	8 (1996)	9 (1996)	23 (1996)
Netherlands	13	40	7	6	17
Austria	16	28	11	9	26
Portugal	29	40	12	13	58
Finland	7	9	5	4	9
Sweden	10	16	6	7	12
UK	39	41	12	16	36 (1996)

Source: European Community Panel Survey 1998; EU Draft report on Social Inclusion (2001)

- If a less relative threshold is used, such as the proportion of children below the US Poverty Standard then the ranking change. Among the EU countries the southern EU countries and Ireland have the highest child poverty rates (UNICEF 2000).
- It is very likely to be the case that where child poverty is persistent it is a harsher experience and with longer-term consequences. Table 2 presents an analysis of the long-term poverty for all households and households with children based on the ECHP. Long-term poverty is

defined here as being in poverty (below 50 per cent of median equivalent disposable income) in each of the first four sweeps (income data 1993-1996) of the ECHP. On this definition long-term poverty is very rare in Denmark and rare in France and the Netherlands but it is higher in UK, Ireland, Belgium and the Southern EU countries.

Table 2   Long term poverty (below 50 per cent median equivalent disposable income in the first four waves of the ECHP)

	All households	Households with children
Austria	2.5	-
Belgium	4.3	6.0
Denmark	0.7	0.1
Finland	1.6	-
France	2.4	1.7
Greece	7.3	5.9
Ireland	3.8	4.3
Italy	4.8	5.3
Netherlands	2.5	2.2
Portugal	8.7	6.4
Spain	3.6	4.6
Sweden	10.5	-
UK	6.5	4.3

Source: Calculations from Koen Vleminckx on the ECHP

Bradbury, Jenkins and Micklewright (2001) have compared the dynamics of child poverty in seven countries (Britain, Germany, Hungary, Ireland, Russia, Spain and the USA). The results are summarised in Table 3. They found that among the countries with a consistent income definition Britain had the highest proportion of children always in poverty in two waves (10%) and five waves (3%) but Russia has the highest proportion ever in poverty in one wave (24%) and in two waves (34%).

Table 3   Persistence of poverty among children

	% children with household income always below half median average				% children with household income ever below half median income			
Current net income	In wave 1	2 out of 2 waves	5 out of 5 waves	10 out of 10 waves	In wave 1	In 2 waves	In 5 waves	In 10 waves
Britain	16.8	10.1	3.3		16.8	22.9	39.3	
Germany	7.7	4.1	1.5		7.7	11.9	15.6	
West Germany	6.8	4.3	1.7	2.2	6.8	10.0	14.5	21.3
Hungary	9.7	4.6	2.1		9.7	11.2	19.5	
Russia	24.1	9.6			24.1	33.5		
Spain	11.9	7.6			11.9	18.1		
Ireland*	15.6	8.3			15.6	21.3		
USA**	24.7	19.3	13.0	6.8	24.7	30.4	37.6	44.7

Source: Bradbury, Jenkins and Micklewright (2001)
Note: Ireland and USA income definitions not comparable: *annual net income, ** annual gross income

- Nine out of the 15 European Union countries have a higher child poverty rate than over 65 poverty rate, including the UK (see Figure 1).[1] Some countries including the UK are special in having comparatively high poverty rates for both children and the over 65s. There need not be a trade-off between child and older people poverty - Luxembourg, the Netherlands, Finland and Sweden achieve low rates of both. However in some countries there may have been a trade off - Denmark has a much lower child poverty rate than older poverty rate and Germany and the UK both have a big gap between their over 65 and child poverty rates. The living standards of their pensioners may have been sustained at the expense of children.
- Not all countries experienced an increase in child poverty between the mid 1980s and the mid 1990s, indeed about half have experienced a reduction (Figure 2). This demonstrates that it is not the case that changes in family form, particularly the increase in cohabitation and lone parenthood, inevitably results in an increase in child poverty. Nor that pressure on the economy from globalisation inevitably results in a deterioration in the living standards of children.

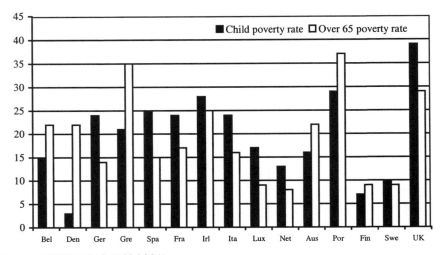

Source: ECHP 1998 (EU 2001)

Figure 1   Child and over 65 poverty rates (1997)

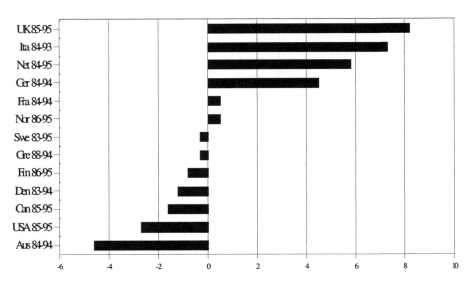

Source: OECD (Oxley *et al.*, 2001)

Figure 2   Trends in child poverty (% point change)

Variations in child poverty are to some extent explainable by variations in *demographic patterns*. It is generally the case that children are more likely to be poor if they live in:

* A *lone parent family*. It can be seen in Table 1, column 2 that the poverty rates of lone parent families are higher in all countries than for two parent families with one or two children. The differential in the poverty rate (between a lone parent and a couple with one child) is largest in Germany, the Netherlands and the UK.
* If there are *many children in the family*. It can be seen in Table 1 that the poverty rates are higher in all countries when there are three or more children in couple families.
  Variations in child poverty are also explainable by variations in the *labour supply of parents*. It is generally the case that children are more likely to be poor if they live in
* A *workless family*. Table 4 shows that along with Ireland, the UK has the highest rate of worklessness among lone parent families and comes close to Ireland with the highest rate of worklessness among couple families.
* A *single earner* family. Table 5 gives the child poverty rates by the number of earners in the family. In all countries there are very low child poverty rates if there are two earners in a couple family. The UK after Italy has the highest child poverty rate among couples with only one earner.

Table 4   Worklessness among families with children 1998

	Rate of worklessness among lone parent families	Rate of worklessness among couple families with children
	%	%
Belgium	51	6
Germany	38	6
Greece	35	3
Spain	39	9
France	34	6
Ireland	61	12
Italy	29	7
Luxembourg	30	2

Table 4 (continued)

	Rate of worklessness among lone parent families %	Rate of worklessness among couple families with children %
Netherlands	55	6
Austria	24	3
Portugal	25	3
Finland	42	7
UK	61	11

Source: OECD (1998) Table 1.7 Data for Denmark, Norway and Sweden not available

Table 5   Child poverty rates (children in families with income below 50 per cent of median income), by number of earners, mid 1990s

	Type of family and number of earners				
	Couple, no earner	Couple, 1 earner	Couple, 2+ earners	Lone parent, no earner	Lone parent, 1+ earners
Australia	18	9	5	42	9
Belgium	16	3	1	23	11
Canada	74	18	4	73	27
Denmark	6	4	-	34	10
Germany	45	6	1	62	33
Greece	22	15	5	37	16
Finland	4	4	2	10	3
Italy	70	21	6	79	25
Netherlands	51	5	1	41	17
Norway	31	4	-	30	5
Sweden	10	6	1	24	4
UK	50	19	3	69	26
USA	82	31	7	93	39

Source: Oxley *et al.* (2001)

However, the impact of the demographic patterns and the variations in employment rates on child poverty can be mitigated by social policies, crucially the tax and cash benefit systems that exist. We have seen that the poverty rate for children living in workless families is much lower in some countries than in others. This is because the system of social protection for workless families is so much better in those countries - it protects children more effectively. Similarly we have seen that the poverty rate for children living in families with one or even two earners is much lower in some countries than in others. This is partly a function of variation in the level of earnings. However it is also the consequence of variations in the level of the tax and benefit package, which exists in each country to support the incomes of families raising children. We know from international comparisons that there are major variations in this child tax/benefit package (Bradshaw *et al.*, 1992 and 1996; Ditch *et al.*, 1998; Kilkey, 2000).

One way of illustrating the importance of the transfer mechanisms is to estimate child poverty rates before transfers - that is the poverty rate that would exist as a result of the market and before any intervention by the state; and after transfers - that is after the impact of taxes and cash benefits (but not services in this example) on market income. The results of such a comparison are presented in Figure 3. The UK starts with a pre transfer poverty rate that is highest of the countries in the comparison. This is a function of demographic patterns, in particular the large number of children in lone parent and workless households in the UK. After the impact of transfers the child poverty rate in the UK falls by 43 per cent to the third highest of the countries in the Figure. The UK's transfer package is more successful at reducing pre transfer poverty than that in the US and certainly Italy (where the tax system results in an increase in child poverty). However, the UK tax and benefit systems are much less successful in preventing child poverty than for example Finland and Sweden which reduce their pre transfer child poverty by 88 per cent or France with a 73 per cent reduction.

It is important to emphasise that this is largely a historical picture of the situation in the mid 1990s. However it demonstrates the importance of social security policy in explaining variations in child poverty rates - and thus the importance of research on the impact of social security policy on children. Hence the theme of the Sigtuna conference.

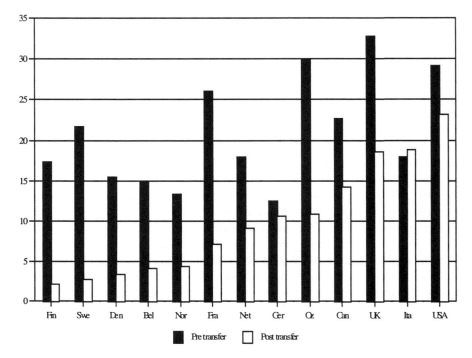

Source: Oxley *et al.* (1999)

Figure 3   Impact of transfers on child poverty rates mid 1990s

Introduction to the papers is this volume

The papers in this volume are organised under three headings.

1. International comparisons of child poverty

We have seen in this introduction that the United States, the richest country in the world, also has the highest child poverty rate. Danziger's paper seeks to explain why this is the case. He argues that when the USA has had a budget surplus providing the resources, a President and Congress with the political will, labour demand making it easier and welfare reform removing the last disincentives, the US has failed to deliver policies that deal with child poverty. This, and public opinion evidence, supports the conclusion that Americans do not care about child poverty. What is it in the American culture that produces this result? There is, after all, no shortage of evidence about child poverty and its effects in the US. Despite having a small welfare state the US has a huge and relatively effective public pension system (Social Security) and highly centrally directed education system. So, it is not just that the pursuit of liberty is not conducive to tackling child poverty. One explanation is that child poverty is very spatially and ethnically concentrated in the US, and therefore does not challenge the white middle class voter as much as it does in European countries. Danziger's conclusions are depressing - given the large tax reductions in 2001, anti poverty policies are not likely to reach the top of the agenda, and welfare reform has made children in the US even more vulnerable to poverty as the recession begins to bite.

In contrast to the United States, in Britain since 1999 child poverty has become the Number One domestic issue - after Tony Blair the Labour Prime Minister, made a commitment to abolish child poverty in 20 years. By the end of the first Parliament in 2001 they had announced tax and benefit reforms that would lift over a quarter of children out of poverty and with labour demand reducing the number of workless families they are well on course to achieving their objective.

The chapter by Middleton and Adelman reviews the results relating to child poverty in a recent British survey of poverty and social exclusion. The survey was undertaken in 1999, too early to be used to evaluate the Government's anti poverty strategy but it is of interest to an international audience in being the first survey to develop a Breadline Britain index of lack of socially perceived necessities especially for children; it contrasts child poverty measured by this index with the conventional income measures; and contrasts these with a variety of indicators of social exclusion. Their most important conclusion however is that employment and activation or welfare-to-work measures cannot be the only remedy for child poverty.

The paper by Gustafsson, Johansson and Palmer underlines again the importance of a strong social protection system for the prevention of child poverty. Their paper traces what happened to child poverty in Sweden during the severe recession in the early 1990s. Their conclusions are that, despite a dramatic increase in unemployment and cuts in welfare state programmes, the child poverty rate increased from only 3.4 per cent in 1991 to 4.4 per cent in 1994 and was down to 4.2 per cent by 1998. Over the whole period 1980 to 1998 relative child poverty increased from 3.7 per cent to 4.2 per cent. (During this period in Britain the child poverty rate increased from 10 per cent to 33 per cent!). They explain how Sweden managed to protect her children - it was a combination of progressive taxation and good unemployment compensation.

The paper by Cantillon and colleagues highlights in rather an alarming way how sensitive estimates of the poverty rate are to the definitions used to measure it. They compare the results of two different data sources used in Belgium to make poverty estimates. Using the same poverty thresholds and equivalence scales, for the same years, they find widely divergent poverty estimates. The period of income measurement turns out to be the main explanation and unexpectedly they find that yearly incomes are more unequal than monthly incomes. However this is to be blamed on problems of recalling annual income and the impact of imputation procedures. These findings have subsequently influenced the conclusions of the Atkinson Report (2001) on *the Indicators of Social Inclusion*.

2. *Child benefit packages*

Every welfare state has some combination of tax deductions, cash benefits and services which help parents with the support of raising children. The value of this 'package' is a measure of the extent to which raising children is seen by different states as a public responsibility rather than purely a private one. Part 2 of this collection is concerned with elements of this package.

Mendelson's paper presented the results of a comparison of the child tax and benefit package in Canada, the USA, Australia and the UK where three countries have converged by adopting an integrated child credit and the USA has an Earned Income Tax Credit. In discussing the harsh system in the USA there are echoes of the Danziger chapter. It was good to see that the UK system appears to be the most generous of the four countries.

Banks and Brewer set out to attempt to answer how generous should financial support for children be? They argue that in order to ensure horizontal equity, households with the same pre transfer income and the same needs should have the same post transfer income. They use equivalence scales to standardise for need and compare horizontal equity in the UK and the USA. Using this method the USA appears to be more generous to families with children than the UK but this is because they are less generous to childless couples who were the base for the comparisons. They also acknowledge that their method assumes that equivalence scales capture households' variation in needs.

We were delighted to include a paper on the New Zealand case by Stephens. Over the last 20 years New Zealand has implemented the most radical reforms of any welfare state - especially for families with children. Though it is difficult to tell much comparatively about child poverty in New Zealand - they do not send their data to the Luxembourg Income Study, there is evidence that New Zealand has experienced one of the sharpest increases in inequality among OECD countries. Stephen's paper traces this, particularly for lone parent families, and shows that the concentration on economic efficiency in place of social justice has harmed the well-being of Maori and Pacific Islander children most. It is good to learn from the paper that New Zealand has begun to give up its role as a neo-liberal test bed and begun to invest resources in its children.

We compared earlier the relative poverty rates of children and older people. Economists have begun to describe life cycle patterns of distribution in terms of inter-generational transactions and we had a number of papers at the Sigtuna exploring this approach. Unfortunately this method has not yet been developed comparatively and Werding's paper applies the approach to the German case, but produces stylised accounts for other countries. One conclusion of the argument is that public investment in children is an essential component if we are to generate the resources from the working population to maintain the income levels of the elderly. The EU has begun to recognise this and it was one of the principle conclusions of the New Architecture of the welfare state prepared by Esping-Anderson *et al.* (2001). Figure 4 reviews how the balance between public spending on the elderly and on children has changed since 1980. It is notable that the southern EU countries, Japan and the USA are spending much more per older person compared with children than other countries and that in those countries there has been a tendency for that share to increase. Quite how those who choose not to have children can begin to understand the importance of investing in them has yet to be tackled in social security policy. Horizontal redistribution from the childless to the child rearing exists in most countries. But is it enough? Perhaps there should be premium in the retirement pensions of those who have reared children during their working lives.

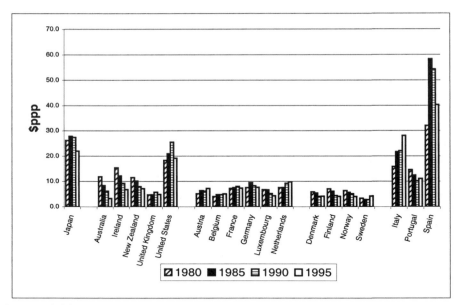

Source: OECD Health Database

Figure 4 $ public expenditure on benefits and services for the elderly per person over 65 for every $ spent on benefits and services for families per child under 20

3. Other aspects of social security provision for children

Scherer's chapter is highly relevant to this debate because it flies in the face of facile assumptions about the pattern of intergenerational obligations, built into different national social security systems. In the comparative social security literature Confucian/Pacific Rim welfare states are characterised as highly generationally interdependent, reflecting the authority and status of the aged. In contrast in western welfare states this generational compact is said to have broken down. However Scherer shows that obligations of children to maintain dependants has always existed and been maintained very strongly in all societies. It is not necessary to invent family obligations but it is necessary to encourage and support them.

Benson's paper compares the development of child support in the US and the UK. UK policy on the obligation of fathers to maintain their absent children was developed with an eye to the US experience (as well as the Australia's). In the past in most countries the maintenance obligation has been a matter of family law, not social security. However in the Anglo Saxon countries, perhaps because more of their lone mothers are dependant on social security benefits rather than the labour market, it has rapidly become an important element in the social security system affecting families with children. Whether social security systems are the best way to handle these highly charged issues seems to be in question from both these country's experiences. Perhaps the lesson to be drawn is that the Anglophone countries have more to learn from continental European experience than from looking at each other - just because they speak the same language.

It was a great development in the FISS seminar that we had papers from South Africa. We chose Vorster's paper which outlines the prevalence of poverty among families with children, the impact of the AIDS pandemic and the shift that has taken place in the South African social security system towards families with children - from a general system of social assistance to a selective system of child benefits for low income families with a children.

The Bengtsson and Middelboe paper is a study in progress concerned with negotiations for help and support between families with a disabled child and social assistance authorities in Denmark. The paper states the case for a consideration of the users perspective in research in social security. It reports the results of a study that collected parent's views about the service offered by the municipality. They conclude that although (in Denmark at least) the financial compensation package is adequate, parents still lack knowledge about how to care for a disabled child and what help is available to them. Views about their case managers are mixed and services have much to learn from listening - and listening styles of research.

The Kucera/Bauer paper is a report of an analysis of the costs and benefits of child care in Zurich. In addition to taking account of the developmental benefits to children, it takes into account the benefits to parents, firms and the general taxpayer. The results are quite startling - child care produces a benefit of at least three times its costs overall. If only the public costs are taken into account, it more than pays for itself in increased tax revenue and lower public subsidies. Given these findings it is quite extraordinary why countries like Switzerland with relatively poor child care provision and low married women's labour participation are not investing heavily in child care. We need studies that validate these results for other countries.

Note

1   These results are highly sensitive to the equivalence scale used.

References

Atkinson, T., Cantillon, B., Marlier, E. and Nolan, B. (2001) *Indicators for Social Exclusion in the European Union*, EU Subgroup on Social Protection.

Bradbury, B. and Jantti, M. (1999) *Child Poverty Across Industrialised Countries*, Innocenti Occasional Paper, Economic and Social Policy Series, No 71, UNICEF International Child Development Centre, Florence.

Bradbury, B., Jenkins, S.P. and Micklewright, J. (2001) 'Child Poverty Dynamics in Seven Nations', Chapter 4 in Bradbury, B., Jenkins, S.P. and Micklewright, J. (eds), *The Dynamics of Child Poverty in Industrialised Countries*, Cambridge University Press, Cambridge.

Bradshaw, J. (ed) (1993) *Budget Standards for the United Kingdom*, Ashgate, Aldershot.

Bradshaw, J. (1999) 'Child Poverty in Comparative Perspective', *Journal of European Social Security,* vol. 1/4, pp. 383-404.

Bradshaw, J., Ditch, J., Holmes, H. and Whiteford, P. (1993) *Support for Children: A comparison of arrangements in fifteen countries*, Department of Social Security Research Report 21, HMSO, London.

Bradshaw, J., Kennedy, S., Kilkey, M., Hutton, S., Corden, A., Eardley, T., Holmes, H. and Neale, J. (1996) *Policy and the Employment of Lone Parents in 20 Countries, The EU Report*, European Observatory on National Family Policies, EU/University of York.

Cornia, G. and Danziger, S. (eds) (1996) *Child Poverty and Deprivation in the Industrialised Countries 1994-1995*, Clarendon Press, Oxford.

Ditch, J., Barnes, H., Bradshaw, J. and Kilkey, M. (1998) *A Synthesis of National Family Policies*, European Observatory on National Family Policies, EC/University of York.

Esping-Anderson, G., Gallie, D., Hemerijck, A. and Myles, J. (2001) *A New Welfare Architecture for Europe*, Report submitted to the Belgian Presidency of the European Union.

Eurostat (1997) 'Income Distribution and Poverty in the EU', in *Statistics in Focus: Population and Social Conditions*, vol. 6.

Eurostat (2001) *European Community Panel Survey 1998. Draft Report on Social Inclusion*, Brussels.

Gordon, D. and Townsend, P. (eds) (2000) *Breadline Europe: The measurement of poverty*, Policy Press, Bristol.

Kilkey, M. (2000) *Lone Mothers Between Paid Work and Care: The policy regime in 20 countries*, Ashgate, Aldershot.

OECD (1998) 'Recent labour market developments and prospects', *Employment Outlook*, June.

Oxley, H., Dang, T., Forster, M. and Pellizzari, M. (2001) 'Income inequalities and poverty among children and households with children in selected OECD countries', in Vleminckx, K. and Smeeding, T. (eds) *Child Well-being, Child Poverty and Child Policy.*

UNICEF (2000) *A League Table of Child Poverty in Rich Nations*, Innocenti Report Card 1, UNICEF, Florence.

Vleminckx, K. and Smeeding, T. (eds) (2001) *Child Well-being, Child Poverty and Child Policy in Modern Nations: What do we Know?*, Policy Press, Bristol.

PART 1

INTERNATIONAL COMPARISONS OF CHILD POVERTY

1.1 After welfare reform and an economic boom: why is child poverty still so much higher in the U.S. than in Europe?

Sheldon Danziger[1]

Economic conditions in the United States in 1999 (the latest year for which data on poverty are currently available) were excellent. Inflation and unemployment were low (2.2 and 4.2 per cent, respectively), and the budget was in surplus (about 2 per cent of GDP). In addition, by 1999, the welfare reform of 1996 had transformed the social safety net, requiring work as a condition of cash assistance, even for single mothers with very young children, and limiting the number of years of eligibility for benefits. Favorable economic conditions led employers to increase labour demand and welfare reform mandated increased labour supply. As a result, the labour force participation rate of single mothers increased and the welfare caseload decreased substantially over just a few years.

Wage rates increased as the labour market tightened, but still remained below levels achieved a quarter century earlier. For example, average hourly earnings (in 1999 constant dollars) in private industry were $13.57 in December 1999, 6.4 per cent above the December 1992 level, but still 7.5 per cent below the December 1973 level, $14.61. Because wage rates of the least-skilled workers and of single mothers are below these averages, the official child poverty rate (an absolute measure) remained high - 16.9 per cent in 1999. Using a relative poverty measure (40 per cent of median adjusted disposable personal income), Smeeding, Rainwater and Burtless (2002), show that the U.S. child poverty rate in the late-1990s (14.7 per cent) was about three times the average rate of 17 other countries in the Luxembourg Income Study (4.8 per cent). When they measure poverty with the U.S. poverty line and 1999 OECD purchasing power parities, the U.S. rate in the mid-1990s remains well above those of France, Canada, Germany, Netherlands, Sweden, Finland, Norway and Luxembourg, and below those of only Australia and the United Kingdom.

The U.S. child poverty rate fell during the 1990s economic boom (it was 22.7 per cent in 1993). However, the 1999 rate was about the same as the 1967 rate (16.6 per cent). Whereas child poverty in 1999 was about the same as in 1967, real per capita money income (before tax, but after cash transfers) was about twice as high, $21,181 vs. $11,309 (in 1999 dollars). This doubling in per capita income did not 'trickle down' to the poor, however, as earnings and family income inequality increased dramatically over this period (Danziger and Gottschalk, 1995).

Do Americans care about poverty?

How should one interpret these trends? I argue that the experience during the economic boom of the 1990s, together with long-standing American choices concerning social policies, implies that child poverty in the U.S., in the foreseeable future, will remain much higher than it is in most of Europe. My hypothesis is that Americans' choices about health, education and welfare policies reveal these preferences - poverty is not as high on their agenda as it is for Europeans, and they are content to live in a society that has more economic hardship than most Europeans would tolerate. For example, a recent survey (Henry J. Kaiser Family Foundation, 2001) found that only about ten per cent of the population considered poverty, welfare or something similar as one of the top two issues government should address, whereas about 20 per cent or more mentioned healthcare, education, and tax reform. Ladd and Bowman (1998, p. 31) report that polls in both the U.S. and Britain have asked, 'In your opinion, which is more often to blame if a person is poor - lack of effort on his own part, or circumstances beyond his control?' In the U.S. in most years, 35 - 40 per cent chose 'lack of effort', whereas fewer than two in ten in Britain selected this choice.

There are several reasons why Americans 'accept' a high level of poverty. First, they prefer a flexible, market economy with relatively little government intervention. In the economic arena, policy-makers in the 1990s successfully managed monetary and fiscal and regulatory policies and the public was pleased with the fact that macro-economic performance surpassed expectations. There was not strong public demand during the economic boom for higher minimum wages, increased health and safety regulations, employer mandates to provide health benefits or paid sick or maternity leave, probably because Americans value labour market flexibility and tend to distrust most government interventions. Europeans seem much more willing to sacrifice some labour market flexibility for policies that raise wages and benefits for their least-skilled workers much closer to those of the median worker than is the case in the U.S. even if these policies reduce overall employment.

Second, Americans seem to have a preference for achieving the best outcomes in a number of socio-economic domains, even if the poorest citizens have little access to minimal levels of resources in these domains. For example, Americans spend a large share of their own income and significant public funds to utilise frontier medical technologies and treatments. The government funds extensive medical research and income tax policy subsidises the purchase of private health insurance and the development of new drugs and treatments, all of which contribute to the availability of new technologies and treatments that are less available in other economies. For citizens with high-quality employer-provided or government-provided health insurance, especially those with sufficient personal resources, America offers the very best health care in the world.

On the other hand, about 14 per cent of American children in the late-1990s had no public or private health insurance, and infant mortality rate and deaths from childhood injury in the U.S. are very high relative to those in most developed countries (just as its child poverty rates are high). For example, between 1991 and 1995, there were 14.1 deaths per 100,000 children ages 1-14 in the U.S. The U.S. ranked 23 out of 26 industrialised nations, below the Czech Republic (12.0), Poland (13.4) and New Zealand (13.7), and far below Sweden, the U.K., Italy, the Netherlands, Norway and Greece, whose rates ranged from 5.2 to 7.6 deaths per 100,000. Child deaths by injury fell substantially in most countries between 1971-75 and 1991-95. However, the rate of decline was higher for many others than it was for the U.S. For example, the U.S. rate fell by 43 per cent, from 24.8 to 14.1 per 100,000, whereas the decline in Canada was 65 per cent, from 27.8 to 9.7. Canada rose in rank from 22 to 18, whereas the U.S. fell from 21 to 23 (UNICEF, 2001). Interestingly, Canadian anti-poverty policy became more aggressive over these decades and its poverty rate declined from a rate that was higher than that of the U.S. in the early 1970s to a rate that was lower by the 1990s.

Americans seem to be getting the public policies that deliver what matters most to most of them. The benefits of having the best technologies available to most citizens dominates any social costs they might experience from living in a society where millions lack access to health care. The American objective seems to be to maximise opportunities for the median voter and those higher in the income distribution, even if that leaves significant gaps between those at the top and those at the bottom.[2] This is consistent with the fact that national health insurance has often been proposed but abandoned over the past 60 years, most recently in the mid-1990s. If Americans cared more about the consumption of the poor, they would have found a way to protect the uninsured, as most European countries did in the aftermath of World War II.

A concern for maximizing the output available to most citizens, even if it leaves the poor with inadequate outcomes is also evident in education. In this domain, Americans also spend lavishly from their family incomes and public funds to support universities with distinguished faculties that include Nobel prize winners and that generate new technologies, employment opportunities and enterprises. At the same time, spending for universal public education at the elementary and secondary levels is based primarily on local property taxes, rather than on a uniform national level of spending per pupil, as is the case in most of Europe. This funding mechanism disadvantages poor children, especially those living in large cities, because their school districts have lower property values per capita than suburban districts. As a result, they attend schools that have less instructional funds per pupil than do affluent children, that have inferior facilities and the least-experienced or least-qualified teachers. In part because of resource differences, the poor children score lower on standardised tests, are less likely to graduate from high school, and are less likely to enroll in college.

Even if poor children score highly on academic tests, however, they are less likely to continue their education than are high-income students. According to Ellwood and Kane (2000), 84 per cent of the children from the top family income quintile who score in the top third of a math test enroll in a four-year college, compared to 68 and 69 per cent of the children in the lowest and second income quintiles. If Americans cared more about equalizing educational opportunities, they would long ago have found a way to reduce funding disparities between poor and nonpoor children and to improve the educational prospects of disadvantaged students.

Certainly, Americans have the resources to purchase public goods that they value. Many new sports stadiums have been built with public funds in the same cities where taxpayers have been unwilling to increase public funding for children who are poor, without health insurance, and/or attend inferior schools.

Given America's private wealth and the large government budget surplus of the late-1990s, and given that Americans seem to have achieved their preferences in many socio-economic domains, it must be the case that they care less than do Europeans about the living standards of their poorest citizens.

The relative inattention to the problems of the poor is also found in the public debate over the federal budget surplus. In mid-2001, Congress had to choose between passing a tax cut or using the funds for other policy purposes and then how to distribute the tax cut across the population. First, that the tax

6

cut was the Bush Administration's top priority reveals a preference for promoting the private consumption of taxpayers rather than addressing other public priorities, such as increasing assistance for the poor or access to health care for the uninsured or reducing funding disparities in public schools.

Second, even the 'liberal' side of the debate was conservative by European standards. The Bush Administration proposed to expand a non-refundable 'per child tax credit'; hence 26 million children in low and moderate income families would not benefit. The opposition Democrats offered a compromise making the credit available to some low-income families so that *only* 10.6 million children would receive nothing. They did not even try to make the credit fully refundable (i.e. to turn the credit into a children's allowance). The policy goal was to benefit only those who paid income taxes, not to reduce child poverty.

In contrast, the Blair government made reducing the UK's high child poverty rate a top priority and instituted policy changes that have increased the incomes of poor families. According to Piachaud and Sutherland (2000), Blair's tax and benefit changes and introduction of the minimum wage 'increased the incomes of the poorest more than those of the better-off and of households with children more than others' (p.16). According to the Centre on Budget and Policy Priorities (2001), the U.S. tax cut, when fully-implemented, would raise after-tax income of the top one per cent of persons by five per cent, that of the middle quintile by 2.2 per cent and that of the lowest quintile by 0.8 per cent. In other words, Blair's policies reduce income inequality and poverty, whereas Bush's increase inequality in after-tax income and provide little for the poor.

In the next section, I review the history of welfare policies from the late-1960s to the present and show that the 1996 welfare reform is consistent with my hypothesis that Americans care relatively little that their poverty rate is so much higher than those in Europe. According to a winter 2001 poll (Henry J. Kaiser Family Foundation, 2001):

Americans who know about the new welfare law like the way it is working ... And the most important reason they give for why it is working well is that it requires people to go to work. Americans appear to value work so strongly that they support welfare reform even if it leads to jobs that keep people in poverty. The vast majority of those who know there has been a major change in the welfare laws (73%) believes that people who have left the welfare rolls are still poor, despite having found jobs (emphasis added).

After welfare reform and an economic boom, child poverty is higher in America than in Europe because Americans want to increase work among the poor and give themselves tax cuts more than they want to reduce poverty. These American preferences are long standing. Ladd and Bowman (1998) review opinion polls from numerous industrialised countries and conclude that Americans 'are inclined to the idea that opportunity is present to those who avail themselves of it. As a result, they are unsympathetic to government redistribution of wealth' (p. 115). They cite a 1992 poll that asked, 'Do you agree or disagree that it is the responsibility of the government to reduce the differences in income between people with high incomes and those with low incomes?' and 'Do you agree or disagree that the government should provide everyone with a guaranteed income?' The percentages reporting 'agree' plus 'strongly agree' were lower in the U.S. (38 and 35 per cent, respectively), than in other western countries -Australia (43 and 51 per cent), Sweden (53 and 46 per cent) the U.K. (66 and 68 per cent) and West Germany (66 and 58 per cent).

Four decades of welfare reform policy

The decade following the War on Poverty was a brief period during which social policy discussion in America took on a European tone:

> We have concluded that more often than not the reason for poverty is not some personal failing, but the accident of being born to the wrong parents, or the lack of opportunity to become nonpoor, or some other circumstance over which individuals have no control. ... Our main recommendation is for the creation of a universal income supplement program financed and administered by the Federal government, making cash payments to all members of the population with income needs.
> (U.S President's Commission on Income Maintenance, 1969)

This willingness to extend cash assistance and the 'structural' views about the causes of poverty are consistent with current European social policies, but were never widely endorsed in America.

Between the mid 1970s and mid 1980s, public dissatisfaction with rising welfare spending increased, and greater attention was paid to promoting work. I suspect most Europeans would not endorse this very-American view about poverty and personal responsibility:

Money alone will not cure poverty; internalised values are also needed. ... The most disturbing element among a fraction of the contemporary poor is an inability to seize opportunity even when it is available and while others around them are seizing it. ... Their need is less for job training than for meaning and order in their lives. ... An indispensable resource in the war against poverty is a sense of personal responsibility.
(Novak *et al.*, 1987)

This emphasis on the personal responsibility of the poor, rather than public responsibility for providing the poor with resources, dominated policy debates and culminated in passage of the Personal Responsibility and Work Opportunity Reconciliation Act of 1996 (PRWORA). The Act ended the entitlement to cash assistance, mandated work and contributed to a dramatic decline in the welfare rolls. In part, caseload decline was rapid because the economic recovery lasted so long, and in part, because states aggressively pursued caseload-reduction strategies (Danziger [ed.], 1999). However, an effective work-based safety net was not put in place - there is no guarantee that a welfare recipient who seeks work, but cannot find a job, will receive any cash assistance or any opportunity to work in return for assistance after she reaches her time limit. In contrast to the safety net in most European countries, many of the nonelderly, nondisabled poor do not receive unemployment insurance or cash public assistance or child care allowances.

I now briefly review the major welfare reform proposals put forward after the 1960s. I emphasise the rise and fall of poverty reduction as a social policy goal and the primacy of personal responsibility as a goal.

The war on poverty

When War on Poverty was declared by President Johnson in 1964, his economic advisers thought that if stable economic growth could be maintained, as it had been since the end of World War II, government programs and policies could eliminate income poverty if sufficient resources were devoted to the task. The Administration's proposals emphasised labour supply policies to raise labour market productivity (Lampman, 1959; U.S. Council of Economic Advisers, 1964). Poverty was thought to be high, because the poor did not work enough or because their skills were insufficient even if they worked hard. Employment and training programs were established or expanded to enhance individual skills, especially for young people. Little attention was focused on welfare dependency because the caseload was small. However, in the aftermath of program liberalizations fostered by the War on Poverty, caseloads increased from about four million recipients in the mid 1960s to about six million by 1969, leading to proposals for welfare reform.

The family assistance plan

In 1969, President Nixon proposed the Family Assistance Plan (FAP) as a replacement for the Aid to Families with Dependent Children Program (AFDC). Although FAP included a work requirement, the president stated '... a welfare mother with pre-school children should not face benefit reductions if she decides to stay home. It is not our intent that mothers of pre-school children must accept work' (Nixon, 1969). FAP and other negative income tax (NIT) plans (Lampman, 1965; Tobin, 1966) would have extended welfare to two-parent families, established a national minimum welfare benefit, and reduced work disincentives arising from AFDC's high marginal tax rate on earnings. After the legislative defeat of FAP, even though a cash NIT for all of the poor never passed, the Food Stamp program evolved into one. By the mid-1970s, it provided a national benefit in food coupons that varied by family size, regardless of state of residence or living arrangements or marital status.

The program for better jobs and income

In 1977, President Carter proposed the Program for Better Jobs and Income (PBJI), a universal NIT with one income guarantee for those not expected to work and a lower guarantee for those expected to work. The latter group would also have been eligible for a public service job (PSE) job of last resort. Whereas the welfare reform debates of the 1990s emphasised time-limiting benefits and enforcing work requirements, PBJI would have both expanded the welfare rolls and provided minimum-wage PSE jobs for recipients who could not find work. As was the case with FAP, a single mother with a child of age six or younger would have been exempted from work. If her youngest was between the ages of seven and fourteen, she would have had to work part-time; if her youngest was over age 14, she would have had to work full-time. By providing jobs of last resort and supplementing low earnings, PBJI would have raised the family income of working welfare recipients. It was thus a precursor of proposals articulated in the U.S. in the late 1980s, and by the Blair government in the U.K. in the 1990s 'to make work pay'. The plan would have increased total federal welfare spending substantially, which was a key reason for its failure to become law.

PBJI provides a benchmark against which later welfare reforms can be evaluated because it called attention to insufficient employer demand for less-skilled workers. It recognised that some welfare recipients would want to work but would not find a job, and that a job of last resort could address involuntary unemployment and be an alternative to welfare. The 1996 Act neglected the demand side of the labour market when it ended the entitlement to cash assistance without offering an entitlement to work. PBJI would also have supplemented low earnings, addressing the falling real wages of the less-skilled, a trend which was just then emerging.[3]

Congress and the public, however, were never enthusiastic about a guaranteed income, not even when PBJI linked the guarantee to work. Nonetheless, even without welfare reform, the income maintenance system expanded between the late 1960s and the late1970s. The number of AFDC recipients increased from about 6 to 11 million and the number of Food Stamp recipients, from about 1 to 19 million over this period. As higher cash and in-kind benefits became available to a larger percentage of poor people, the work disincentives and high budgetary costs of welfare programs were challenged. The public and policy makers came to view increased welfare receipt as evidence that the programs were subsidizing dependency and encouraging idleness (Anderson, 1978; Murray, 1984). What followed was an era of welfare retrenchment that made caseload reduction and increased work among single mothers the primary goals.

The Reagan years

The Reagan Administration proposed that welfare become a safety net, providing cash assistance only for those unable to secure jobs. Public employment was considered an unnecessary intrusion into the labour market, and the PSE program of the 1970s, the Comprehensive Employment and Training Act, was abolished. The Omnibus Budget Reconciliation Act of 1981 changed welfare benefits and eligibility criteria. After four months of welfare receipt, benefits were reduced by one dollar for every dollar earned. This reform reduced caseloads, but contributed to public dissatisfaction because it removed most working recipients from the caseload. As the percentage of recipients who did not work increased, nonwork became a key focus of welfare reform (Mead 1992).

While inflation-adjusted spending on cash welfare for non-workers was trimmed in the 1980s, spending on the working poor increased. Given the high value placed on work, Congress found no contradiction in reducing assistance for the nonworking poor, while increasing it for the working poor. The Earned Income Tax Credit (EITC), enacted in 1975, provides working poor families with a refundable income tax credit. The maximum EITC was $400 in 1975, $550 by 1986, and $953 by 1990. The number of families receiving credits increased from about 5 million a year in 1975 to more than 11 million by 1988.[4]

Because the EITC supplements low earnings, policy makers began to emphasise welfare reforms that could place recipients into any job, rather than training them for 'good jobs'. If a nonworking recipient took a low-wage job, a substantial EITC could make work pay as much as a higher-wage job would have paid in its absence. For example, by the mid 1990s, the income of a single mother with two children working half-time at the minimum wage plus her EITC exceeded welfare benefits, in most states and the maximum EITC, about $3500, raised the after-tax income of a minimum wage worker who worked full-time, full-year to about the poverty line (Ellwood, 2000).

The Family Support Act

The Family Support Act (FSA) of 1988 reflected a bipartisan consensus in which liberals achieved a broader safety net and conservatives achieved stronger work requirements (Baum, 1991; Haskins, 1991; Mead, 1992). The Job Opportunities and Basic Skills Training Program (JOBS) required states to provide a variety of training and support services. It was based on welfare-to-work demonstrations that were undertaken in response to the Reagan Administration's welfare reform legislation. Evaluations of these programs (Gueron, 2001; Friedlander and Burtless, 1995) were promising enough that, by the late 1980s, support for moving welfare recipients into employment was widespread (Novak *et al.*, 1987; Ellwood, 1988).

The Family Support Act reflected a commitment to mutual responsibility: recipients were required to exercise personal responsibility and take advantage of education, training, and work opportunities which the government had the responsibility to provide. States had to implement welfare-to-work programs, extend them to a greater proportion of the caseload and offer a range of education, skills training, job placement, and support services for such items as child care and transportation.

Policy-makers soon questioned the need for education and training, in part, because a JOBS program with a high employment rate for recipients (Riverside, California), implemented a 'work first' program. Work First programs adopt the philosophy 'that any job is a good job and that the best way to succeed in the labour market is to join it, developing work habits and skills on the job rather than in a classroom' (Brown, 1997, p. 2). This allows a greater percentage of recipients to be served with a fixed budget. Work First programs were to become the dominant model after the 1996 Act.

JOBS also raised work expectations and provided sanctions for recipients who did not co-operate with welfare agencies. It lowered the age of the child at which a welfare recipient was expected to participate. Once her youngest child reached age three, she had to participate for up to 20 hours per week; once that child reached age six, she could be required to participate for up to 40 hours per week. Any recipient who complied with JOBS requirements continued to receive welfare; any failure to comply without good cause could reduce the monthly grant to reflect a family with one fewer person.

The FSA took effect as the economic expansion of the 1980s ended. When the welfare rolls jumped in the late-1980s and early-1990s, from about 11 to about 14 million recipients, dissatisfaction with welfare again increased. Even though JOBS had not yet been fully implemented, it had come under enough criticism that Candidate Clinton saw political gain in placing welfare reform at the top of his policy agenda.

Welfare as we now know it

PRWORA replaced AFDC with Temporary Assistance for Needy Families (TANF). Each state can now decide which families to assist, subject only to a requirement that they receive 'fair and equitable treatment'. PRWORA also reduced the total amount of spending required from the federal and state governments. The federal contribution changed from a matching grant to a block grant that is essentially capped for each state at its fiscal year 1994 spending level. Increased costs associated with population growth, recessions or inflation will be borne by the states or by the poor. Moreover, states are only required to spend 75 per cent of what they spent in 1994 on AFDC, JOBS, child care, and Emergency Assistance.

States that have both the funds and the desire can choose to provide a more supportive safety net than existed before. Each state can pursue whatever it chooses, including mutual responsibility reforms that increase its commitment to help recipients find jobs. In practice, however, most states have worked harder to cut caseloads than to provide either work opportunities or services to recipients, including those who have been unable to find work (Pavetti, 2002).

States may not use federal funds to provide more than a cumulative lifetime total of 60 months of cash assistance. However, they can grant exceptions to the limit for up to 20 per cent of the caseload. States also have the option to set shorter time limits. The extent of work expectations has increased. Single-parent recipients with no children under age one are expected to work at least 30 hours per week. States can require participation in work or work-related activities regardless of the age of the youngest child. Whereas President Nixon called for work exemptions for mothers of children under age six, some states now exempt a mother for only 13 weeks following childbirth.

PRWORA offers no opportunity to work in exchange for welfare benefits when a recipient reaches her time limit.[5] Although the labour market prospects for less-skilled workers have greatly eroded since early 1970s, the government is no longer responsible for providing a cash safety net. Although states can exempt 20 per cent of recipients from the time limit, a greater percentage of post-reform recipients is likely to need such extensions or a last resort work-for-welfare opportunity. This is because their personal attributes (for example, a high prevalence of health, mental health and skill problems) compromise their employment prospects (Danziger, 2002).

We have learned four key lessons to date about the effects of PRWORA. *First*, it 'ended welfare as we knew it' more decisively than most analysts expected when the legislation was signed - welfare caseloads dropped so dramatically, that by mid-2000, the number of recipients had fallen to 5.8 million, about the same number as in 1968.

Second, economic conditions, federal government policy changes and state welfare policy changes have increased the financial rewards of moving from welfare to work. The welfare trap has been sprung in many states through a combination of an expanded Earned Income Tax credit, a higher minimum wage, the passage in 1997 of the Children's Health Insurance Program (CHIP), increased funding for child care subsidies, and increased earned income disregards within welfare. As a result, the caseload decline has not caused the surge in poverty or homelessness that many critics of the 1996 Act predicted because most former recipients are finding jobs. Even though many welfare leavers are not working full-time, full-year, and many are working in low-wage jobs, a significant number are earning at least as much as they had received in cash welfare benefits and some now have higher net income because of the income supplements mentioned above.

Third, the national poverty rate has fallen rather little. Many who have left welfare for work remain poor. The extent of economic hardship remains high, because, given their human capital and personal characteristics, many recipients have limited earnings prospects in a labour market that increasingly demands higher skills. Thus, much uncertainty exists about the long-run prospects for escaping poverty of both welfare stayers and welfare leavers.

Fourth, we do not yet know how welfare reform will play out during a recession. Because PRWORA placed a five year, lifetime limit on the receipt of cash assistance, women still receiving welfare (stayers), who have more barriers to employment than those who have left the roles (leavers), are at risk of 'hitting their time limits' in 2002, possibly during a recession. At present, we do not know whether the possible termination of cash assistance during a recession might produce increased child poverty and extreme hardships, or whether Congress and the states might respond by expanding exemptions from or extensions to federal time limits or by providing work-for-welfare community service employment or by creating state-funded programs for those reaching time limits.

What have these policies accomplished?

Table 1.1.1 presents trends over the past three decades on the work effort, welfare receipt and economic well-being of single mothers with children; Table 1.1.2, trends in poverty rates for all children, and for subgroups classified by the marital status and race/ethnicity of their mothers. The data reinforce the view that child poverty in America, regardless of economic conditions or welfare policies, remains higher than in Europe.

Consider the top panel of Table 1.1.1. The percentage of single mothers with children under the age of 18 who worked at some point during the year was about 70 per cent for most of the period from the late 1960s to the late 1980s. After the economic boom and the welfare reform of the 1990s, this employment rate increased to 85 per cent. Between 1989 and 1999, the employment of white single mothers increased by nine percentage points, that of black single mothers by 17 points and that of Hispanic single mothers by 18 points. Increases in employment were greatest for the race/ethnic groups which relied most on welfare. Over most of the period about one quarter of white single mothers, but about half of black and Hispanic single mothers received cash welfare at some time during the year. Between 1979 and 1999, there was a 27 percentage point decline in welfare receipt among black single mothers, a 31 point decline among Hispanic single mothers, and a 13 point decline among white non hispanic mothers. Most of the increased employment and reduced welfare receipt occurred after the mid-1990s and can be attributed to the economic boom, welfare reform and interactions between them.

15

Table 1.1.1   Trends in work, welfare receipt and poverty, single mothers with children, by race/ethnicity, 1969-1999

Year	All	White non-hispanic	Black non-hispanic	Hispanic
% reporting earnings during the year				
1969	70	72	65	n.a.
1972	65	75	56	43
1979	72	80	63	52
1989	72	80	66	57
1999	85	89	83	75
Median earnings (1999 constant) $				
1969	14,163	15,888	n.a.	10,731
1972	15,735	17,621	11,857	11,997
1979	15,859	17,511	14,318	13,326
1989	16,941	18,541	13,167	16,123
1999	16,000	19,000	14,000	14,500
% reporting welfare income during the year				
1969	32	23	50	n.a.
1972	41	27	60	64
1979	34	23	49	53
1989	30	22	39	42
1999	16	10	22	22

Table 1.1.1 (continued)

Year	All	White non-hispanic	Black non-hispanic	Hispanic
Median welfare benefits (1999 constant) \$				
1969	8,716	8,997	8,262	n.a.
1972	8,143	7,102	8,039	11,400
1979	6,425	6,246	5,948	7,690
1989	4,434	4,176	4,299	6,030
1999	2,834	2,712	2,184	4,289
Official family poverty rate (%)				
1969	43.9	36.4	59.4	n.a.
1972	44.4	30.3	62.7	59.5
1979	40.4	28.8	55.9	59.0
1989	44.4	33.7	55.1	62.0
1999	37.4	27.7	48.5	47.3

Source: Computations by author from March Current Population Survey Computer Tapes
Note: Single mothers include women between the ages of 18 and 54 who are never married, divorced, separated or widowed and reside with at least one child under the age of 18. Each family is counted once; data are weighted.
n.a.: The Census Bureau did not make detailed data on Hispanics available until 1972.

The median inflation-adjusted welfare benefit fell over the entire period. The median annual cash benefit for all single mothers in 1999 was only about one-third of its 1969 value. As reviewed above, the extent of welfare receipt (the third panel in Table 1.1.1) was the focus of public debate from the late 1960s onwards. Little attention was focused on the declining real value of welfare benefits (panel 4) or the very high poverty rates of single-mother families (bottom panel).

Table 1.1.2 shows that the child poverty rate in the U.S. is similar to that in Europe for white non-hispanic children living in married-couple families, ranging from five to seven per cent over the 30 year period. However, the rate for all children is substantially higher. It rose from 14 to 20 per cent between 1969 and 1989, and fell only slightly to 17 per cent in 1999 due to the combined effects of the economic boom and welfare reform. Poverty did fall substantially for children in single mother families between 1989 and 1999, from 53 to 44 per cent. However, even if poverty for minority children and children of single mothers were to continue to decline at the rate achieved during the past decade, it would be decades before their rates reached European levels.

Table 1.1.2   Trends in child poverty rate by race/ethnicity and mothers' marital status, 1969-1999

Year	All	White non-hispanic	Black non-hispanic	Hispanic
A. All children				
1969	14	10	40	n.a.
1972	15	8	43	29
1979	16	10	40	29
1989	20	11	44	35
1999	17	9	34	30
B. Children living with single mothers				
1969	55	44	70	n.a.
1972	54	36	71	64
1979	49	34	65	63
1989	53	39	64	68
1999	44	32	55	55
C. Children living with married mothers				
1969	9	7	27	n.a.
1972	9	5	24	23
1979	9	6	18	20
1989	10	7	19	25
1999	9	5	12	23

Source: Computations by author from March Current Population Survey Computer Tapes
Note: Children under 18 years of age living in a family where the head is over 18 and is in the civilian population. Married mothers have spouse present or absent; single mothers are never married, separated, divorced or widowed. Each child is counted once; data are weighted.
n.a: The Census Bureau did not make detailed data on Hispanics available until 1972.

Conclusion

Any welfare system produces errors of commission and omission. The pre-1996 welfare system was biased toward 'false positives' because it provided cash assistance to some recipients who could have found jobs. Some of these 'false positives' might have been unwilling to look for a job; others might have been offered jobs and turned them down because the wages were low or because they did not provide health insurance.   American taxpayers increasingly came to expect that welfare recipients, regardless of the age of their children, take available jobs, regardless of how little they might pay in wages or benefits.

PRWORA has virtually eliminated 'false positives' by terminating benefits for people who will not search for work or co-operate with the welfare agency. But the labour market experiences in recent years for millions of low-skilled workers who do not receive welfare and the experience of former recipients in the five years following welfare reform suggest that the new policy is generating many 'false negatives'. Many recipients who reach the time limits or who are sanctioned for not finding a job are being denied cash assistance simply because they cannot find any employer to hire them.

Because I support a work-oriented safety net, I am not suggesting America return to the pre-1996 welfare system. Welfare recipients who have no serious impairments should have the personal responsibility to look for work, but if they diligently search for work without finding a job, they should be offered an opportunity to perform community service in return for continued cash assistance. A more costly option, but one that would have a greater antipoverty impact, would be to provide them with low-wage public service jobs of last resort. Welfare recipients who were willing to work could then combine wages with the Earned Income Tax Credit and support their families even when there was little employer demand for their skills. For recipients with extensive personal problems, there remains a need to expand social service and treatment programs to experiment with sheltered workshops and to consider increased exemptions or extensions of time limits.

If poverty is to be significantly reduced in the near term, Americans must demonstrate a greater willingness to spend public funds to complete the task of turning a cash-based safety net into a work-oriented safety net. This would be consistent with the high value Americans place on personal responsibility, but it would also bring our poverty rate closer to those in Europe. What are the prospects for making such changes following the very popular welfare reform of 1996? Americans are very pleased with the dramatic caseload reductions and increased employment of the past five years that were highlighted in Table 1.1.1. Given the large tax reductions of 2001, and this satisfaction with welfare reform, I suspect that antipoverty policies are not likely to reach the top of the political agenda in the near future. Indeed, they have not been very high on the political agenda since the mid-1970s. As I stated at the outset, this suggests that Americans have revealed a willingness to tolerate a child poverty rate that would be considered unacceptable in most European countries.

Notes

1   This research was supported in part by a grant from the Ford Foundation. Kristine Witkowski provided research assistance, Barbara Ramsey, clerical assistance, Scott Allard, Jonathan Bradshaw, Robert Haveman, John Hills, Julian Palmer, Peter Scherer, Kristin Seefeldt and Jane Waldfogel, comments on a previous draft.

2   At the conference, Peter Scherer pointed out that a smaller percentage of Americans vote than Europeans vote and that the percentage voting increases more rapidly with income in the U.S. Hence, the median voter in the U.S. has an income that is well above that of the median person.

3   The earned income tax credit, enacted in 1975, now serves this earnings-supplementation function.

4   The EITC was substantially expanded again in 1990 and 1993. By 1997, total spending on the EITC, about $27 billion, exceeded federal cash welfare payments, about $17 billion. The number of families benefiting from the EITC increased to more than 18 million in the late 1990s (U.S. House of Representatives 1998). The EITC served as a model for the Blair government's working families tax credit.

5   Seven states set lifetime time limits for adults (or the entire family) of less than 60 months, ranging from 21 months to 48 months. However, another 12 states have time limit policies in which adults or the family are ineligible for assistance for a period of time after receiving benefits for a certain number of months (e.g., the family may receive benefits for up to 24 months but then may not receive additional assistance until 36 months have passed). (State Policy Documentation Project, 2002.)

References

Anderson, M. (1978) *Welfare: The Political Economy of Welfare Reform in the United States*, Hoover Institution Press, Stanford, CA.

Baum, E.B. (1991) 'When the Witch Doctors Agree: The Family Support Act and Social Science Research', *Journal of Policy Analysis and Management*, vol. 10 (Fall), pp. 603-15.

Brown, A. (1997) *Work First: How To Implement An Employment-Focused Approach To Welfare Reform*, Manpower Demonstration Research Corporation, New York.

Centre on Budget and Policy Priorities (2001) 'Who Would Benefit from the Tax Proposal Before the Senate?', Washington DC, website address: http://www.cbpp.org/5-15-01tax.htm.

Danziger, S. (ed.) (1999) *Economic Conditions and Welfare Reform*, Upjohn Institute for Employment Research , Kalamazoo, MI.

_____ (2001) 'Welfare Reform Policy from Nixon to Clinton', in D. Featherman and M. Vinovskis (eds), *Social Science and Policy Making*, University of Michigan Press, Ann Arbor MI, pp. 137-64.

_____ (2002) 'Approaching the Limit: Early National Lessons from Welfare Reform', in B. Weber, G. Duncan and L. Whitener (eds), *Rural Dimensions of Welfare Reform*, Kalamazoo, Upjohn Institute for Employment Research, MI.

Danziger, S. and Gottschalk, P. (1995) *America Unequal*, Harvard University Press, Cambridge, MA.

Ellwood, D.T. (1988) *Poor Support: Poverty in the American Family*, Basic Books, New York.

———— (2000) 'Antipoverty Policy for Families in the Next Century: From Welfare to Work - and Worries', *Journal of Economic Perspectives*, vol. 14, no. 1, pp. 187-98.

———— and Thomas Kane (2000) 'Who is Getting a College Education? Family Background and the Growing Gaps in Enrollment', in S. Danziger and J. Waldfogel (eds), *Securing the Future: Investing in Children From Birth to College*, Russell Sage Foundation, New York, pp. 283-324.

Friedlander, D. and Burtless, G. (1995) *Five Years After: The Long-Term Effects Of Welfare-To-Work Programs*, Russell Sage Foundation, New York.

Gueron, J. (2001) 'Welfare Reform At The State Level: The Role Of Social Experiments And Demonstrations', in D. Featherman and M. Vinovskis (eds), *Social Science and Policy Making*, University of Michigan Press, Ann Arbor, MI, pp. 165-86.

Haskins, R. (1991) 'Congress Writes A Law: Research And Welfare Reform', *Journal of Policy Analysis and Management*, vol. 10 (fall), pp. 616-32.

Henry J. Kaiser Family Foundation (2001) *National Survey on Poverty in America*, http://www.kff.org.

Ladd, E. and Bowman, K. (1998) *Attitudes Toward Economic Inequality*, American Enterprise Institute, Washington DC.

Lampman, R. (1959) *The Low-Income Population And Economic Growth*, U.S. Congress, Joint Economic Committee, Study Paper No. 12. Washington DC, GPO.

———— (1965) 'Approaches To The Reduction Of Poverty', *American Economic Review*, vol. 55, no. 2, pp. 521-29.

Mead, L.M. (1992) *The New Politics Of Poverty: The Non-Working Poor in America*, Basic Books, New York.

Murray, C. (1984) *Losing Ground: American Social Policy, 1950-1980*, Basic Books, New York.

Nixon, R.M. (1969) 'Welfare Reform: A Message From the President of the United States' House Document No. 91-146, *Congressional Record*, vol. 115, no. 136, The House of Representatives, 91st Congress, First Session, H7239-7241.

Novak, M. *et al.* (1987) *The New Consensus On Family And Welfare: A Community Of Self-Reliance,* Marquette University, Milwaukee, WI.

Pavetti, LaDonna. (2002) 'Welfare Policy in Transition: Redefining the Social Contract', in S. Danziger and R. Haveman (eds), *Understanding Poverty*, Harvard University Press, Cambridge, MA.

Piachaud, D. and Sutherland, H. (2000) *How Effective Is the British Government's Attempt to Reduce Child Poverty?*, UNICEF, Innocenti Research Centre, Working Paper 77, Florence, Italy.

Smeeding, T., Rainwater, L. and Burtless, G. (2002) 'United States Poverty in a Cross-National Context', in S. Danziger and R. Haveman (eds), *Understanding Poverty*, Harvard University Press, Cambridge, MA.

State Policy Documentation Project (2000) *Time Limits on TANF Cash Assistance.* A joint project of the Centre for Law and Social Policy and the Centre for Budget and Policy Priorities, www.spdp.org.

Tobin, J. (1966) 'The Case For An Income Guarantee', *Public Interest*, vol. 4, (summer), pp. 31-41.

UNICEF, Innocenti Research Centre (2001) *A League Table of Child Deaths by Injury in Rich Nations*, UNICEF, Innocenti Research Centre, Report Card No. 2, Florence, Italy.

U.S. Council of Economic Advisers (1964) *Economic Report Of The President*, GPO, Washington DC.

U.S. House of Representatives, Committee on Ways and Means (1993, 1998) *Background Material And Data On Programs Within The Jurisdiction Of The Committee On Ways And Means: Green Book*, GPO, Washington DC.

U.S. President's Commission on Income Maintenance (1969) *Poverty Amid Plenty: The American Paradox*, U.S. Government Printing Office, Washington DC.

1.2 The poverty and social exclusion survey of Britain: implications for the assessment of social security provision for children in Europe

Sue Middleton and Laura Adelman

Introduction

Poverty and social exclusion are growing concerns in Britain, and in Europe as a whole. The targets for abolishing both have become a major part of the policy agenda of national Governments and of the European Commission. The Lisbon European Council Summit and subsequent European Council Meeting in Nice requires Member States to develop priorities for the combating of poverty and social exclusion, and to 'submit by June 2001 a national action plan covering a two-year period and to define indicators and monitoring mechanisms capable of measuring progress' (EC, 2000).

However, despite such actions, poverty and social exclusion remain contested terms. There are numerous methods for measuring poverty. In the case of social exclusion, although it is a widely used term in Europe, what it means and how it should be measured, has never been clear-cut. One particular area of omission has been the consideration of social exclusion experienced by children.

The detailed and accurate measurement of both poverty and social exclusion are vital for achieving their abolition or minimisation. A new survey, the Poverty and Social Exclusion Survey of Britain (PSE), aimed to alleviate some of the problems associated with their measurement. The new survey has its roots in two earlier 'Breadline Britain' surveys,[1] which measured poverty as the inability to afford items perceived as necessities by the majority of the public. However, the original questionnaires have been expanded into a new and unique survey that attempts to operationalise the concept of social exclusion, including questions on access to local services, social networks, and civic engagement.[2] The survey also includes a range of poverty measures and explores how poverty is distributed within households.

This paper uses data from the PSE survey first to consider material deprivation among children and how this compares with the material deprivation of their parents. Second, the paper offers some first thoughts on how children's social exclusion might be measured. The conclusion describes how these more wide-ranging and imaginative measures of children's poverty and social exclusion can be used throughout Europe to assess the effectiveness of social security provision.

The PSE measure of poverty - children's material deprivation[3]

The PSE measure of poverty broadly measures a lack of 'socially perceived necessities'. To define socially perceived necessities a representative sample of adults were asked in a first survey to say which of a list of items and activities for children, and a second list for adults, they considered everyone should be able to afford in Britain today and which they should not have to go without. The 30 items in the children's list and 54 items in the adult's list were drawn from extensive and careful research, including a programme of focus groups (Bradshaw *et al.*, 1998).

In the subsequent PSE survey respondents were asked to say which of the items and activities they or their children had, which they did not have but did not want and, finally, which they did not have and could not afford. Therefore, deprivation was measured not simply because children or adults did not have items but because they could not be afforded.

The PSE measure of poverty is particularly well-suited to measuring children's poverty as it is democratically decided (by parents) and can produce a poverty line specifically related to children rather than to adults or their households. It does not assume that poverty is shared out equally among household members. Finally, it allows us to describe what poverty actually means for children's lives. What do poor children go without that non-poor children do not? The meaning of poverty in their lives can, therefore, be better understood.

Which necessities do children lack?

Only a small proportion of children had parents who could not afford each socially perceived necessity. (The relevant percentages are shown in the second column of Table 1.2.1.) They were least likely to go without items that the largest percentages of parents thought to be necessary - food, environmental and developmental items - and most likely to lack participation items and activities.

Nearly all parents thought that new, properly fitted shoes, a warm waterproof coat and fresh fruit and vegetables daily were necessities, yet one in 50 children did not have these because of lack of money. One in 25 went without each of the following highly endorsed necessities: celebrations on special occasions, educational games, a meat, fish or vegetarian equivalent twice daily, and access to a garden.

How many children fall below the child poverty threshold?

To construct a poverty threshold for this measure of children's poverty, only items and activities that more than 50 per cent of parents said were necessary were included. A range of statistical techniques was used to ensure that the full list of items was a valid and reliable measure, and then to determine a threshold for childhood necessities deprivation (see further Gordon *et al.*, 2000).

The conclusion was that children who went without two or more of the items or activities on the list were defined as poor - 18 per cent of children.

Which children fall below the child poverty threshold?

A number of characteristics were particularly likely to lead to a child being poor. For example, children were at a greater risk of being poor if they lived: in lone parent families, with large numbers of children in the household, with a long term sick or disabled parent, in local authority housing, with unemployed parents and with families who were receiving means-tested benefits.

Many of these characteristics are related to each other - being unemployed and receiving benefit is just one example. Logistic regression modelling was therefore undertaken to determine which children were most likely to be poor once all other characteristics were held constant. Compared to children in households where two adults were in full-time work, or more than two adults were in employment, children in households with:

- one full-time and one part-time paid worker were five times more likely to be deprived;
- one full-time paid worker were eight times more likely to be deprived;
- one or more part-time paid workers were 11 times more likely to be deprived;
- no paid workers were nine times more likely to be deprived.

The only other significant characteristic was tenure. Children in local authority housing were three times, and those in the 'other' rented sector over twice as likely, to be deprived as children living in owner-occupied housing.

Table 1.2.1   Necessities and 'necessities deprivation'

	Percentage of parents regarding item as 'necessary'	Percentage of children who lack item because their parents cannot afford it	
		All children	Children who lack at least two of the 27 necessary items
Food			
Fresh fruit/vegetables daily	93	1.8	9
Three meals a day	91	(0.9)	(5)
Meat/fish/vegetarian twice daily	76	3.7	21
Clothes			
New, properly fitted shoes	96	2.3	12
Warm, waterproof coat	95	1.9	11
School uniform*	88	2.0	12
Seven + pairs underpants	84	1.9	11
Four + pairs of trousers	74	3.1	18
Four + jumpers/cardigans	71	2.8	16
Some new, not all 2nd hand, clothes	67	3.1	18
Participation and activities			
Celebrations on special occasions	92	3.6	20
Hobby or leisure activity*	88	3.2	18
School trip at least once a term*	73	1.8	(10)
Swimming at least once a month	71	7.1	34
Holiday away from home at least one week a year	63	21.8	68
Leisure equipment*	57	3.1	17
Friends round for tea/snack fortnightly*	53	3.7	21

Table 1.2.1 (continued)

| | Percentage of parents regarding item as 'necessary' | Percentage of children who lack item because their parents cannot afford it | |
		All children	Children who lack at least two of the 27 necessary items
Developmental			
Books of own	90	(0.1)	(1)
Play group at least once a week (pre-school age children)*	89	(1.3)	(7)
Educational games	84	4.2	21
Toys (e.g. dolls, play figures)*	85	(0.5)	(3)
Construction toys	66	3.3	19
Bike: new/second-hand*	60	3.4	18
At least 50p a week for sweets	45	1.6	-
Computer suitable for school work	38	35.7	-
Computer games	13	13.2	-
Environmental			
Bed and bedding to self	96	(0.6)	(3)
Bedrooms for every child of different sexes*	76	3.3	10
Carpet in bedroom	75	(1.4)	(5)
Garden in which to play	68	3.5	8
Base	560	792	139

Key: Brackets - less than 20 unweighted cases;   * age-related items

How poverty is shared within households[4]

Most poverty measures operate at the household level. In other words they assume that if a household is poor, all members of the household will share equally in that poverty. Yet earlier research suggests that this is not an accurate reflection of what actually happens in families. Children seem to have first call on available resources, with men second and women last in the queue.[5]

The PSE survey investigated the distribution of poverty within households by asking a series of questions about things that respondents, their partners and their children had gone without in the previous 12 months because of lack of money. Children were very much less likely than their parents to lack individual items that can be directly compared; clothes, shoes, food, a hobby, or a holiday.

Further analysis compared the extent to which children went without in households where parents were going without (Figure 1.2.1). For four of the items, in almost 90 per cent of households where parents went without their children did not. Even in the case of a holiday, 51 per cent of children were able to have one although their parents could not.

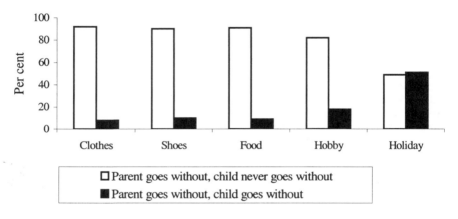

Figure 1.2.1 Comparison of parent and child deprivation

However, there was a small percentage of households in which parents were not protecting their children from deprivation. Further analysis showed that it was the depth of poverty being experienced by households where both parents and children went without which prevented parents from protecting their children from deprivation. Compared to all parents, these parents were:

- three times more likely to have been disconnected from utilities and to lack five or more essential social activities;
- two and a half times more likely to have considered themselves currently in poverty 'all of the time';
- twice as likely to feel that they had been in poverty 'often' or 'most of the time' in the past and to have had to cut back on the amount of utilities used; and
- one and a half times more likely to have had incomes below 40 per cent of the median and to be necessities deprived.

Therefore, for parents to go without their poverty need not be severe, but to let poverty impact on their children parents had to be suffering very severe poverty indeed.

Children's social exclusion

As far as we are aware this is the first survey that has attempted to operationalise the concept of social exclusion and to measure it. It is not suggested that the results presented are conclusive, but they do throw light on children's experiences in a way that other evidence has not.

For these first thoughts on social exclusion in childhood, exclusion has been defined as falling into three main categories. First, service exclusion, that is the extent to which children were excluded from relevant services. Second, exclusion from social relations or social participation - measured as a lack of activities in the deprivation index described earlier. Finally, exclusion during education - defined as exclusion from adequate resources in school, bullying and being bullied, being suspended from school, having special educational needs. In this section the experiences of social exclusion amongst poor and non-poor children are compared (using the PSE definition of poverty).

Exclusion from children's service[6]

The PSE survey asked parents whether their child had access to a range of services. Their response could be one of the following five, their child:

- used the service and thought it adequate;
- used the service and thought it inadequate;
- did not use the service because it was not relevant or not wanted;
- did not use the service because it was unavailable or unsuitable; or
- did not use the service because the parents could not afford it.

Therefore children could be excluded from these services either through a lack of availability or inability to afford services. For simplicity, these two responses have been combined and not relevant responses have been removed (Figure 1.2.2).

Play facilities: Poor children were almost twice as likely to be excluded from play facilities as non-poor children; 42 compared to 23 per cent.

School meals: Poor children were almost three times more likely to be excluded from receiving school meals - 19 per cent compared to seven per cent of non-deprived children (although it should be noted that numbers were small). This is because access to free school meals is severely restricted under present legislation, excluding many children who would be identified as poor under most poverty measures.

Youth clubs: Although numbers were small, among those for whom youth clubs were relevant, poor children were, again, more likely to be excluded than non-poor children. One half of poor children were excluded from youth clubs compared to one-third of non-poor children.

After school clubs: After school clubs have recently been encouraged by the British Government. Their availability was seen as one route to allow parents to go to work without the use of private child care. However, those most likely to benefit from such schemes were also least likely to have access to them. Poor children were far more likely to be excluded from after school clubs - over two-thirds of poor children, compared to one-third of non-poor children.

Public transport to school: Of those for whom public transport to school was relevant or wanted, slightly more poor children were excluded from this service, 20 compared to 16 per cent (numbers were small).

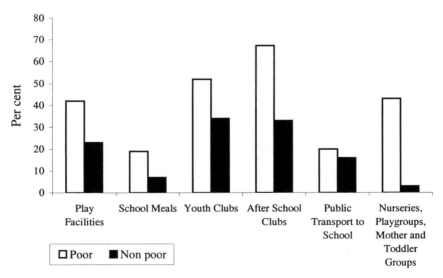

Figure 1.2.2   Children's services

Nursery, playgroup or mother and toddler groups: Poor children were far more likely to be excluded from one of these groups than non-poor children. Forty-three per cent of poor children were unable to attend these groups, compared to just three per cent of non-poor children.

Exclusion from social relations or participation

The deprivation measure for children included a range of activities. (The following analysis excludes these activities from the deprivation measure so that it compares children who lack none or one of the *items* with children lacking two or more.) Children lacking two or more items were significantly more likely to be excluded from each of the activities (Table 1.2.2). Perhaps most striking is the fact that whilst just one per cent of children lacking one or no items could not afford a hobby or leisure activity this affected 20 per cent of children lacking two or more items.

Table 1.2.2   Exclusion from social activities

Activity	Children lacking none or one item	Children lacking two or more items	All children
Hobby or leisure activity*	(1)	20	3
Celebrations on special occasions*	(3)	(8)	4
Swimming at least once a month*	4	33	7
Play group at least once a week (pre-school age children)*	(1)	(5)	1
Holiday away from home at least one week a year*	19	45	22
School trip at least once a term*	(1)	(8)	2
Friends round for tea/snack fortnightly*	(2)	23	4

Key: Brackets - less than 20 unweighted cases; * significant difference (p<0.05).

Exclusion during education[7]

Problems at school: Parents in the PSE survey were asked whether their children had experienced a number of problems at school in the past 12 months.

Although, in general, differences were small, it seems that poor children were more likely to be in schools that were short of computers (30 compared to 20 per cent) and with other problems resulting from a lack of resources (20 compared to 13 per cent). Non-poor children, in contrast, were more likely to have experienced none of the seven problems (46 compared to 41 per cent) but were slightly more likely to suffer from specific shortages - missing classes because of a teacher shortage or having to share books in key subjects.

Bullying and being bullied: Although differences were small it seems that poor children were both slightly more likely to be bullied and to be accused of bullying. Forty-four per cent of poor children were bullied compared to 41 per cent of non-poor children, whilst 12 per cent of poor children had been accused of bullying compared to nine per cent of non-poor children.

Suspensions from school: Children in the UK can be suspended from school for varying periods and, indeed, permanently if their behaviour is considered sufficiently bad. Poor children were almost six times more likely to have been suspended from school than non-poor children, 17 compared to just three per cent.

Although numbers were small, the differences between the length of time children had been suspended from school were also stark. Of non-poor children who had been suspended, the length of suspension on the last occasion was most likely to have been five days or less (93 per cent, only seven per cent had been suspended for more than five days). In contrast among poor children over two-fifths had been suspended for more than five days on the last occasion (43 per cent).

Special educational needs: Poor children (39 per cent) were almost three times more likely than non-poor children (14 per cent) to have special educational needs, that is, to have physical or learning disabilities or behavioural problems (Figure 1.2.3).

Poor children were also more likely to be 'statemented'. The system of statementing thoroughly investigates the needs of children with difficulties, and recommendations are made for their education. It guarantees additional help and the final document, or statement, is legally binding on the education authorities and other professionals. The process of statementing is expensive since it requires the involvement of many professionals.

However, proportionately fewer poor children with special educational needs were statemented than non-poor children with such needs. Therefore, not only were poor children more likely to have special educational needs, but they were less likely to have access to the additional resources guaranteed by a statement to help meet those needs.

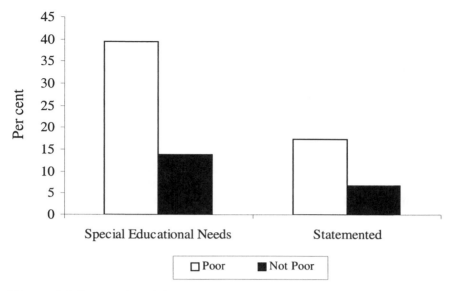

Figure 1.2.3   Special educational needs

Conclusions

In addition to recommendations for detailed policy change at the national level, lessons for all countries can be drawn from these different methods of looking at poverty and social exclusion among children.

Income poverty should not be confused with social exclusion. Income measures are inadequate on their own if the meaning of poverty and social exclusion is to be fully understood, and if governments are to properly evaluate the success of policies to remove children from poverty and social exclusion.

In particular, this paper has highlighted the need to take account of local and education services in the lives of children. Poverty and social exclusion are not simply the result of lack of resources within the family. Too often a pre-occupation with household income means that the vital contribution made by these services to children's well-being are ignored.

Another important finding has been that most parents do their best, prioritising the needs of their children above all else. It is simply that for the most materially poor it is simply not possible to provide adequately for children, and it is these families that most urgently need policy attention.

This paper has also shown that employment cannot be the only answer to ending child and adult poverty, the remedy that many governments seek. For children, even having just one parent in work is not enough. For those families where one worker is all that is possible, either through being a lone parent family or having a sick or disabled person in the family, for example, or where it is not possible for any family member to be in work, poverty will remain. For these families security out of work through increased social security provision must be provided.

There is a clear necessity for national and international surveys to include measures of poverty and social exclusion such as those presented and, in particular, measures that focus on children separately, rather than simply through the lens of the family. This leads to an inadequate and distorted picture of children's lives, poor children's lives in particular. These measures will allow governments to ensure that their policies to combat poverty and social exclusion - including their social security provisions - are working by exploring poverty and social exclusion in all their dimensions.

Notes

1   Gordon, D. and Pantazis, C. (1997); Mack, J. and Lansley, S. (1985).
2   Further details about the survey's method and contents can be found in Gordon, D. *et al.* (2000) or on the survey's website: www.bristol.ac.uk/poverty/pse.
3   This section is a summary from the chapter on children's poverty in the main report Gordon, D. *et al.* (2000).
4   For further details on this analysis see Adelman, L. and Middleton, S. (2000).
5   See, for example, Goode, J., Callendar, C. and Lister, R. (1998); Middleton, S., Ashworth, K. and Braithwaite, I. (1997); Vogler, C. (1994).
6   Respondents were asked these questions about all their children. Obviously each service will only be relevant to children of specific ages. Therefore responses have been adjusted to include only those children for whom each service would be age appropriate. The age groups are:
-   Less than 5 years old for playgroups, nurseries or mother and toddler groups;
-   2 years to 13 years for play facilities;
-   5 years and over for school meals, after school clubs and public transport to school; and
-   11 years and over for youth clubs.
7   These questions were asked to parents about all their children, so that even though only one child in the family may have experienced the problem, all children in the family would be counted as experiencing it. This may over-estimate the proportion of children affected. This has been compensated for to some extent by only including children of school age in the analysis.

References

Adelman, L. and Middleton, S. (2000) *Management of Household Finances and Intra-Household Poverty*, PSE Working Paper No. 23.

Bradshaw, J., Gordon, D., Levitas, R., Middleton, S., Pantazis, C., Payne, S. and Townsend, P. (1998) *Perceptions of Poverty and Social Exclusion 1998*, Report on Preparatory Research, Townsend Centre for International Poverty Research, Bristol.

European Council (2000) *Presidency Conclusions. Nice European Council Meeting 7-9th December 2000.*

Goode, J., Callendar, C. and Lister, R. (1998) *Purse or Wallet? Gender Inequalities and Income Distribution within Families on Benefits*, Policy Studies Institute, London.

Gordon, D., Adelman, L., Ashworth, K., Bradshaw, J., Levitas, R., Middleton, S., Pantazis, C., Patsios, D., Payne, S., Townsend, P. and Williams, J. (2000) *The Poverty and Social Exclusion Survey of Britain*, Joseph Rowntree Foundation, York.

Gordon, D. and Pantazis, C. (1997) *Breadline Britain in the 1990s*, Ashgate, Aldershot.

Mack, J. and Lansley, S. (1985) *Poor Britain*, Allen and Unwin, London.

Middleton, S., Ashworth, K. and Braithwaite, I. (1997) *Small Fortunes: Spending on Children, Childhood Poverty and Parental Sacrifice*, Joseph Rowntree Foundation, York.

Vogler, C. (1994) 'Money in the household', in Anderson, A., Bechhofer, F. and Gershuny, J. (eds), *The Social and Political Economy of the Household*, Oxford University Press, Oxford.

1.3 Economic well-being of children in the deep Swedish recession of the 1990s

Björn Gustafsson, Mats Johansson and Edward Palmer

1. Introduction

Recent comparative research as summarised in Vleminckx and Smeeding (2001) indicates that Sweden has performed better, and in fact much better, than most other OECD countries when it comes to child well-being and child poverty. High labour market participation among parents, particularly mothers, and generous public programmes facilitating parenthood are very important reasons for this good record.

In the beginning of the 1990s, this 'paradise' was hit by a severe recession. From 1991-1994, unemployment skyrocketed and cutbacks in many public programmes were undertaken in order to make ends meet. How was the economic welfare of children affected? This is the overriding research question posed in this paper. Using the Household Income Survey from Statistics Sweden, we examine what happened to equivalent income of children in the 1990s.

The questions we ask are: How did average income change and was it more or less affected than income of the total population? Were children in various parts of the distribution of child income affected differently by the downturn? How were children living in single parent households and households with two parents affected? To what extent did taxes and transfers counteract inequality-increasing forces from the labour market?

2. Changes in the Swedish labour market and social policy during the 1990s

Sweden was hit more severely by the slowdown in the world economy in

1990 than other OECD countries. The slowdown in economic activity ruptured a financial loan and property market bubble that had been expanding during the 1980s, and sent the Swedish economy into a downward spiral. From a low of two per cent open unemployment and another two per cent of the labour force in active labour market measures in 1989, the sum of open unemployment and persons in labour market measures skyrocketed, and in 1993 these had reached 14 per cent of the labour force. The level of GDP fell by five per cent in 1990-1994, and Sweden went almost overnight from a period of sustained growth from 1983 into its deepest recession since the 1930s.

The large increase in the unemployment rate is only one part of the story of the labour market. Another, and also very important reason, is that the labour force shrank. While 84.5 per cent of the population aged 16-64 were in the labour force at the end of the 1980s, participation fell to only 78.2 per cent in 1995.

Although the downturn affected all groups in the population, there were clear differences in the scope and depth (Gustafsson and Palmer, 2001). Above all, there was a very clear age-pattern. Young entrants into the labour market encountered substantial difficulties in finding jobs, while unemployment among younger workers became very high for Sweden, and, consequently, employment of young adults fell very rapidly. At the other end of the age spectrum, however, the labour-market effects were not as harsh. Older workers, protected by last-in first-out rules, were less likely to become unemployed.

The financial impact of the recession varied between ages. Persons already established in the labour market, and who lost employment, were entitled to unemployment benefits, while young adults with no or insufficient employment history were left outside this income replacement system. Not surprisingly then, social assistance payments increased most rapidly among young adults.

From 1990 through 1995, public expenditures increased as the costs of unemployment exploded, tax revenues fell with income, and the public-sector budget deficit increased rapidly. In order to control the expanding deficit, many public programmes were cut back and the tax rate was increased for persons with higher income. In addition, employee contributions to social insurance were reintroduced, and gradually increased to 6.95 per cent of earnings in 1998.

Child allowances, one of the main support instruments for families with children, went through their own cycle in the 1990s. In 1990, the child allowance had been increased from 560 kronor (about 56 USD) per month per child to 750 kronor (about 75 USD) per month per child, where it remained throughout the recession. A supplementary benefit to families with three or more children was taken away in 1995, however. Remarkably, with the upturn in the economy in 1996, the allowance per child was decreased to 640 kronor (about 64 USD), and by 1997 the total amount paid in allowances to families with children was 20 per cent lower per child than in 1994. In 1998, per capita amounts were increased once again to their level in 1990.

In addition, the rules for the child support benefit for single parents, which guarantees a minimal amount of child support per child for separated parents, were changed in order to increase the collection of debts from the non-custodian parent. The means-tested housing allowance was redesigned too in 1996, leading to a drop in the number of eligible claimants for households with two adults and children by 25 per cent, and by almost 20 per cent for single-parent households. In addition to this, the earnings replacement rate for parents who leave employment for child care in the home, as well as the earnings replacement rate while at home caring for a sick child were reduced. On the other hand, the supply of day-care facilities increased, implying that day-care became less of an impediment for job seekers. Financial resources did not increase with the increase in places, however, which means there were fewer public resources being spent per child.

As GDP started to increase once again in the mid-1990s, the unemployment rate started to decrease, although at first very slowly. In 1990-1998, Sweden was close to the bottom in economic growth in OECD, with an average annual growth rate of only 1.0 per cent. Sweden outperformed only Switzerland, Hungary and the Czech Republic. The GDP growth rate in Sweden was only half as high as in Australia, Canada, the United Kingdom and Spain and only one-third of the growth rate of the United States.

After ten years, as Sweden entered the new millennium, the economy was back on track, and GDP growth was higher than in most other OECD countries. In fact, the unemployment rate had become so low that labour shortages were arising in many sectors, especially in the larger metropolitan areas. Public finances were now in good shape, and social policy began to return to pre-recession generosity, although once again a new recession seemed to be lurking around the door in the autumn of 2001.

3. Measurement of child income

Data for this study come from the Swedish Household Income Survey (HINK) compiled by Statistics Sweden. This is an annual survey of around 10,000 households conducted since the mid-1970s. The present study focuses on the period 1991 to 1998, but we also use data from earlier years to compare the outcome in the 1990s with the preceding decade. There is a methodological problem that arises in comparing the years before 1991 and from 1991 and after, because the tax base was broadened from 1991. The resultant definitional change led to an increase in household factor income of about five per cent.[1]

A HINK household consists of adults and children up to the age of 18. Multi-family households are treated as separate households, as are children 18 years old and older living at home. Information on earnings, taxes and most transfers is obtained from public registers, and is supplemented by additional information obtained through telephone interviews.

The main unit of measurement in this study is equivalent disposable income. Equivalent disposable income is obtained by dividing disposable income by an equivalence scale, which follows social assistance norms including housing costs (see Gustafsson, 1987 for a detailed description of the procedure used). 'Norm' housing costs are based on the size of the household and region of the country where people reside. Individuals constitute the unit of analysis in the study. We assume consumption opportunities are equally shared within the household, which means that all household members share the household income. An equivalent income value of 1.0 means that the income of members of the household, considered separately, is exactly equivalent to the norm for a single person living in their region of the country.

In this way, we obtain values of child income for all children, compute the average for various years, compare child income with the income of other persons and analyse inequality in the distribution of child income. The approach also makes it possible to study child poverty for all children, and for children living in different households. We are thus able to present a detailed picture of how child welfare and child poverty changed during the 1990s.

4. The development of average child income during the 1980s and 1990s

Since the mid-1970s, Sweden has experienced two deep recessions, the first in 1978-1982 and the second in 1991-1995. From the end of the first recession in 1983 through 1990, the equivalent disposable income of children increased steadily (Figure 1.3.1), along with the general trend in the development of earnings. Similarly, from 1991, the equivalent disposable income of children fell through 1995, and did not turn up again until 1997.

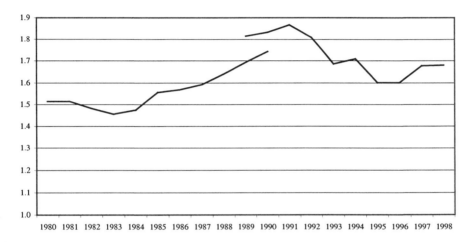

Figure 1.3.1 **Development of equivalent disposable income among children 0-17 years. Ratio to the social assistance norm with housing costs. 1980-1998**

During the first recession, according to Table 1.3.1a, child income decreased by 3.8 per cent. The decline was slightly more for the youngest children and less for school-age children. The decrease in income was marginally lower than for the population as a whole. As the economy recovered and average child income increased annually, in 1990 the level income per child was 20 per cent higher than in 1983, and 15 per cent higher than in 1980. Similar results can be noted for the entire population during the expansion of the 1980s.

41

Table 1.3.1a also shows that the development of average child income during the 1980s was not the same for children of all ages. Average child income developed more favourably for school-aged children than for younger children, probably reflecting the overall development of earnings for younger adult workers.

Also according to Table 1.3.1a, average child income decreased by 9.7 per cent from 1991 to 1993, when open unemployment reached its maximum. Average child income continued to fall even though the labour market situation gradually started to improve, and in 1996 it was as much as 14.2 per cent lower than in 1991. The recessionary labour market had the first and deepest consequences for child income, but cuts in benefits in 1995-96 added considerably to this. Average child income increased again after 1996, by 4.9 per cent. However, in 1998, when our time series ends, average child income was still ten per cent lower than in 1991.

In the 1990s, average income for school-age children fell more dramatically than for non-school-age children, the opposite of what characterised the 1980s. Our data show that single parents fared slightly worse than couples with children during the recession itself (1991-95), but while couples saw improvements after 1995, single parents did not. Finally, the data show that single persons without children fared the worst of all, and that persons over 64 years old - old-age pensioners - were the only ones more or less protected from the fall in income during the deep recession.[2]

Table 1.3.1a   Mean equivalent disposable income* for children 0-17 years old. Ratio to the social assistance norm with housing costs. 1980 and 1991-1998

	1980	1991	1992	1993	1994	1995	1996	1997	1998	Percentage change			
										1995/ 1991	1998/ 1995	1998/ 1991	1998/ 1980
Children													
Children 0-7 years	1.485	1.751	1.731	1.611	1.613	1.543	1.535	1.634	1.642	-11.9	6.4	-6.2	10.6
Children 8-17 years	1.531	1.966	1.878	1.755	1.797	1.655	1.662	1.714	1.708	-15.8	3.2	-13.1	11.6
Children 0-17 years	1.514	1.867	1.810	1.686	1.709	1.601	1.601	1.677	1.679	-14.3	4.9	-10.1	10.9
Sweden	1.682	2.043	1.994	1.867	1.925	1.801	1.826	1.897	1.858	-11.8	3.2	-9.1	10.5

* The tax-reform of 1990-91 broadened the income-tax base by on average about 5%. The change affected mainly persons in the higher deciles. For this reason measured income is not fully comparable before and after the reform.

Table 1.3.1b   Relative income of children 0-17 years old. 1980 and 1991-1998

Relative Income of children to:	1980	1991	1992	1993	1994	1995	1996	1997	1998
All	90.0	91.4	90.8	90.3	88.8	88.9	87.7	88.4	90.4
Singles 0 children	89.5	103.3	102.0	105.3	105.5	103.7	101.9	105.4	110.2
Couples 0 children	67.1	65.4	65.9	65.3	62.3	63.6	62.2	61.5	63.2
HH over 64 years old	103.5	105.6	99.9	96.7	91.5	91.1	88.7	92.4	95.4

5. A closer look at the distribution of child income

In this section we look at how child income developed in the various quintiles of the distribution during the 1990s. Before looking at the observed values we perform a thought experiment and look at how large child income would have been at various parts of the income distribution if there had been no public sector transfers or income taxes. This enables us to investigate to what extent inequality increasing forces have come from the labour market and the capital market. The major part of factor income is wages and salaries. However, factor income also includes interest, dividends and net capital gains. Many households in Sweden had capital gains from the increase in stock market values of equities in the 1990s, and those gaining were largely people with medium high or high earnings.

In 1991, in the first quintile, child income derived from factor income was only a little over one-third of the social assistance norm for children 0-7 years. Figure 1.3.2a shows that it had dropped two-thirds by 1994, where it more or less remained through 1996. In 1998 first quintile income had increased to a level around two-thirds of that in 1991. Both the fall and the subsequent gain reflect largely, then, the relative employment success of younger parents.

The story for the first quintile of factor income among school-age children is similar. At the outset of the recession in 1991, the factor income of the first quintile of households with school-age children was about half that needed to reach the social assistance norm. It dropped by about half during the recession and began to slowly move upwards in 1997-98.

Turning to the rest of the distribution, we note first that factor income for non-school-age children is right on the social assistance norm in quintile 2, but is increasingly higher in the three higher quintiles. The factor income of school-age children is higher than that of non-school-age children in all of quintiles 2-5, once again reflecting the earnings curve.

Average factor income in quintiles 2-5 for non-school-age children fell during the recession, but turned up in 1995. Average income in quintile 2 was close to the social assistance norm to start out with, but dropped below the norm in 1993-96. This quintile was once again above the norm in 1997-98, but still below its level for 1991. The average factor income for families with school-age children in quintiles 2-5 fell through 1995, and then turned up, albeit with quintiles 2-5 ending up slightly worse off in 1998 than in 1991. We can also note that for both groups factor income in quintile 5 was higher in 1997 than in 1998, which can be traced back to realised capital gains.

What happens when we put taxes and transfers into the picture, and examine average real disposable income? Disposable income was above the social assistance norm in all quintiles in 1991. For both under-school-age and school-age groups it fell gradually below the norm for quintile 1 as the recession progressed. In fact, both quintile 1 groups were still slightly below the norm in 1998, well after the recovery. Average disposable income in all quintiles was lower in 1995 than in 1991, and with one exception (quintile 5 with children 0-7) had not regained its 1991 level even by 1998. The results for quintiles 3-5 for families with children 8-17 suggest a considerable redistribution of income to other groups. The data show that whereas there was a considerable difference in average disposable income between families with younger and older children in 1991, there was not much difference in 1998. This reflected relative gains in factor income for younger families in quintiles 3-5, and the increased impact of direct taxes on the highest quintiles - especially quintile 5 with older children. The analysis indicates that, to a large extent, transfers and income taxes reduced the inequality generating forces coming from the market. This can be tested formally by computing inequality indices. Here, we examine the Gini-coefficient for each year and under-school-age and school-age children. The results are reported in Table 1.3.2. Clearly there is a tendency towards increased inequality among families with children 0-7 years. The Gini-coefficient for children 0-7 was 2.9 percentage units higher in 1998 compared to 1991. (Index values for 1997 were influenced by a large realisation of capital gains in that year.) By the end of the period the Gini-coefficient indicated about the same degree of inequality for non-school-age and school-age children. There was no notable tendency towards changed inequality for families with school-age children.[3]

Overall, it can be concluded that the Swedish welfare state was relatively successful in keeping inequality in child income from changing during the deep recession of the 1990s, albeit inequality did increase among younger families, owing mainly to relative improvements in the factor income in the highest quintiles. It is interesting to note in this context that, in an international comparison, inequality in child income in Sweden is low. Oxley *et al.* (2001) report that, together with Denmark, Sweden has the lowest child income inequality in the mid-1990s. The same study also notes that child income inequality in Sweden is small in comparison to inequality within the entire population.

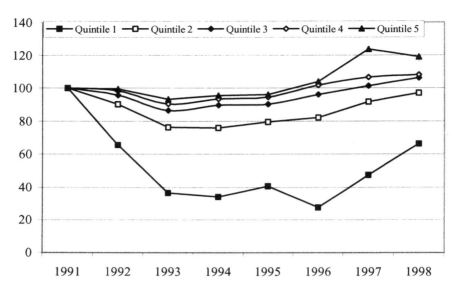

Figure 1.3.2a   Quintile values for factor income among children 0-7 years. Index 1991=100. 1991-1998

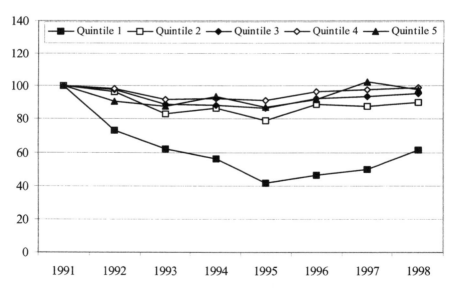

Figure 1.3.2b   Quintile values for factor income among children 8-17 years. Index 1991=100. 1991-1998

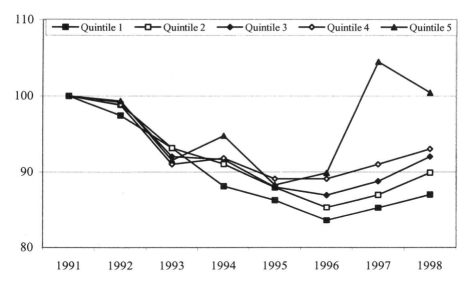

Figure 1.3.3a   Quintile values for equivalent disposable income among children 0-7 years. Index 1991=100. 1991-1998

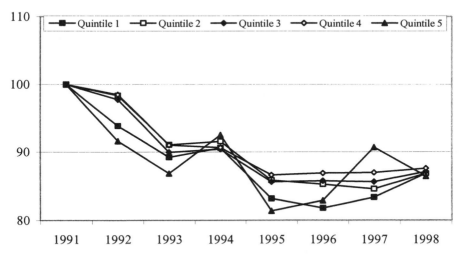

Figure 1.3.3b   Quintile values for equivalent disposable income among children 8-17 years. Index 1991=100. 1991-1998

Table 1.3.2 **Gini-coefficient for equivalent disposable income for children 0-7 and 8-17 years of age. 1991-1998**

	0-7 years of age	8-17 years of age
1991	0.178	0.212
1992	0.181	0.200
1993	0.174	0.202
1994	0.192	0.215
1995	0.182	0.202
1996	0.193	0.209
1997	0.224	0.230
1998	0.207	0.209

6. Single parents and their children

Generally, results from recent comparative research indicate that poverty among single parent households is a considerably less serious problem in Sweden than in other countries. In fact, in a recent study by Bradbury and Jäntti (2001) lone mothers in Sweden had the lowest relative poverty rate in the 25 countries examined. In a study comparing Italy, the United Kingdom and Sweden, Solera (2001) shows that the fact that most single parents in Sweden are employed while those in UK are not is a very important reason why the poverty rate among single parents is much lower in Sweden. Generous transfers, on the other hand, constitute the main reason why single parent poverty in Sweden is lower than in Italy.

While the economic welfare of single parent families in Sweden appears to be good in international comparisons, this is not the entire story. Health of lone mothers in Sweden is poor, as in Britain. Whitehead *et al.* (2000) find that the magnitude of the differential between lone mothers and mothers living with partners is of the same magnitude in both countries. We also know that single parents were hit harder in Sweden by rising unemployment in the first half of the 1990s than most other groups. For example, Lundborg (2000) shows that, while about ten per cent of single parents were unemployed in 1990, almost a third were unemployed in 1997. This can be compared with an increase in unemployment among couples with children from about five per cent in 1990 to about ten per cent in 1994. In addition, single parents in Sweden have a lower probability than married parents of finding a new job in the 1990s. Nordmark (2000) finds that this can be attributed in part to the fact that single parents are less well educated.

Table 1.3.3 shows the distribution of factor income of single parent households. The first quintile has practically no factor income, and factor income is so low in quintiles 2-3 that it is generally not sufficient to push these households over the social assistance norm. Only quintiles 4-5 are self-sufficient in this sense. The first quintile lost what little factor income it had during the recession, and the second quintile dropped dramatically, as the level was down by about half already in 1993. The trend for the second quintile was downwards all the way through 1997, at which point it appears to have turned back up. Still in 1998 the level of average factor income in the second quintile was 26 per cent lower than in 1991. Factor income for single parent families in quintiles 3-5 fell by less and, as opposed to quintiles 1-2, had recovered fully by 1998.

Table 1.3.3   Mean factor income for single parent households in quintiles. Ratio to the social assistance norm with housing costs. 1991-1998

	Quintile 1	Quintile 2	Quintile 3	Quintile 4	Quintile 5
1991	0.037	0.491	0.974	1.424	2.399
1992	0.021	0.385	1.016	1.448	2.527
1993	-0.026	0.257	0.832	1.277	2.257
1994	-0.005	0.149	0.748	1.262	2.081
1995	0.008	0.264	0.807	1.283	2.176
1996	-0.004	0.198	0.864	1.471	2.530
1997	-0.003	0.187	0.847	1.377	2.243
1998	0.009	0.365	1.002	1.485	2.390

Turning to the average disposable income of single parents the picture is much better. First, we can note that only quintiles 4-5 rose above the social assistance norm on the basis of their own earnings. With the help of net transfers, however, quintiles 2 and 3 are also clearly above this norm. Quintile 1 is not, although net transfers bring their level up to 85-90 per cent of the norm. Second, while the second quintile in the distribution of factor income experienced a rapid deterioration of its resources during the first years of the recession, disposable income declined only moderately (for example 13 per cent from 1991 to 1995). Transfers also cushioned the fall in disposable resources for the higher quintiles.

Table 1.3.4   Mean equivalent disposable income for single parent households in quintiles. Ratio to the social assistance norm with housing costs. 1991-1998

	Quintile 1	Quintile 2	Quintile 3	Quintile 4	Quintile 5
1991	0.933	1.310	1.450	1.604	2.153
1992	1.026	1.326	1.484	1.655	2.315
1993	0.897	1.230	1.374	1.520	2.019
1994	0.832	1.158	1.331	1.500	1.974
1995	0.845	1.140	1.295	1.447	1.934
1996	0.859	1.133	1.298	1.456	2.045
1997	0.849	1.125	1.277	1.435	1.822
1998	0.904	1.146	1.291	1.433	1.863

The good news is thus that the disposable income of single parents was not hit harder than that of other groups in the recession of 1991-95. They were well insulated by net transfers. The bad news is that they have not participated to the same extent as other groups in the recovery of the labour market in the second half of the 1990s, the result being that a larger proportion of single parents and their children remained dependent on public transfers.

7. Child poverty

In this section we take a look at child poverty. There is no official poverty line in Sweden. To study 'poverty', two different approaches are normally used, and both are examined in this study. This will show that the choice of approach matters very much.

First, following the approach used in most comparative research, the poverty line can be defined as a fraction of median or mean income of the entire population examined. In much comparative research the poverty line is set at 50 per cent of the median of overall equivalent income. This is a relative measure. It means that the general level of income in a country does not affect the poverty assessment. What matters is only the shape of the income distribution. We have observed a weak tendency for inequality in child income to increase in Sweden during the 1990s. Using this relative-poverty approach there is only a weak tendency towards increased child poverty in Sweden, as Table 1.3.5 shows. For example the relative child poverty rate increased from 3.4 per cent in 1991 to 4.4 per cent in 1994, and was at 4.2 in 1997-98. Thus, Sweden continued to have a fairly low child poverty rate according to this measure.[4]

While child poverty rates defined using the relative approach have increased in some countries in the 1990s, this is not the case for Sweden. In fact, the proportion of children falling below 50 per cent of the median in 1998 was very close to that observed about twenty years earlier in 1980. However, this is not the entire story. There is a long run tendency for transfers to be ever more important for children in Sweden to escape poverty, as we have already noted above for the development in the 1990s. This can also be seen in Table 1.3.5 where we make the thought experiment of setting all transfers and income taxes equal to zero and then compute how many children fall under the poverty line for a specific year. We find 14 per cent in 1980. From this we conclude that transactions with the public sector had thus taken ten per cent of the children out of poverty. In 1991, 16 per cent of children would have fallen under the poverty line without public net transfers, and the fraction increased to 21 per cent in 1993, when the unemployment rate had reached its highest level. The poverty-reducing effect of public transfers increased during the recession, holding poverty low. In 1997-98, once again, factor income (earnings) began to become more important.

Table 1.3.5   Proportion of children 0-17 years falling under 50 per cent of median of equivalent disposable income. Factor income and equivalent disposable income. 1980 and 1991-1998

	Factor income	Equivalent disposable income	Difference: factor income - equivalent disposable income
1980	13.8	3.7	10.1
1991	19.5	3.4	16.1
1992	22.1	3.7	18.4
1993	24.6	3.6	21.0
1994	24.3	4.4	19.9
1995	24.8	3.8	21.0
1996	23.7	4.5	19.2
1997	21.5	4.2	17.3
1998	20.8	4.2	16.6
Difference 1995/1991	5.3	0.4	
Difference 1998/1996	-4.0	0.4	
Difference 1998/1991	1.3	0.8	
Difference 1998/1980	7.0	0.5	

In times of strong changes in average income the relative poverty approach means that the purchasing power of the poverty line changes. In periods of rapid growth the poverty line grows rapidly too, and vice versa, as in Sweden during the recession of the 1990s. Consequently, the finding that child poverty has increased in such circumstance need not mean more than that children in the bottom of the distribution are experiencing slower increases than others.[5] For this reason, it might be more reasonable to apply a poverty line with constant in purchasing power. This is also the approach taken when computing official estimates of poverty in the United States.[6] Following this approach we base the poverty line on the recommendation issued by the Swedish National Board of Health and Social Welfare for scales used in processing social assistance applications (see Gustafsson, 2000 for a more detailed explanation).

Table 1.3.6 Proportion of children 0-17 years falling under 75, 100 and 125 per cent of Swedish national board of health and welfare's poverty line. Factor income and equivalent disposable income. 1980 and 1991-1998

	Factor income			Equivalent disposable income			Difference: Factor income - equivalent disposable income		
	< 0.75	< 1.00	< 1.25	< 0.75	< 1.00	< 1.25	< 0.75	< 1.00	< 1.25
1980	12.9	18.4	29.6	3.2	10.4	29.3	9.7	8.0	0.3
1991	15.0	20.9	28.9	1.5	4.7	12.8	13.5	16.2	16.1
1992	17.1	23.5	31.7	1.9	5.1	13.4	15.2	18.4	18.3
1993	21.1	28.3	38.0	2.2	6.7	18.6	18.9	21.6	19.4
1994	21.6	27.8	36.4	2.8	7.6	20.2	18.8	20.2	16.2
1995	22.2	29.6	37.4	2.6	8.3	24.5	19.6	21.3	12.9
1996	21.6	26.5	33.9	2.6	9.6	27.1	19.0	16.9	6.8
1997	19.6	25.5	32.5	2.7	9.9	26.2	16.9	15.6	6.3
1998	18.1	24.6	30.9	2.4	8.6	23.0	15.7	16.0	7.9
Difference 1995/1991	7.2	8.7	8.5	1.1	3.6	11.7			
Difference 1998/1995	-4.1	-5.0	-6.5	-0.2	0.3	-1.5			
Difference 1998/1991	3.1	3.7	2.0	0.9	3.9	10.2			
Difference 1998/1980	5.2	6.2	1.3	-0.8	-1.8	-6.3			

We have seen that average child income fell substantially in Sweden during the 1990s, and that there was some tendency towards increased inequality in child income. The first change should lead to more and more children being pushed under a poverty line specified as a constant basket of goods. This is also what is reported in Table 1.3.6. While 4.7 per cent of the children were considered as poor in 1991 the proportion increased yearly until 1997 when it was as high as 9.9 per cent. In fact, child poverty measured in this way thus doubled and reached a level close to that in 1980, which is of course a very disappointing development. It means that gains in the reduction of child poverty during the 1980s were wiped out during the 1990s.

It is also interesting to compare the change in the child poverty rate defined as above with what happened with child poverty in the United States, keeping in mind that we now apply the same procedure for updating the line. While child poverty in Sweden doubled from 1991 to 1997 it fell by one quarter in the USA during the same number of years from 1992 to 1999 (Freeman, 2000).[7] As income inequality in the United States did not show large changes towards decreases (rather the opposite), this difference between the two countries must be the outcome of a much more favourable change in average child income in the US during the 1990s, compared to Sweden.

More can be said on the basis of the information in Table 1.3.6. First, the estimated number of poor is rather sensitive for relatively small changes in the level of the poverty line. There are many children living in a household having disposable income only marginally lower or higher than the poverty line. Reducing the level of the poverty line by 25 per cent leaves us with a very low proportion of poor, while increasing it by 25 per cent more than doubles the fraction. Comparing how the time series develops we find the largest changes (both evaluated as percentage and percentage points) for the most generous alternative, and the smallest for the less generous alternative. While 13 per cent of the children were under 125 per cent of the poverty line in 1991 the proportion had increased to 27 per cent in 1996.

We can also make the same kind of thought experiment as in Table 1.3.3 by replacing the observed disposable income by factor income and see how many children were taken out of poverty by public sector transfers and how this proportion has changed over time. Again we find that the poverty reducing effects were rather large in the beginning of the 1990s. However, as the recovery of the economy took place the poverty reducing effect became smaller, and the effect of factor income greater.

This pattern is particularly true for the number of children falling under 125 per cent of the poverty line. In 1993, without transfer payments, 38 per cent of all children would have been in poverty with the 125 per cent definition. However, the observed rate was 18 per cent, a difference of 20 percentage points. By 1998 the economy had recovered so much that 31 per cent of children would have been in poverty with the 125 per cent definition. However, after transfers, the rate was 23 per cent, which is actually higher than in 1993.

8. Why inequality in child income changed so little

Why was the change in the inequality in child income so small in the deep recession of the 1990s? The frame for the analysis is slightly different from that in the previous sections, as we will restrict the analysis to people living in households whose head is age 25-54. We will examine changes in the distribution measured by the Gini-coefficient.

Table 1.3.7 reports the various income sources for the years 1975, 1991 and 1998 - the level, their relative shares of equivalent disposable income and their concentration coefficients based and the contribution of each source of disposable income to total income inequality in a particular year (see Rao, 1969; Pyatt et al., 1989 for the methodology).

The largest share is accounted for, not surprisingly, by the earnings of men, followed by the earnings of women and capital income.[8] The highest concentration coefficients are reported for capital income during 1991 and 1998. All concentration coefficients are larger than the Gini-coefficient. In other words, all three components are inequality increasing. However, for female earnings the difference between the concentration coefficient and the Gini-coefficient in 1991 and 1998 is small, indicating neutrality.

Next we look at taxes and transfer. We distinguish between transfers subject to income taxes, other transfers and income taxes. 'Other' (non-taxed) transfers consist mainly of child allowances and non-taxed, but means-tested social assistance and housing allowances. Unemployment compensation is an important taxable transfer, which made up only 0.6 per cent of equivalent disposable income in 1975 but 6.4 per cent in 1998.

Table 1.3.7 Decomposition of equivalent disposable income (EDI) by source in families with household head 25-54 years of age. 1975, 1991 and 1998

	1975				1991				1998			
	Ratio to social assistance norm with housing	Per cent of EDI	Gini- and concentration -coefficient	Contribution to Gini-coefficient	Ratio to social assistance norm with housing	Per cent of EDI	Gini- and concentration -coefficient	Contribution to Gini-coefficient	Ratio to social assistance norm with housing	Per cent of EDI	Gini- and concentration -coefficient	Contribution to Gini-coefficient
Factor income	2.065	132.2	0.280	0.370	2.438	113.4	0.333	0.378	2.384	125.5	0.365	0.458
Earnings of men	1.412	90.4	0.236	0.213	1.401	65.2	0.327	0.213	1.382	72.7	0.375	0.273
Earnings of women	0.567	36.3	0.380	0.138	0.785	36.5	0.253	0.092	0.822	43.3	0.292	0.126
Capital income	0.086	5.5	0.342	0.019	0.252	11.7	0.614	0.072	0.180	9.5	0.620	0.059
Taxable transfers	0.135	8.7	0.083	0.007	0.356	16.5	-0.012	-0.002	0.342	18.0	-0.127	-0.023
Pensions	0.027	1.7	0.022	0.000	0.070	3.3	0.091	0.003	0.068	3.6	-0.015	-0.001
Unemployment	0.009	0.6	-0.191	-0.001	0.056	2.6	-0.172	-0.004	0.121	6.4	-0.236	-0.015
Others	0.099	6.3	0.126	0.008	0.229	10.7	-0.004	0.000	0.153	8.0	-0.091	-0.007
Untaxed transfers	0.123	7.9	-0.255	-0.020	0.176	8.2	-0.307	-0.025	0.166	8.7	-0.346	-0.030

Table 1.3.7 (continued)

	1975				1991				1998			
	Ratio to social assistance norm with housing	Per cent of EDI	Gini- and concentration-coefficient	Contribution to Gini-coefficient	Ratio to social assistance norm with housing	Per cent of EDI	Gini- and concentration-coefficient	Contribution to Gini-coefficient	Ratio to social assistance norm with housing	Per cent of EDI	Gini- and concentration-coefficient	Contribution to Gini-coefficient
General	0.084	5.4	-0.198	-0.011	0.137	6.4	-0.246	-0.016	0.121	6.4	-0.239	-0.015
Means tested	0.039	2.5	-0.376	-0.009	0.038	1.8	-0.528	-0.009	0.045	2.4	-0.636	-0.015
Total transfers	0.258	16.5	-0.078	-0.013	0.531	24.7	-0.110	-0.027	0.508	26.7	-0.199	-0.053
Gross income	2.323	148.7	0.241	0.358	2.969	138.1	0.254	0.351	2.892	152.2	0.266	0.405
Taxes	-0.761	-48.7	0.331	-0.161	-0.820	-38.1	0.324	-0.124	-0.992	-52.2	0.327	-0.171
EDI	1.562	100.0	0.196	0.196	2.149	100.0	0.227	0.227	1.900	100.0	0.234	0.234
Number of persons	4 966 739				5 336 586				5 373 390			
No. of observations	22 690				15 291				15 637			

The concentration coefficients for the various transfers at each point in time are all lower than the Gini coefficient, and many are negative. This means they are inequality decreasing. Table 1.3.7 also shows that the concentration coefficients vary considerably across the various transfers. The largest negative concentration coefficient is not surprisingly for means tested transfers, i.e. housing benefits and social assistance. These are thus the benefits that most strongly helped decrease inequality.

Turning finally to income taxes, we find that the concentration coefficient is higher than for disposable income. This means people at the top of the distribution pay a larger proportion of their income in taxes compared to those at the bottom of the distribution, which reflects the progressive construction of the Swedish tax-system.

Based on this decomposition we can now ask how different income sources have contributed to keeping the Gini-coefficient stable. Each component can affect the development through changed relative share as well as through a changed concentration coefficient. The development of the Gini-coefficient from 1991 to 1998 can be followed between each pair of years. The decomposition gives numbers on concentration coefficients and relative shares for each component each year under study. We organise the information in Figure 1.3.4, which shows how the three components of market income have affected the development in the Gini-coefficient for disposable equivalent income with 1991 as base year, and Figure 1.3.5, which provides the corresponding information for various transfer payments and income taxes.

According to Figure 1.3.4 earnings of both females males pushed the Gini-coefficient upwards and with roughly equal force. There was a temporary halt in the expansion in 1994 just when the unemployment rate started to go down, and changes since 1996 are small. Comparing years 1991 and 1998 we find that male earnings as well as female earnings make up larger shares of average disposable equivalent income the latter year, and in addition, we see that their concentration coefficients have both increased.

The development of capital income has also had an effect on income inequality. This component is responsible for spikes observed in the data series for year 1994 and 1997 and can in the data be traced to realised capital gains. However, there is much less of a trend in how this component has affected inequality as measured by the Gini-coefficient.

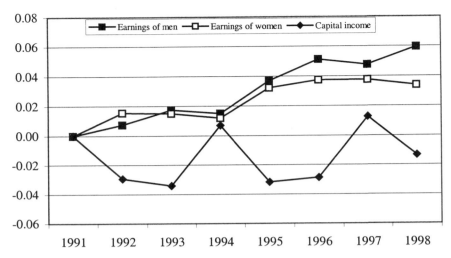

Figure 1.3.4 **Contributions to changes in the Gini-coefficient in families with household head 25-54 years of age since 1991-1998**

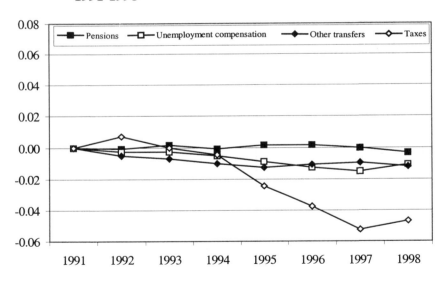

Figure 1.3.5 **Contribution to changes in the Gini-coefficient in families with household head 25-54 years of age since 1991-1998**

We now turn to how changes in transfers have affected the development of the Gini-coefficient. Out of the four components all but pensions (disability and survivor benefits), which had a more or less neutral effect, contributed towards counterbalancing increases in income inequality. Unemployment compensation and other transfers both worked towards less inequality up to the mid-1990s. The effect of income taxes came later, in the phase of moving towards a budget surplus. The figure shows that from 1994 to 1997 the effect of income taxes was to forcefully reduce income inequality, which we have also concluded in Gustafsson and Palmer (2001). The increased income inequality reducing effect of income taxes reflects an increase in taxes pressure. As can be computed from Table 1.3.7, in 1998, households with a head 25-54 years old paid 37 per cent more in income taxes compared to year 1991. During the same period their disposable equivalent income decreased by 12 per cent.

9. Conclusions

Using data from the Household Income Survey we have analysed what happened with the economic well-being of children in Sweden during the 1990s, a period with declining national income and a dramatic increase in unemployment, followed by recovery. There are several conclusions to draw.

First, we have shown that the loss of child income during the recession of the 1990s was much more severe than that experienced at the end of the 1970s and beginning of the 1980s. The largest loss occurred when employment fell and unemployment increased rapidly in the first half of the 1990s. This was followed by a brief phase during which public programmes directed at child support were cut back.

Strikingly, although it improved after 1996, average child income in 1998 was still ten per cent lower than in 1991, when average child income was not substantially higher than in 1980. Although the child poverty situation in 1998 was not very different from that in 1980 there was one important change. In 1998 a larger proportion of families with children depended on public transfers to escape poverty. Income from work played a larger role in 1980. In this sense income marginalisation has increased among children in Sweden.

Second, the drop in income during the period studied was not unique for families with children. Old-age pensioners were winners, as their income was hardly affected by the recession. Among households under 64, winners and losers were to be found in another dimension - namely those within and outside the labour market

This leads to the third conclusion. The lower part of the child income distribution was strongly affected by decreased earnings. Increased joblessness was a strong force working towards increased inequality in child income through this mechanism. However, to a large extent public sector transfers counteracted this development, especially during the first phase of the process. Nevertheless, there was a tendency for inequality in child income to increase, especially among households with younger children. During the recovery, income taxes played a large role in keeping inequality in child income from increasing more - by reducing the income of the wealthiest.

A fourth conclusion is that, although the economic situation of single parents in Sweden continues to be good in international comparisons, as in many other countries there are clear signs of developing storm clouds. The labour market situation of single parents deteriorated more and for a longer period during the 1990s than for other parents, which other evidence suggests is connected with the relatively low educational level of single parents.

The fifth conclusion is that if Sweden were to adopt an official goal of reducing child poverty, how the goal is formulated can make a difference. Applying a relative approach in defining the poverty line makes the child poverty record of the 1990s look far from alarming. However, this means the fact that average income fell is disregarded. Instead, based on a poverty line representing the same purchasing power throughout the decade, the situation looks rather alarming. This measure of child poverty actually doubled during the studied period, while the same sort of measuring rod shows that child poverty in, for example, the United States decreased substantially in the same period. This suggests that the economist's usual medicine for alleviating poverty, economic growth and increased labour force participation, places transfers in a position of second best.

Notes

1   There are also other changes in methodology over the years, for example sample size has changed. However, most likely they are of less importance for the results.

2   Oxley *et al.* (2001) report that average child income in Sweden (in real terms) increased by 7.8 per cent from 1983 to 1995. This percentage is similar to what can be obtained from our data. Thus, the severe reduction during the 1990s was smaller than the preceding increase from the mid-1980s through 1990.

3   We have also computed the Theil index and the MLD index. The results show that while the three indices do not always move in the same direction from one year to another, they show the same pattern.

4   Our estimate of relative child poverty for 1992 (3.7 per cent) is identical to the one of Bradbury and Jäntti (2001). While Oxley *et al.* (2001) report a relative poverty rate for Sweden 1995 of 2.7 per cent, our estimate for the same year is 3.8 per cent.

5   See for example Nolan (2001) who discusses how poverty in Ireland developed during the 1990s using this approach.

6   However, this approach has also been criticised, mainly because during long periods of economic growth a poverty line that represents constant purchasing power runs a risk of becoming outdated. In the middle of the 1990s, a panel at the National Academy of Sciences discussed various issues in changing the official definition. One of their recommendations was to ' ... re-evaluate the official US poverty measure to take account of both a new resource concept and the real growth in consumption that has occurred since the official threshold was first set 30 years ago. ...' (Citro and Michel, 1995, p. 106).

7   It should be understood that, as poverty lines are defined differently, poverty rates are not comparable across countries.

8   In case there is no male/female in the household, the corresponding income source is set equal to zero for this household. Capital income includes imputed rents from owner occupied housing, interests, dividends, as well as capital gains.

References

Bradbury, B. and Jäntti, M. (2001) 'Child Poverty Across the Industralised World: Evidence from the Luxembourg Income Study', in Vleminckx, K. and Smeeding, T. (eds), *Child Well-Being, Child Poverty and Child Policies in Modern Nations*, Policy Press, Bristol.

Citro, C. and Michael, R. (1995) *Measuring Poverty. A New Approach*, National Academy Press, Washington DC.

Freeman, R. (2000) 'The Rising Tide Lifts...?', *Focus*, vol. 21, no. 2, pp. 27-31.

Gustafsson, B. (1987) *Ett decenium av stagnerande realinkomster*, Statistics Sweden Levnadsförhållanden Rapport 54, Stockholm.

Gustafsson, B. (2000) 'Poverty in Sweden: Changes 1975-1995, Profile and Dynamics', in Gustafsson, B. and Pedersen, P. (eds), *Poverty and Low Income in the Nordic Countries*, Ashgate, Aldershot.

Gustafsson, B. and Palmer, E. (2001) 'Was the Burden of the Deep Swedish Recession Equally Shared?', Paper to the University of Göteborg and National Social Insurance Board.

Lundborg, P. (2000) 'Nittiotalets förlorare', *Arbetsmarknad & Arbetsliv*, vol. 6, pp. 235-48.

Nolan, B. (2001) 'The Evolution of Child Poverty in Ireland', in Vleminckx, K. and Smeeding, T. (eds), *Child Well-Being, Child Poverty and Child Policies in Modern Nations*, Policy Press, Bristol.

Nordenmark, M. (2000) 'Familjesituation och arbetsmarknadsstatus. Vad förklarar ensamstående föräldrars låga sannolikhet att erhålla ett arbete?', *Arbetsmarknad & Arbetsliv*, vol. 6, pp. 97-111.

Oxley, H., Dong, T-T., Förster, M. and Pellizzasro, M. (2001) 'Income Inequalities and Poverty Among Children and Households With Children in Selected OECD Countries', in Vleminckx, K. and Smeeding, T. (eds), *Child Well-Being, Child Poverty and Child Policies in Modern Nations*, Policy Press, Bristol.

Pyatt, G., Chan, C.N. and Fei, J. (1980) 'The Distribution of Income by Factor Components', *Quarterly Journal of Economics*, vol. 95, pp. 451-73.

Roa, V.M. (1969) 'The Decomposition of the Concentration Coefficient', *Journal of Royal Statistical Society*, vol. 132, pp. 418-25.

Solera, C (2001) 'Income Transfers and Support for Mothers' Employment: The Link to Family Poverty Risks', in Vleminckx, K. and Smeeding, T. (eds), *Child Well-Being, Child Poverty and Child Policies in Modern Nations*, Policy Press, Bristol.

Vleminckx, K. and Smeeding, T. (eds) (2001) *Child Well-Being, Child Poverty and Child Policies in Modern Nations*, Policy Press, Bristol.

Whitehead, M., Burström, B. and Diderichsen, F. (2000) 'Social Policies and the Pathways to Inequalities in Health: A Comparative Analysis of Lone Mothers in Britain and Sweden', *Social Science & Medicine*, vol. 50, pp. 255-70.

1.4 Child poverty à la carte? The effects of measurement period for income on poverty estimates

Bea Cantillon, Rudi Van Dam,
Bart Van Hoorebeeck, Karel Van Den Bosch

Abstract

In Belgium, two main different datasets are used for comparative (child) poverty research. One data source has been providing data for the Luxemburg Income Study since 1985 (further referred as LIS-Belgium). Another has provided data for the European Community Household Panel since 1994 (hereafter ECHP-Belgium). Using the same poverty thresholds and equivalence scales, poverty estimates differ strongly according to the different sources.

In this paper we explore possible reasons for these differences. We consider sampling, methods of data collection, household definitions, income components and measurement periods for income and data treatment. We find the most important structural difference being the period for income measurement.

Contrary to what one expects in theory we find that yearly incomes are more unequally spread than monthly incomes. This is probably due to measurement errors (non-response and inconsistencies), which are more substantial in the yearly income measurement of ECHP-Belgium than in the monthly approach of LIS-Belgium. In addition, the impact of imputation procedures, which differ for the two data sources, is very significant.

How many children are poor in Belgium?

The starting point of this paper is the measurement of the child poverty rates in Belgium, on the basis of three datasets resulting from two different data sources. The first set is the Belgian Socio-Economic Panel (BSEP, which has been providing data for the LIS since 1985 (hereafter LIS-Belgium). The second is the Panel Study of Belgian Households PSBH).

The final source is the Belgian contribution to the European Community Household Panel (hereafter ECHP-Belgium). Data for the ECHP-Belgium originates from the PSBH. The difference between the two related datasets lies in the data treatment (weighting and imputation procedure): the PSBH is treated by a Belgian research team, while the ECHP is processed by Eurostat.

We use the Eurostat-procedures, in which the poverty line is set at 50 or 60 per cent of the overall median disposable household income, standardised according to the modified OECD-scale, whereby every additional adult (14 years and above) is equated to 0.5 and every younger child to 0.3. Subsequently, in order to calculate child poverty rates, all individuals under the age of 18 were filtered out of the data.[1]

Table 1.4.1   Child poverty* rates in Belgium according to different sources (%)

	1992	1993	1994	1995	1996	1997
PSBH						
50% median	5.5			10.2		
60% median	13.7			16		
LIS-Belgium						
50% median	4.4					7.3
60% median	12.3					13.4
ECHP-Belgium						
50% median		11.4	10.9	12.7	11.8	
60% median		18.9	19.3	21	16.2	

* Child poverty rate is defined as the relative number of persons under 18 years of age, living in a household with a standardised household income below the overall poverty line.

Table 1.4.1 indicates that LIS-Belgium recorded an increase in child poverty between 1992 and 1997 especially if one applies the 50 per cent of the median income poverty line. The ECHP-Belgium figures 1993-1996 do not hint at a trend, but they yield a considerably higher poverty rate throughout.

Such discrepancies in findings regarding child poverty are not unique to Belgium.[2] In Table 1.4.2, child poverty rates and consequent ranking are compared for those countries where both ECHP and LIS data are available. The threshold applied in the LIS-figures is 50 per cent of the median poverty line, while in the ECHP estimates the poverty line is 60 per cent of the median. ECHP-figures are based on the modified OECD-scale standardisation. Consequently, child poverty as measured by ECHP is typically 1.5 to 2 times higher than LIS-estimates. However, in Belgium, Luxemburg and Austria the child poverty rate according to LIS figures is three times higher, while Danish child poverty registered by ECHP is *lower* than the LIS-registration. In other words, the ranking of countries vary for the two measurement methods. The discrepancy between the respective rankings is most significant for Belgium, the Netherlands and Austria.

Table 1.4.2   Child poverty figures in 12 European countries according to ECHP and LIS

Country	% ECHP	Rank ECHP	% LIS	Rank LIS
Belgium	20	5	6.1	9
Denmark	5	12	5.9	10
Germany	20	5	11.6	5
Spain	24	2	13.1	4
France	19	7	9.8	6
Ireland	24	2	14.8	3
Italy	23	4	21.2	2
Luxemburg	18	9	6.3	8
Netherlands	15	10	8.4	7
Austria	19	7	5.6	11
Finland	8	11	3.4	12
United Kingdom	25	1	21.3	1

Sources: Dirven *et al.* (2000), who provide ECHP-figures for 1995 (using 60 per cent of the median net available household income poverty line); Bradbury and Jäntti (1999), who offer figures from the most recent LIS wave available to them, varying form 1989 to 1995 depending on the country (with 50 per cent of the median net available household income poverty line).

Table 1.4.3 provides a further indication of differences in income measurement. According to these figures, overall mean household incomes, income inequality and poverty rates are considerably higher according to ECHP-Belgium than LIS-Belgium. However, LIS-Belgium uses a higher standardised median household income and therefore higher poverty thresholds.

Robustness assessment report of the data sources

Results of different surveys may diverge because of sample designs, sample fluctuations, non-response, data treatment and divergent questions designs. They may also diverge simply because of *sample fluctuations*. Sampling merely allows one to draw conclusions about a characteristic of the population with a certain degree of (un)reliability. The accuracy and reliability of sample-based estimates depends primarily on the sample size and design. There are, however, other elements that may cause survey results to vary. Such factors as the research objectives, the design of the fieldwork, the expertise and supervision of the interviewers, the length and the adequacy of the questionnaire, and the processing of the data may affect the quality of the measurement or the representativeness of the sample, and can thus give rise to divergent results.

An important aspect of surveys is the degree of non-response. Almost inevitably, a number of interviewees will not participate in the survey, or they may be either unreachable or untraceable. First and foremost, this implies fewer available cases, and therefore less efficient sample-based estimates. Moreover, to the extent that *non-response* is selective, i.e. that its occurrence within a specific category is more than proportional, it will provide biased estimates. This problem is particularly apparent in panel surveys, as with each wave there is inevitably some attrition. In order to correct for non-response biases, weighting factors are to be incorporated (each respondent is allocated a certain weight which is inversely proportional to the probability that the respondent will be included in the sample). Certainly in the case of panel surveys, these factors can be estimated fairly accurately, as the previous wave will always provide a great deal of information about both the respondents who participated and those who did not. The degree of (selectivity in) attrition and the adequacy of the *weighting procedure* may influence the survey results.

Table 1.4.3 Income and poverty in Belgium according to different sources

	PSBH 92*	LIS-Be 92	ECHP-Be 93	ECHP-Be 94	ECHP-Be 95	ECHP-Be 96	LIS-Be 97
Measured income volume (bill.fr.)	3.600	3.683	4.574	4.578	4.203	4.425	3.994
Household income							
- mean	910.783	938.484	1,140.257	1,147.230	1,063.227	1,120.477	1,010.328
- median	803.880	863.832	892.100	907.000	824.814	856.500	873.996
Standard household inc.							
- mean	530.330	521.676	668.287	668.893	656.789	685.757	543.912
- median	479.165	473.004	535.559	538.664	526.338	550.587	492.000
Inequality measurement							
- Gini	24.7%	25.2%	36.9%	39.1%	34.2%	34.1%	24.5%
- D9/D1	2.91	2.86	3.62	3.73	3.55	3.56	3.04
Poverty line (calculated among individuals)							
50% median	242.857	234.000	266.899	276.365	263.847	276.354	279.282
60% median	291.428	280.800	320.297	331.638	316.617	331.625	335.146
Poverty rate with 60% median							
- household	5.6%	10.0%	16.6%	15.3%	15.9%	15.3%	13.0%
- individual	12.4%	10.9%	16.5%	17.4%	16.4%	14.8%	12.6%

* No data on income from capital available

67

It is invariably the case in surveys that a number of respondents fail to answer certain questions. Situations where respondents either refuse or are unable to answer particular questions that apply to them are referred to as *item non-response*. Questions which respondents experience as sensitive or difficult to answer tend to generate greater item non-response. This is often the case with questions about income. Item non-response reduces the number of cases that can be included in the analysis. Moreover, if item non-response is selective, it can give rise to biased estimates. If item non-response is systematically greater within specific population segments (for example, large households, the self-employed, high income households, etc.), it may cause biased income and poverty figures.

For this reason, it is common practice in income surveys to correct by means of so-called *imputation procedures* for item non-response on income variables. In such imputation procedures, a respondent with non-response on an income variable is attributed a value on the basis of (similar) respondents who have indicated an income. There are various imputation procedures of varying quality. The higher item non-response is, the more important the quality of the imputation procedure.

A further problem is that survey results may be disproportionately affected by outliers: for example, very high or low (negative) values for income or other variables. These outliers may simply arise on account of sampling variability, but they may also suggest shortcomings in the data. A self-employed person, for instance, may record a substantial loss in a particular period, but this may merely be a reflection of a particular accounting practice. Large incomes or large losses may be purely transitory. For these reasons, it is a common practice to apply top-coding or bottom-coding to income and other data.

The research objectives, the design of the fieldwork, the expertise and supervision of the interviewers, the length and adequacy of the questionnaire, and the processing of the data may also affect the quality of the measurement or the representativeness of the sample, and can thus also give rise to divergent results.

Given the complexity of income poverty statistics and the degree of error or uncertainty of the results, information about the sample and question design and about weighting and imputation procedures should be made available. To this end the Canberra Group (2001) developed a Robustness Assessment Report (RAR) which encapsulates the information needed to ensure that comparable and consistent information is available on each statistical output from which the user can judge their fitness for purpose. Such RARs were made on on ECHP-Belgium and LIS-Belgium. We indicate the most important conclusions we can draw on the basis of the RARs for Belgium.[3] They are summarised in Figure 1.4.1.

The LIS-B survey is administered by a university-based research centre (CSP-University of Antwerp). The ECHP-B survey, on the other hand, is administered by two university-based research groups: one for the Flemish part of the country (PSBH-University of Antwerp) and one for the Walloon part (PSBH-University of Liège). LIS-B data is treated by the CSP, while ECHP-B data is processed by Eurostat. The methodological characteristics of both surveys are largely identical. In both surveys, a two-stage sampling procedure is used, in which the National Register or population registers serve as the sampling frame. The two samples differ in that, in LIS-B, first stage sampling units are stratified by socio-economic characteristics, while this is not the case in ECHP-B. Both surveys generated a low initial response rate (<50 per cent), which appears to be a common problem in Belgium.[4] In spite of these low response rates, comparison with external data shows no serious representativity problems with regard to socioeconomic and demographic variables. The sampling units and methods of data collection are also identical. The ECHP questionnaire is considerably longer than that used in the LIS-B survey. The main purpose of the latter is to measure income and socio-economic variables, while the ECHP-B questionnaire has a broader scope. It not only collects income data, but also data required in other research fields (for example, sociology of the family, mobility, voluntary work etc.). The two surveys differ fundamentally in terms of the income concept that is measured. LIS-B measures current income (i.e. income for the previous month), while in the ECHP-B survey respondents are asked to report income for the previous calendar year. Both datasets are weighted to correct for differential response probabilities in the successive waves and for differential selection probabilities due to panel follow-up rules. Imputation procedures are applied in either survey to correct for item non-response on the income variables. The procedures used are designed not to reduce the variance.

Comparison of the respective data with external sources indicates that unemployment benefits are underestimated in both surveys: by 35 per cent in LIS-Belgium, and by 19 per cent in ECHP-Belgium. Pensions, disability and family benefits are overestimated in ECHP-Belgium (respectively by 16, 42 and 31 per cent). By contrast, such benefits are slightly underestimated in LIS-Belgium (by 8, 9 and 5 per cent) (see Table 1.4.4).

Estimates of wages are approximately the same in the two sources, but self-employment income is more underestimated in ECHP-Belgium than in LIS-Belgium.

---

1. Sampling: sampling frame is identical. LIS-B: two stage sampling design with stratification of first stage units, ECHP-B: two stage design without stratification of first stage units.
2. Purpose: LIS-B: measurement of income and socio-economic variables and poverty indices is only purpose; ECHP-B questionnaire is designed to cover other research domains besides income and socio-economic and poverty indices.
3. Method and data collection: no major differences.
4. Household definition: no differences.
5. Income components: no differences.
6. Measurement period for income: ECHP-B: N-1 (previous year), LIS-B: current monthly.
7. Data treatment:
   - In general: data treatment of ECHP-B by Eurostat, data treatment of LIS-B by university team CSP.
   - Imputation of household income: full for 4 per cent of households, partial 34.4 per cent in ECHP-Be (1996); in LIS-Be (1997) 55 per cent of the households have some income component imputed, without income from capital this drops to 21 per cent.
8. Employment and demographic patterns as compared with external sources: no major differences.
   Sample size and non-response: ECHP-B (1996) contains 3,210 households, LIS-B (1997) contains 4,632 households, consisting of 2,257 panel households and 2,375 households from a new sample. The initial response rate of the ECHP-B sample was 41 per cent. The initial response rate of the LIS-B sample was not adequately documented but is estimated to be below 40 per cent. The response rate of the supplementary sample was 46 per cent.

Figure 1.4.1   RAR: Major differences between ECHO-Belgium and LIS-Belgium

Not only is there differential income underreporting between survey types, this underreporting can also differ between different countries, and be corrected for by different procedures in any of them. A cross-national comparison could shed more light on this phenomenon and its impact on (child) poverty figures.

Table 1.4.4   Income estimates from LIS-B and ECHP-B as % of amounts from administrative sources

Income	ECHP 1996 (1995) %	ECHP 1997 (1996) %	BSEP 1997 (1997) %
Unemployment benefit	81	83	65
Retirement benefit*	102	116	92
Sick/invalid benefit	129	142	91
Family allowances	120	131	95

* The BSEP retirement amount contains the first pension pillar and early retirement schemes. In the ECHP other retirement schemes are also taken in account.

The higher income estimates in ECHP-Belgium are due to the fact that more people reported such incomes and, in the case of retirement, disability and child benefits also from higher average amounts (Table 1.4.5).

Table 1.4.5   Proportion of people receiving various income components, mean and standard deviation of those components as measured by ECHP-Belgium 1996 and LIS-Belgium 1997

Income	ECHP-Belgium 1996			LIS-Belgium 1997		
	%	mean	st.dev.	%	mean	st.dev
Salary	34.3	584.150	394.298	30.2	643.524	287.184
Self-employment	4	578.440	787.870	5.1	754.548	656.136
Unemployment benefit	7.8	189.671	208.876	5.5	230.484	118.680
Retirement benefit	19	473.385	524.417	18.5	414.876	201.900
Family allowances (among hh.)	34.5	156.102	196.928	36.1	108.072	83.868

Comparison of the grossed-up LIS-B (1997) income data with fiscal statistics shows a close correspondence in average gross income. The survey-average is 101 per cent of the fiscal statistics-average. Comparisons of (simulated) LIS-B gross earnings with data from the National Office of Social Security (RSZ) also show a reasonable correspondance. For private sector employees average gross earnings, as measured in LIS-B, are 107 per cent of the RSZ-data. The difference is somewhat higher for the public sector employees (110 per cent) (Verbist *et al.*, 2001). As the simulation program to gross-up survey net-incomes is not adapted to the ECHP-data, a similar comparison is not (yet) available for these data.[5]

The Robustness Assessment Report indicates that there is little difference between the two surveys in terms of purpose, sampling, method of data collection, household definition and income components between the two surveys. However, the measurement period for income is a potentially significant factor. We shall highlight the impact of this aspect in the following sections.

The observation period: in theoretical perspective

The approaches of LIS-Belgium and ECHP-Belgium differ in terms of the *observation period* that is applied for measuring income. LIS-Belgium gauges monthly incomes, whereas in ECHP-Belgium the observation period is the calendar year prior to the year in which the survey is conducted (N-1).

Theoretically, a longer reference period will result in less income inequality. A short observation period (for example, monthly income) might register coincidental fluctuations which would have been evened out over a longer period. Consider the following example: if a respondent happens to be asked about his monthly income during a short spell of unemployment, the income registered in the survey will be 'unrealistically' low in comparison to his annual income. Conversely, a short observation period may register incomes that are 'exceptionally high' in comparison to the respondent's annual income. Thus, if the objective is to measure income inequality, and if one accepts that the majority of the population is able to spread out its income in order to compensate for a temporary drop in income, then a longer observation period may be called for. Therefore, the Canberra Group recommends that the accounting period to be used for income distribution analyses should be one year.

Which observation period is most appropriate in poverty research will depend on the assumptions made regarding the effect of short-term income fluctuations on the economic well-being of individuals and households. Some households will be able to maintain their consumption level during short spells of lower income by using their savings, by borrowing or postponing some expenditure. However, this is likely to be more problematic for households at the lower end of the income scale. There are empirical indications that persons whose income in a given month is below the poverty line have a limited capacity to dissave. Ruggles and Williams observe in the United States that 'the majority of those with sub-annual spells of poverty are in fact unlikely to be able to maintain their consumption levels, even though their poverty spells may be quite short' (Ruggles and Williams, 1989). This observation suggests that monthly income is a relevant indicator for measuring poverty. If the objective is to determine the number of poor, and assuming that it is more difficult for low-income groups to spread their income out evenly over a year with a view to retaining a minimum level of spending, then it may be more appropriate to observe monthly incomes. Moreover, annual income is not a very useful measure for governments as most benefits are paid in weekly or monthly amounts. Measuring income on a yearly basis will make it difficult to assess to what extent monthly benefits are targeted at low-income households.

An annual income-approach poses serious methodological difficulties, as respondents are often unaware of their overall annual income. As the most important income components (earned income, social transfers) are usually received on a monthly basis, these are the amounts that respondents are most familiar with. Other types of income (such as interests, holiday pay and scholarships) are received annually, so that for these components respondents may be asked to indicate a yearly amount. This can subsequently be calculated back to a monthly sum. These amounts can be incorporated in the monthly income insofar as households may be assumed to take this income into account in their monthly spending. Alternatively, one could conduct a survey that runs through all sources of income for every month during a whole year. This would, however, increase the interview burden considerably. Moreover, such an approach may yield unreliable data.

The observation period in practice: a direct comparison of methods of income data collection

The PSBH offers a unique opportunity to compare the two methods of data collecting. In 1993 (as in 1992), the interviewer mentioned a range of income sources, and asked the respondent whether he/she had received this source of income in the *previous month*. If the answer was affirmative, the interviewer asked the respondent which amount he/she had received. In 1994 the PSBH was incorporated into the ECHP, and the income part of the questionnaire was changed accordingly. The interviewer now asked whether income sources had been received in the *previous calendar year*. If the answer was affirmative, he asked the respondent which monthly amount had been received and for how many months. Consequently, we have at our disposal income data for the same persons, households and year, but collected through different methods. Yet, the measurements are independent of each other in the sense that they were carried out at different in points in time and may therefore be assumed not to have been affected by memory effects and the like. Using this unique database, we were able to formulate a tentative explanation for the unexpected finding that yearly incomes are more unequally distributed than monthly incomes.

The annual approach generates neither higher income volumes nor a more equal distribution of incomes. The overall income volume that is captured by the monthly measurement is some 12 per cent higher than in the case of the annual measurement. Differences are more pronounced for pensions and disability benefits. Volumes of earned income are affected to a lesser degree by the measurement period for income (see Table 1.4.6). For all income components, the standard deviation is higher in the annual approach than in the monthly approach.

These findings are contra-intuitive. As a shorter observation period might be assumed to register coincidental fluctuations which would have been evened out over a longer period, one would expect the annual approach to generate less dispersion than the monthly approach.

Furthermore, the main reason that Eurostat opted for the N-1 annual approach was that it allows respondents to use their annual pay strips or tax declaration at the moment of the interview. It was assumed that this would reduce memory failure and thus increase the captured income volumes.

A possible reason for our contra-intuitive findings is measurement errors. We shall highlight this aspect in the next subsections. First, we shall consider non-response on income questions. Subsequently, we shall look at the degree of consistency between 1993 and 1994 to the filter questions about whether an income source is received at all. In the third subsection, we shall analyse the consistency between both measurement approaches in the amounts given.

Table 1.4.6 **Income volumes for 1993 measured by two methods: (1) income in month prior to the survey *12 and (2) average monthly income in previous calendar year * number of months this income was received, PSBH data, waves 1993 and 1994. Basis = all adults present in both waves (n=6715)**

Sum in 1000000 BEF. (rounded)	Measurement 'month' (1)	Measurement 'year' (2)	Difference (1) / (2)
Labour income *			
- a. (n=2588)	1530.1	1565.3	97.8
- b. (n=3194)	1636.5	1646.5	99.4
- c.	1876.4	1796.8	104.4
	(n=3191)	(n=3226)	
Unemployment benefits			
- a. (n=395)	73.0	67.5	108.1
- b. (n=615)	83.5	84.1	99.3
- c.	100.7	91.3	110.3
	(n=567)	(n=590)	
Pensions			
- a. (n=809)	367.0	325.7	112.7
- b. (n=1028)	402.8	346.2	116.4
- c.	554.0	384.7	144.0
	(n=1291)	(n=985)	
Sickness and disability allowances			
- a. (n=181)	47.4	49.4	95.9
- b. (n=376)	67.2	62.3	108.0
- c.	81.5	66.4	122.9
	(n=328)	(n=297)	
Total income from the above sources			
- a. (n=3586)	1956.1	1954.9	100.1
- b. (n=4033)	2067.5	1976.9	104.6
- c.	2612.7	2339.2	111.7
	(n=4880)	(n=4588)	

a. = sum over all adults with two complete measurements for this item,
b. =sum over all adults with no item non-response on the two measurements and complete income information on at least one of the two measurements
c. = all adults with a complete measurement in one of the two surveys
* Includes wages, salaries, self-employment income, income from secondary job.
Wages and salaries are all net amounts for method (1), in method (2) 95 respondents report only gross amounts. These gross amounts are included in the figures. Consequently method (2) slightly overestimates earned and total income compared with method (1).

Table 1.4.7   Average and median personal income from different sources and standard deviation, 2 methods of income measurement, respondents with two complete measurements on the respective income sources, PSBH data waves 1993 and 1994

	Average		Median		Standard deviation	
	Monthly	Annual	Monthly	Annual	Monthly	Annual
Earned income	591,218	604,821	540,000	540,000	339,825	429,232
Unemployment benefits	184,746	170,928	144,000	138,000	109,466	116,825
Pensions	453,649	402,561	408,000	390,420	277,094	184,664
Sick/invalid	261,922	273,118	258,000	240,000	204,343	484,906
Total income	545,761	545,149	510,000	486,000	335,722	393,640

* 'monthly' and 'annual' refer to the measurement period. In this table the 'monthly' amounts were transformed to annual amounts by multiplying by 12

Non-response

Table 1.4.8 shows that, for most income components (except self-employment), non-response is much higher for yearly incomes than for monthly incomes. In the case of yearly incomes, non-response is recorded when either the amount or the number of months is not given. Except for wages and salaries, item non-response is primarily due to respondent's failure to indicate during how many months the income was received.

Table 1.4.8   Non-response for various income sources* in the monthly and yearly income measurements, PSBH data waves 1993 and 1994

	Monthly (%)	Annual (%)
Wages and salaries	3.8	10.3
Self-employment inc.	24.8	26.1
Unemployment benefit	8.2	24.8
Survivors pension	19.5	29.6
Old-age pension	14.4	29.3
All pension**	9.9	28.5
Sickness and disability allowances	12.3	34.4

* Percentages within groups answering positively to filter questions about the income source; ** Including early retirement pensions.

76

Consistency in answers to the question whether particular income sources were received at all

Consistency requires that a respondent who reports reception of a certain income source for a certain month in 1993 should also mention this income source in 1994. Conversely, a respondent who says in 1994 that he received income from a certain source throughout 1993 should have mentioned this in the 1993 survey. Table 1.4.9 shows the extent of such inconsistencies in respondents' answers. While inconsistencies appear especially significant in relation to self-employment income, they are not negligible in the case of social transfers either. In relative terms, the degree of inconsistency in answers regarding wages and salaries is smaller. However, the absolute number of cases involved is in fact much larger than for any of the other income components.

The income amounts that are undetected in the 1994 (yearly) survey due to these inconsistencies are not negligible. The 1993 monthly income amounts that were 'forgotten' in 1994 are, on average, only slightly smaller than the corresponding income amounts of respondents from whom no inconsistencies were recorded. Likewise, in the case of respondents who reported a particular income in 1994 but failed to do so in 1993, the 'forgotten' amounts are smaller than the corresponding average amounts for respondents without inconsistencies, though here the differences are slightly greater. In any case, the average undetected amounts approximate to the average amounts that were detected. They are, moreover, quite substantial.

Consistency in amounts

As incomes from a particular source may change or fluctuate in the course of a year, differences between the amounts mentioned in 1993 and 1994 are not necessarily indications of inconsistency. Yet, it seemed worthwhile to compare these amounts. For this comparison, we only took account of persons stating an exact amount in both surveys. This implies that we excluded the (rather large) group of persons who did not give an amount, but merely indicated an income bracket.

Table 1.4.10 provides an overview of means and standard deviations for the various income components. At this aggregate level the differences are small.

Table 1.4.9 **Inconsistencies in income reporting: percentage of adults who report an income in one method but not in the other method, PSBH data waves 1993 and 1994**

	All labour income	Wages and salaries	Income from self-employment	Unemployment income	Pension	Disability allowance
A % 'forgotten' incomes in method 2 *	6.6 (3.4)	4.2	35.3	15.7 (1.4)	12.8 (2.7)	29.0 (1.6)
B % 'forgotten' incomes in method 1*	3.1 (1.7)	4.7	20.7*	5.2 (0.6)	4.9 (1.0)	7.6 (0.5)

A. Adults who report an income in method 1 but not in method 2 in % of respondents reporting an income in method 1

B. Adults who report having received an income for 12 months in 1993 (method 2), but who didn't report an income in method 1 in percentage of respondents reporting an income in method 2

* For self-employment income it is not asked whether this income was received during the whole year, so this figure is not completely comparable

() Between brackets percentages on all respondents present in the two waves (n=6715)

Table 1.4.10 **Comparison of mean 'income in previous month' (method 1) and mean 'average monthly income in previous year' (method 2)*, PSBH data waves 1993 and 1994**

	Average income		Standard deviation	
	Income previous month	Average monthly income in 1993	Income previous month	Average monthly income in 1993
Wages and salaries	47,754	46,424	20,680	20,442
Unemployment allowances	16,695	15,442	10,043	9,033
Pensions	33,020	33,592	15,647	15,440

Table 1.4.11 concerns the individual differences in wages and salaries between the two measurement methods. It appears from column 2 that only 17 per cent of respondents indicated exactly the same amount; in 30 per cent of all cases, the amounts given diverge by over BEF 5,000 while in 15 per cent of all cases, the difference exceeds BEF 10,000. In the other columns of Table 1.4.11, the analysis is narrowed down to subgroups, where the likelihood of changes and fluctuations in income may be can be expected to be smaller: i.e. those working full-time, and in particular tenured civil servants working full time. Even among the latter group, the differences are significant: in 21 per cent of these cases, the difference exceeds BEF 5000.

Table 1.4.11   Individual differences in wages and salaries between two measurement methods*, PSBH data waves 1993 and 1994

Difference in BEF.	All cases (%)	Respondents working full time in both waves (%)	Tenured civil servants working full time (%)
0	17.0	16.7	14.2
1-999	9.2	8.9	12.7
1000-4999	44.2	45.5	52.2
5000-9999	15.0	15.0	11.2
>=10000	14.6	13.8	9.7
N	1473	1143	268

* Only cases that report exact amounts (no income bracket-answers) in both waves

Table 1.4.12 indicates that similar differences were recorded for unemployment benefits and for pensions.

Table 1.4.12   Individual differences in unemployment benefits and pensions between two measurement methods

	Unemployment benefits (%)	Pensions (%)
0	20.2	18.1
1-999	15.1	21.4
1000-4999	46.0	38.8
5000-9999	10.3	11.8
>=10000	8.9	10.0
N	470	1102

The effect of data treatment

As non-response is apparently higher in the annual approach, imputation is likely to be more important than in the monthly approach. Therefore, we shall now consider the impact of differences in data treatment on income estimates. To this end we shall compare PSBH 1995-estimates with ECHP 1995-estimates.

PSBH constitutes the data-source of ECHP-Belgium. Income data from the PSBH is treated by the same research group that processes the LIS-Belgium data. The data treatment procedure is identical in both cases. Eurostat treats the PSBH-data following standardised procedures for all member states' data sets. After this treatment PSBH becomes ECHP-Belgium. By comparing PSBH and ECHP-Belgium one can thus immediately assess the effect of divergences in data treatment on income and poverty measurement. Such a comparison was made for the data collected in 1996 regarding incomes from 1995.

Table 1.4.13 shows that, after data treatment by Eurostat, the overall income volume increases by some 10 per cent. Most affected are unemployment benefits, disability and old age pensions, which increase by between 20 and 24 per cent. The volume of other income sources (mainly capital income) is inflated by over 200 per cent. Average household income increases by 10 per cent, while the median remains unchanged. Income dispersion as measured by the Gini-coefficient rises from 26.8 per cent in the original PSBH-dataset to 34.2 per cent after Eurostat's data treatment. Consequently, poverty (measured by the 2/3 of median threshold) increases slightly from 15 to 16.4 per cent.

Table 1.4.13 **Income volumes, mean and median household income, Gini-coefficients, poverty lines and poverty rates: comparison in PSBH-income 1995 and ECHP-income 1995***

	ECHP-income 1995	PSBH-income 1995
Measured income volume (bill.fr.)	4.203	3.791
Household income		
- mean	1,063.227	959.016
- median	824.814	822.744
Standard household income		
- mean	656.789	566.304
- median	526.338	513.240
Gini (standard household income persons file)	34.2%	26.8%
Poverty line (calculated among individuals)		
- 50% median	263.847	264.762
- 60% median	316.617	317.714
Poverty rate with 60% median (calc.am.indiv.)		
- households	15.9%	16.6%
- individuals	16.4%	15%

* ECHP- and PSBH-income data are collected in the 1996-wave

Table 1.4.14 **Population income volumes reported by ECHP-income 1995 and PSBH-income 1995, in billion Belgian francs***

	ECHP-income 1995	PSBH-income 1995
Salary	1,992	2,061
Self-employment	270	366
Unemployment benefit	153	139
Retirement benefit**	825	666
Sick/invalid benefit	130	108
Family allowances	195	169
Other	638	282
Total	4,203	3,791

* ECHP- and PSBH-income data are collected in the 1996-wave
** The BSEP retirement amount contains only the first pension pillar and early retirement schemes. In the ECHP other retirement schemes are also.

Conclusion

On the basis of the comparison of the Belgian data-sources for comparative poverty research we draw the following conclusions.

First, survey data should be handled with great care. It seems to us that comparative poverty research should put more emphasis on the assessment of data quality and comparability. Though often neglected, we found in particular the impact of data treatment procedures on poverty and income inequality estimates to be particularly significant. Given the complexity of survey statistics and the level of error or uncertainty of the results, information about the sample and question design, as well as the weighting and imputation procedures, should be made available. To this end, in the case of income distribution, the Robustness Assessment Report (RAR) developed by the Canberra Group is very useful.

Second, the choice with regard to the observation period (monthly or annual income) is very important. Belgian poverty and income distribution estimates were found to be affected to a large extent by the use of different approaches taken. Contrary to what one would expect in theory, the annual income approach used by Eurostat (ECHP) does not produce higher income volumes, nor does it yield less inequality in the income distribution. Comparison of the results obtained through the annual approach taken by ECHP-Belgium and the monthly approach of LIS-Belgium revealed that income volumes were more or less the same, while income dispersion was more pronounced in the annual approach than in the monthly approach. Non-response and inconsistencies in reported income by respondents were found to be more substantial in the annual approach, which is probably due to the questionnaire being more burdensome.

Third, the ECHP annual income approach most likely does not measure income accurately. Moreover, as the reference period is the preceding calendar year, the income data and other measures (household composition, labour market situation and social exclusion indicators) refer to different moments in time. It may be the case, for example, that a person became unemployed just a few months before the time of the interview and is consequently registered as unemployed, while the income recorded in the survey actually relates to earnings from a year ago, when he or she was still working. This is particularly problematic in the case of households where fieldwork takes place in the latter part of year N. The quality of this approach should therefore be studied in greater detail.

In view of these problems, we recommend that consideration be given to the alternative concept of *current modified income*, i.e. annualised current regular income components (wages, regular social benefits, pensions - multiplied by 12 if paid monthly) and - for irregular components or those best collected on an annual basis - figures for the most recent and appropriate period (for example, self-employment income, income from capital, annual bonuses). The income data would then be timely (they would relate to the current year), and there would be greater consistency between the income variable and other indicators.

In addition to this model, which has in fact been used in the UK for many years, some other elements might contribute to a more all-encompassing view on households' state of poverty. For this purpose some thinking about a proper valuation of non-market household production is called for (Smeeding and Weinberg, 2001). Given the real impact and considerable transnational variations for this factor, the inclusion of this component is essential for any serious international comparison. Another element meriting more attention in household income measurement is non-monetary assets, i.e. command over goods and services (Van den Bosch, 1998, 1999).

Notes

1   The standardisation method used by Bradbury and Jäntti (1999, p. 11) yields slightly higher child poverty rates: using 50 per cent of the median household income as the threshold, yields a poverty rate for 1992 of 6.1 per cent compared to 4.4 per cent for the SEP (LIS-Belgium), and 6.6 per cent compared to 5.5 per cent for PSBH.
2   Such differences are also found for published overall poverty figures, see Cantillon *et al.* (1999), Dirven *et al.* (2000), Van Hoorebeeck *et al.* (2000), Eurostat (2001).
3   Key information on the issues dealt with here can be found in Eurostat, 1997a, 1997b, 1999, 2000 and on the website - http://lisweb.ceps.lu/techdoc.htm.
4   Response rates in the Family Expenditure Survey are about 30 per cent.
5   The use for reseach purposes of the net/gross ratios which are included in the ECHP User Database is advised against by Immervol and O'Donoghue (2001), mainly because the method used to obtain these ratios is not sophisticated enough to reflect the complexities of the tax and contribution systems.

References

Bradbury, B. and Jäntti, M. (1999) *Child Poverty across Industrialised Nations*, Innocenti Occasional Paper, Economic and Social Policy Series no.71.

Canberra Group (2001) *Expert Group on Household Income Statistics. Final Report and Recommendations*, Ottawa, Canberra Group.

Cantillon, B., De Lathouwer, L., Marx, I., Van Dam, R. and Van den Bosch, K. (1999) 'Sociale Indicatoren 1976-1997', *Belgisch Tijdschrift Sociale Zekerheid*, vol. 41, no. 4, pp. 747-800.

Dirven, H.J., Linden, G., Mikulic, B., Schiepers, J., Siermann, C. and de Wreede, W. (2000) *Social Reporting: Reconciliation of Sources and Dissemination of Data. Recommendations on the Measurement of Social Exclusion and Poverty and a Blueprint for a Periodic Publication – Task 3*, Den Haag, CBS.

Eurostat (1997a) *The European Community Household Panel: Data Quality*, DOC.PAN 90/97, European Commission Luxemburg.

Eurostat (1997b) *Response rates for the first three waves of the ECHP*, DOC.PAN 92/97, European Commission, Luxemburg.

Eurostat (1999) *ECHP Data Quality*, DOC.PAN 108/99, European Commission, Luxemburg.

Eurostat (2000) *Imputation of Income in the ECHP*, DOC.PAN 164/00, European Commission, Luxemburg.

Eurostat (2001) *European Social Statistics. Income, Poverty and Social Exclusion*, European Commission, Luxemburg.

Immervoll, H. and O'Donoghue, C. (2001) 'Imputation of Gross Amounts from Net Incomes in Household Surveys. An Application Using EUROMOD', EUROMOD Working Paper, No. EM 1/01, June 2001.

Ruggles, P. and Williams, R. (1989) 'Longitudinal Measures of Poverty: Accounting for Income and Assets over Time', *Review of Income and Wealth*, vol. 35, no. 3, pp. 225-43.

Smeeding, D.H. and Weinberg, D.H. (2001) 'Toward a Uniform Definition of Household Income', *Review of Income and Wealth*, vol. 47, no. 1, pp. 1-24.

Van den Bosch, K. (1998) 'Poverty and Assets in Belgium', *Review of Income and Wealth*, vol. 44, no. 2, pp. 215-28.

Van den Bosch, K. (1999) *Identifying the Poor, Using Subjective and Consensual Measures*, Ph.D. dissertation, Universiteit Antwerpen, Antwerpen.

Van Hoorebeeck, B., Van Dam, R. and Van den Bosch, K. (2000*) Findings from an explorative study of differences in poverty estimates between the Eurostat ECHP-UDB and the original Belgian data (PSBH)*, CSB-bericht, Antwerpen, Centrum voor Sociaal Beleid – UFSIA.

Verbist, G., Van den Bosch, K. and Cantillon, B. (2001) *MISIM. A micro simulation model of income tax and social security contributions for Belgium*, Centre for Social Policy (University of Antwerp), February 2001.

PART 2

CHILD BENEFIT
PACKAGES

2.1 Cash benefits for children in four Anglo-American countries

Michael Mendelson[1]

Child benefits in Anglo-American countries

There is a fundamental and well-recognised contradiction between an adequate income security system and the competitive labour market: an adequate income security system must provide benefits according to family size, but a competitive labour market cannot adjust wages according to the number of children in a worker's family. Therefore, where wages are low and family size large, income security benefits may be greater than those from work, and wages from work will likely be inadequate to support the family.

Beveridge struggled with this contradiction while writing *Social Insurance and Allied Services* (HMSO, 1942), a report that formed an important underpinning for post World War Two social reforms in much of the Anglo-American world. At first Beveridge argued that the solution was a universal flat rate child benefit paid on behalf of all children, whether or not their parents were working. But it soon became clear that such a universal payment, if adequate, would be prohibitively expensive for the treasury, and if affordable, would be wholly inadequate. Beveridge sought a compromise. Without undertaking the bothersome task of collecting empirical evidence, he concluded that wages were adequate to raise one child, so that the universal benefit need only be paid to families with two or more children (Timmins, 1996).

By the 1970s more satisfactory solutions to Beveridge's dilemma were becoming possible. In 1946, when the UK first launched Family Allowances following the Beveridge report, even the comparatively simple task of paying out universal flat rate benefits stretched administrative resources to the limit. Indeed, the UK almost missed its deadline for the first payment, requiring the distribution of 'order books' and an emergency flight of 150 addressing machines from Germany (Timmins, 1996, p.138). In 1946 it would have been impossible to administer a non-demeaning income test to millions of working families, and inexpensively process the resulting cheques; however, by the 1970s advances in information processing technology began to open up new alternatives.

The UK introduced the Family Income Supplement in 1972. The American Earned Income Tax Credit followed in 1975. Both of these programs paid benefits exclusively to working families on a sliding scale according to the recipient's family income. Canada initiated a similar refundable child tax credit in 1978, except Canada's benefit was payable whether the recipient's were working or not (a 'refundable' tax credit goes to everyone qualified whether or not they have a positive tax liability; i.e. a refundable credit functions as a negative tax and not just as a tax reduction). Australia implemented its Family Income Supplement in 1983. What all these programs had in common was: 1) their benefits were paid to families who were working (and in some countries, also paid to those who were not working); 2) the amount of benefits paid to a family was related to the income of the family; and 3) the programs themselves were 'stand-alone' and were not a payment on behalf of children embedded within another social security program, such as social assistance or unemployment insurance. In three out of four countries the income tax system was used to administer the new programs – the exception being the UK with its unique (among Anglo-American countries) 'Pay-As-You-Earn' income tax system that does not require most wage earners to fill out an annual tax form. Over the next decades these stand-alone, income-related child benefit programs evolved considerably, so that by 2001 they have become the centrepiece of government income security programs for families with children in all four Anglo-American countries.

In Australia, the new Family Tax Benefit parts A and B has entirely replaced previous Family Allowances, Family Income Supplement and all tax exemptions. The Australian Family Tax Benefit is a truly 'integrated child credit' in that it pays the same amount to all families strictly dependent upon their income, and not on their workforce status, and provides for a family size benefit adjustment for all income security programs. With relatively generous benefits to low-income families, Australia has solved Beveridge's dilemma through its Family Tax Benefit.

In Canada, the Canada Child Tax Benefit is in the process of replacing benefits paid through social assistance and other programs for families with children. To date, four Canadian provinces have implemented fully integrated child credits through adding provincial supplements to the national Canada Child Tax Benefit.

The UK will be introducing an Integrated Child Credit in 2003, constructed on top of the universal (now including first children) flat rate Child Benefit. The UK plan calls for the Integrated Child Credit and the Child Benefit combined to provide child related benefits to all families based only on their income, whether or not they are working, and to replace all other child related cash benefits.

In the United States the situation is different, since the US seems to have 'solved' Beveridge's dilemma by an alternative that has not even been considered in the other Anglo-American countries - the US simply does not pay adequate, or often any, benefits to families who do not have income from work. Perhaps *because* it does not pay any money to those who are not working, the Earned Income Tax Credit has grown rapidly over the decades since its introduction until it is now by far the largest cash transfer program for low-income parents in the US.

This paper reviews the structure of these 'stand-alone' child benefit programs in Australia, Canada, the United Kingdom and the United States. This paper draws its findings from the research results in *Benefits for Children: A Four Country Study* (Battle and Mendelson, 2001), a study on the design and delivery of programs providing cash benefits on behalf of children in these four major Anglo-American countries.

Comparing programs

It is notoriously challenging to compare social programs among countries. A myriad of differences between programs inevitably make it difficult to compare 'apples to apples' rather than 'apples to oranges.' As well, language itself can be confounding, as even among English speaking countries ordinary words such as 'welfare' may have quite different meanings. For instance, in the UK and Australia 'welfare' refers to the whole system of income security, while in Canada and the US 'welfare' means only the narrow set of programs paying benefits as a last resort when all other financial resources have been exhausted. But even if these challenges have been overcome, there remains the formidable obstacle of identifying any *adaptable* ideas for program design in another country, as the institutional and political contexts are almost always so different amongst nations.

Benefits for Children: A Four Country Study (Battle and Mendelson, 2001) selected the four largest Anglo-American countries partly to assist in overcoming these obstacles. These four countries do share a language, although there may be subtle differences in usage to trap the unwary;

moreover, they share many common institutions, and all have similar ways of organizing their income security system, relying upon the state to pay benefits largely from tax or tax-like revenue. Indeed, the similar trajectory of all four countries in regard to the evolution of their child benefits systems demonstrates that there is much in common between these four countries. Therefore, lessons learned in any one of these countries might be more readily adaptable to another of the countries.

In addition, given the similarity between the four countries of this study, it is possible to do more than simply look at inputs and outcomes of the systems. One can delve into the details of the programs themselves to determine how they are structured, designed and delivered; and this investigation is here greatly assisted by the development of a single, quantitative model of the 'new' type of child benefits in all four countries. The model, and discussion in the following sections, is of the following programs:

Australia
Family Tax Benefit Parts A and B.

Canada
The national government's Canada Child Tax Benefit (comprised of the basic Child Tax Benefit and the National Child Benefit Supplement), and for lone-parent families, the Equivalent to Married non-refundable tax credit, payable on behalf of the first child.

United Kingdom
The existing universal Child Benefit and the Integrated Child Credit (to be introduced in 2003, assuming that the government after the next election continues with these plans, and assuming benefits are set at current levels).

United States
The national government's Earned Income Tax Credit, non-refundable child tax credit and preferences for families with children that are embedded in the income tax system.

Before discussing the findings, there are several features of the model that should be noted:

First, as the results discussed are restricted only to the programs noted above, the comparisons do not show which country's overall system of income security is more or less generous. For example, Australia has substantial housing assistance built into its income security system, and the US has a large food stamp program to provide in-kind benefits both to families and to single individuals, but neither program is reflected here.

Second, to compare programs across countries it is necessary to convert to a common currency. The model uses Purchasing Power Parity as of 2000 to convert to US dollars, with one Australian dollar worth $0.77 US, one Canadian dollar worth $0.85 US and one United Kingdom pound worth $1.49 US (Organization for Economic Co-operation and Development, 2000). Distinct from the exchange rate, Purchasing Power Parity is the amount of money in each national currency needed to buy a common basket of goods and services. The exchange rate is not a good measure of comparative purchasing power, as it is highly responsive to other influences, such as short-term flows of investment capital. Purchasing Power Parity is a better way to estimate the relative purchasing capacity resulting from different benefit levels in each country. As well, Purchasing Power Parity will usually change much less quickly than the exchange rate among countries with similar rates of inflation, since the exchange rate reflects the price of currency exchange at the margin, while Purchasing Power Parity reflects the price level for the whole economy of a country.

Third, in the integrated model of child benefits upon which the results reported below are based, the value of child benefits in US$ is exactly comparable across all four countries, at least to the extent that Purchasing Power Parity can be treated as a reliable means of conversion. However, the related levels of income cannot be made quite so precisely comparable. Income levels in US$ are used to determine a given level of child benefits across all four countries, but each country uses somewhat different definitions of 'income'. For example, Canada pays its Canada Child Tax Benefit not according to total or gross income, but rather according to a definition of 'net income' that allows for certain commonplace deductions (for example, private pension contributions and child care expenses) from gross income. It is this net income in Canada that the level of child benefit is related to, not gross income.

Similarly, the other countries all have slightly different deductions netted out from gross income; for example, the UK at present subtracts income tax, which the other countries do not. As well, the Canadian and American income definitions are retrospective, using last year's income as assessed on the income tax form. Australia's income definition, in contrast, is prospective using an estimate of income in the coming year. In addition, there are other inconsistencies in detail in the definition of income according to which each country sets its benefit levels. Overall, however, the differences should be relatively small and do not effect the basic structure of benefits as discussed below.

One-parent families

Figure 2.1.1 shows child benefits for a one-parent family with one child under age five. Although the figure only shows income up to US$80,000, in fact all four countries' benefits continue beyond US$80,000. The continuation of child benefits to higher income families is due to the universal Child Benefit in the UK, the Family Tax Benefit Part B for single earners in Australia, the Equivalent to Married non-refundable tax credit for lone parents in Canada and the preferences built into the US income tax system for families with children (there are no longer analogous tax preferences in the other three countries, with one exception in Canada of the Equivalent to Married tax credit).

The planned Integrated Child Credit in the UK and existing Child Benefit results in a three-tiered structure, with three ranges of income over which benefits do not change, forming three 'plateaux' on Figure 2.1.1, and two much smaller ranges of income connecting the three plateaux within which there are very high reduction rates (a 'reduction rate' is the rate at which benefits are withdrawn as income increases, so that, for example, if $10 of benefit is withdrawn when income increases by $100, the reduction rate is 10 per cent). Median income for one-parent families in the UK is equivalent to about US$15,000, so most one-parent child benefit recipients will find themselves on the first plateau.

The Australian structure of benefits for lone-parent families is very similar to that planned in the UK (which might come as a surprise to the planners in the UK). Australia also has three plateaux connected by slopes. About the only difference between the Australian and UK child benefits for this family type is the amount: British benefits for the poorest families are higher than benefits in Australia, as are benefits for other income ranges as well.

Unlike Australia and the UK, Canada and the United States have some tax preferences built into their systems. In Canada's case there is just one remaining tax preference, as all the others have been removed through various reforms over the last decades: an Equivalent to Married non-refundable tax credit is provided for lone-parents so that they can treat their first child the same as a dependant spouse for the purposes of claiming a reduction in federal and provincial income taxes. It is an arguable point whether this should be counted as a child benefit: we do so here because the Equivalent to Married credit is only available where there is a child in the family, so on a rigorous definition of child benefits it should be counted as such. In the US, there is a $500 per child non-refundable tax credit (as this paper is being written there is a tax Bill before Congress that would raise the credit to $1,000, but the credit would remain non-refundable) as well as preferences for families with children embedded within the exemption and rate structure of the tax system. As a result of these elements, both the Canadian and US systems provide tax-delivered child benefits that extend income tax savings to upper-income families, though only in the case of one-parent families in Canada. Because of these tax measures, child benefits for lone-parent families in both countries *increase* after the tax system cuts in at roughly US$7,000 to US$8,000.

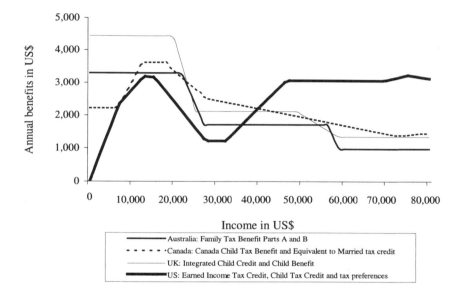

Figure 2.1.1   Lone parent, one child under 5

The US child benefit structure is unique among these four countries, as it provides no benefits for families without any income. In the US, child benefits increase from zero up to a pronounced peak, followed by a decline and a valley, only to have benefits increase again starting at about US$32,000. With median income for female lone-parent families of about US$20,700, most lone-parent families are likely on the downward slope of the benefits structure.

Australian, Canadian and UK per capita Gross Domestic Product in 2000 (in US dollars converted using Purchasing Power Parity) was in a cluster of

US$24,192, US$25,179 and US$21,673 respectively. US per capita GDP is much higher at US$32,184. There is no obvious pattern of benefits related to per capita GDP.

Two-parent families

Figure 2.1.2 shows child benefits for two-parent *single-earner* families with two children (one under five years of age and the other between seven and thirteen). Canada is alone in not paying child benefits to high-income single-earner couples: the Canada Child Tax Benefit ends at net family income of about US$69,000 for one or two children. (While a Canadian two-parent single-earner family will be entitled to the same non-refundable tax credit as the Equivalent to Married credit, in respect of the non-earning spouse, this tax break is available regardless of whether children are present, so this credit cannot be counted as a child-related benefit.) The UK's benefits extend into the upper income ranges because of the universal Child Benefit payment. Australia's Family Tax Benefit Part B provides flat rate universal assistance to all single-earner families with dependent children, so Australia also pays benefits through this program to those in higher income ranges - though not in the case of two-earner families. In the US, the $500 per child non-refundable tax credit is phased out at US$100,000 income for a family with two children, and disappears entirely at US$120,000 income, but this is offset by the tax preferences for families with children, which are more advantageous to those with higher incomes since their value increases in a progressive income tax system with increasing marginal tax rates. Some of the US tax preferences also phase out at very high incomes.

In Australia and the UK, child benefits for two-parent families show the same common structure as child benefits for lone-parent families. It is probably not just coincidental that Australia and the UK share a benefit structure and both pay relatively generous benefits to low-income families. A 'stepped' shape (for example, three plateaux and two sharp slopes) limits costs in systems that pay relatively large benefits to lower-income families. If they were to use the Canadian model, which reduces benefits more gradually for non-poor families, the result would be a substantial increase in benefits for all families between about US$20,000 and US$60,000. This modification would doubtless be very expensive due to the large number of families in that income range. In other words, if a country is going to have high benefits for those with little or no incomes, it will likely have to decrease those benefits fairly sharply through a short range of income, if it is to avoid very generous benefits for those with moderate to middle incomes.

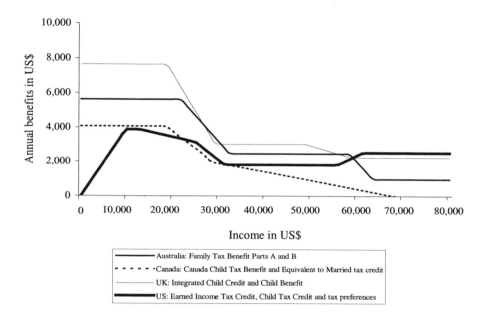

Figure 2.1.2   Two parents, one earner, one child 7 to 13, one under 5

Were Canadian benefits to be increased to the levels in the UK or Australia, with no change in design, the result would be a much more costly system than in Australia or the UK. But there are advantages to the Canadian structure as opposed to the more abrupt reduction rates in the Australian and UK systems.

In the Canadian design, families do not experience such high marginal tax rates - although the other side of this coin is that in the Canadian design many more families experience some increase in marginal tax rates, as is discussed more extensively below. There may also be greater vertical inequities in the UK and Australian design since families of very similar incomes may receive very different amounts of child benefit if they happen to fall at the end and beginning of two plateaus. The reverse is also true: families at either end of each plateau receive similar amounts even though their incomes are very different. In short, as in almost all areas of public policy, there is a trade-off between what might be a theoretically preferable design (Canadian) were budgets unconstrained, and what might be an achievable design given the reality that budgets are constrained (UK and Australia).

The US system, as usual, is unique: child benefits are a roller coaster. The US system provides nothing for the poorest, relatively high benefits for a narrow range of the working poor, less for middle-income groups and more for high income families. At the upper income ranges, the US provides the most generous child benefits of the four countries.

A peculiarity of the Australian system is that it treats single-earner families more generously than two-earner families. This differential treatment resulted from the historical evolution of tax exemptions into the existing system, which provides a refundable tax credit of the same amount to all single-earner families as a way to distribute tax breaks without favouring the wealthiest. However, while accurate, Figure 2.1.2's illustration of preferential treatment for single-earner families does not give a representative view of the Australian system overall, since in reality only a minority of two-parent families in the middle and upper income ranges have just one earner, at least for any length of time.

Figure 2.1.3 provides a view of child benefits for two-parent, two-earner versus two-parent, single-earner families in Australia. In Figure 2.1.3, the second parent begins earning an income at about US$15,500 (i.e. when the first earner is making roughly A$20,000, the second earner begins to add to the family income, so that at about A$40,000 both are making about A$20,000), after which all additional income is attributed to the second parent.

As can be seen, for two-earner families, the Australian system is even more clearly progressive in its distribution of benefits, with one of the three plateaux lopped off, and no payments to upper income families. This is a more representative two-parent family in all four countries. Thus, claiming that 'universal benefits' go to high income families in all four countries may be misleading: in reality, both Canada's and Australia's high end benefits are quite limited provisions (given few rich lone-parents and few wealthy single-earner two-parent families) stemming mainly from efforts to rationalise the tax system. In the US, the universal aspect of high benefits, while fully tangible as an income transfer to the wealthy, is also buried obscurely in the tax system and is not often recognised as part of the child benefit system by US commentators. Thus, in some sense, the UK is the only one of the four countries with a recognised and truly universal child benefit remaining.

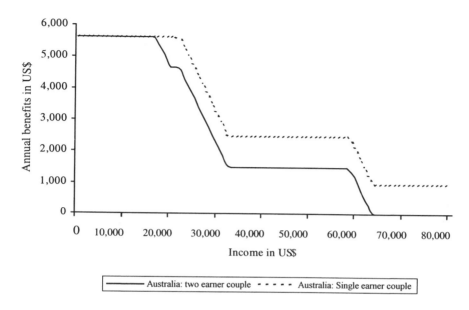

Figure 2.1.3 **Australian Family Tax Benefit Parts A and B, two parents, two earners versus one earner**

State and provincial programs

The central government is exclusively responsible for income security programs in the UK and Australia, but in both Canada and the US, sub-national governments also play important roles in the income security system, including child benefits.

In Canada, every province and territory except for one provides some income-tested child benefit programs or employment earnings supplements for families with children. Fully integrated child benefit programs - replacing most social assistance payments on behalf of children and extending provincial child benefits to the working poor and, in some instances, modest-income families - are now operating in four of ten provinces representing 42 per cent of the population. In the US, in 1999, 15 states had supplements to the federal Earned Income Tax Credit, and many others also maintained some preferences for families with children in their tax systems.

Benefit reduction rates in the child benefit programs

Figure 2.1.4 shows reduction rates for one-parent, one-child families. Neither Australia nor the UK have any areas of positive reduction rates (a 'positive' rate being an *increase* in benefit as income increases), because neither has any programs in which the amount of child benefit increases with income. However, both Canada and the US have some income ranges over which there are positive reduction rates.

In Canada's case, this is a relatively small range of low income that is entirely due to the phasing-in of the Equivalent to Married non-refundable tax credit for lone-parent families. In the US, reduction rates are more varied than for any of the other countries, with substantial income ranges of positive rates due to the Earned Income Tax Credit, the child tax credit and, in upper income ranges, the tax system's exemptions and higher tax thresholds for families with children.

Australia and the UK both concentrate their negative reduction rates in two very narrow bands of income, from about US$20,000 to US$25,000, and again between roughly US$50,000 and US$60,000. This is a reflection of the 'three plateau' structure in Australia and the UK. In contrast, Canada is the only country with a small negative reduction rate for a very large range of income (i.e. for all non-poor families that receive the basic Child Tax Benefit).

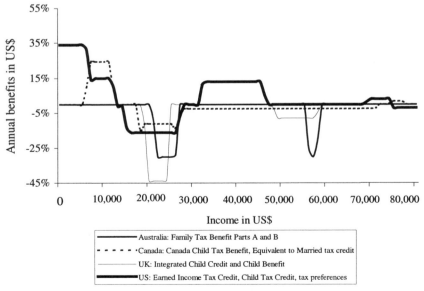

Figure 2.1.4   Reduction rates, lone parent, one child under 5

98

The relationship of child benefit reduction rates to the broader income security and tax systems, particularly social assistance, is not shown here. The highest effective marginal tax rates (i.e. the percentage of additional income that is actually lost or gained as a result of all income-tested social programs, including non-cash benefits such as food stamps in the US, and income and payroll taxes) traditionally have been found in the transition from social assistance to work, where social assistance and related benefits are wholly or largely eliminated as employment earnings increase.

With child benefits in Australia being available at the same rate for families whether or not they are working, and with the implementation of the fully portable Integrated Child Credit in the UK that will also allow child benefits to be maintained whether working or on assistance, effective marginal tax rates for families moving from assistance to work are (or, in the UK, will be) much lower than they would be were child benefits to be unavailable to those who are working. Similarly, the barriers to work in Canada have been lowered by the increased Canada Child Tax Benefit, and lowered most in those provinces with a fully integrated child benefit. Essentially, the biggest decrease in reduction rates is that which occurs as a result of the structural change implemented through the introduction of an integrated tax credit, which is exactly the dilemma to which Beveridge was seeking a solution.

Convergence and divergence

What is striking about this review of child benefits is the convergence of three out of four of the countries - Australia, Canada and the UK - in adopting the same approach to child benefits in their income security systems; namely, an integrated child credit. Although there doubtless may be many wonderfully subtle and complex explanations for this convergence, the most straightforward and simplest hypothesis is usually the best - an income-related integrated child credit comes closest to solving a long-standing problem in the design of income security systems, within acceptable budget constraints. Perhaps the reason this solution is coming into maturity now is that until about the mid-1970s it was not administratively feasible and only recently has become technically possible. At the risk of seeming hopelessly naïve in actually attributing the formation of public policy to a search for sensible, perhaps optimal, solutions to public problems, it is difficult to see how the convergence can be otherwise explained. Indeed, so similar are the child benefit policies of these three countries that what cries out for explanation are the remaining differences, rather than the similarities. But providing such explanations is not difficult - most of these differences are readily attributable to identifiable national characteristics.

In Canada, the endlessly complicated arrangements between national and sub-national governments prevented earlier implementation of an integrated child credit. The national government was reluctant to proceed with increasing its child benefit when the provinces could simply reduce their payments to social assistance recipients and pocket the savings. Indeed, it was an agreement negotiated between the federal and provincial governments, according to which the provinces agreed to spend all savings on programs for children and families, that finally unlocked the door and lead to a rapid increase in the Canada Child Tax Benefit (assisted by improved federal fiscal balances).

The structure of child benefits in Australia and as planned in the UK is virtually identical, but among the three countries working towards an integrated child credit, Canada's structure is unique. The simple explanation, as noted in the preceding discussion, may be found in Canada's so-far less generous benefits. As long as there is a significant budget constraint, it is very likely that an increase in the levels of Canadian benefits will find Canada inexorably moving towards the Australian and British 'three plateaux and two slopes' design. Otherwise, a substantial increase for those with the lowest incomes will be difficult to afford. In short, convergence of benefit levels will likely promote convergence of benefit structures.

In the UK, the development of an integrated child credit has been impeded by a strong political tradition of support for the universal Child Benefit. For better or worse, support for the universal Child Benefit has made it difficult to introduce a fiscally neutral tax credit that will improve benefits to those with low incomes by redistributing benefits from those with high incomes. Only now when the edifice of supplementary benefits to working families has grown to a substantial size, is it fiscally possible to introduce an integrated child credit which equalizes child benefits for all those with low incomes, whether working or not.

The UK also faces a practical administrative impediment not shared by the other three countries in this study. As noted above, Britain has a 'PAYE' (Pay-As-You-Earn) tax system, which does not require an annual reconciliation period during which almost all citizens fill out detailed tax forms. The PAYE system has many advantages, not the least being the ease and invisibility of the income tax system for the average citizen, but it is difficult to see how this tax system can be used as a delivery vehicle in the same way as the tax systems in

Australia, Canada and the US. The UK is now figuring out how to deliver their Integrated Child Credit given their tax system. The UK must find administratively efficient solutions that also meet policy goals (such as not forcing working poor families to make applications that require they stigmatise themselves as 'poor'). Modern information technology should assist the UK in this endeavour.

But even in 2003 when the UK introduces its integrated child credit it will still have a structure different than that of Canada and Australia in respect to two earner families: the UK will retain a universal Child Benefit going to families of all incomes. If the theory of convergence towards the same optimal policy solution in all three countries is correct, we may make a prediction regarding the UK. If the integrated child credit is operating smoothly and is an acceptable non-stigmatizing form of benefits for many working families in the UK, at some point in the future the universal Child Benefit will be sacrificed in favour of a redistributive increase in the by then well-accepted income-related child credit. This policy change will present a quandary for the social policy community, most of which is deeply attached to the concept of a universal Child Benefit. The same quandary was faced by the social policy community in both Australia and Canada: in Canada, at least, many in the social policy community have still not reconciled themselves to the loss of universal benefits, but this is not at all a wider public issue and no political party promises to reintroduce universal child benefits (despite a minor resurgence of support for universality among intellectuals of the moderate right, as the fact that income-related benefits are quite redistributive gradually sinks in).

The US remains the exception in the movement towards an integrated child credit. The American child benefit system is counter-redistributive, with large benefits to upper-income families and nothing at all to those with no earned income. The US pays its largest child benefits to the working poor and to the wealthy, and less to others. To our knowledge, American commentators on child benefits almost always overlook the important role of their income tax system, perhaps assuming that tax preferences for families with children are not 'real' child benefits and not as tangible as the Earned Income Tax Credit - despite the experience of the other three countries in this study, which publicly debated the regressive effect of their old tax preferences for children and eventually replaced them with progressive benefits. In its unique design, the child benefit system in the US reflects a different philosophy of income security than the other countries: the American income security system is almost entirely focused on employment, and its child benefits system is designed mainly to bolster families' ties to the labour market and recognise the horizontal equity claims of taxpaying parents, rather than to provide benefits to those with little or no earned income.

The outstanding question is how America's body politic can support such a harsh system, while the other three Anglo-American countries cannot. The answer to this question obviously goes far beyond the child benefit system and the purpose of this paper, but it may nevertheless be observed that many of the institutional and cultural attitudes in the US have been formed in a crucible of a deeply divided population, one in which 'people on welfare' are very much seen as 'the other.' Rather than promoting solidarity as exists to at least some extent in the other three Anglo-American countries, this cultural inheritance promotes division. Whereas in Australia, Canada and Britain excluding the poorest, especially single women with children eventually becomes politically insupportable; in America *including* the poorest is politically insupportable - and this is directly reflected in the divergence of the US child benefit system from those in the other Anglo-American countries.

Note

1   The research presented here was supported by the Caledon Institute of Social Policy in Canada, the Joseph Rowntree Foundation in the UK, and the Departments of Finance and Human Resource Development in Canada, and is based on papers on child benefits in Australia, Canada, the UK and the US respectively by Peter Whiteford, Ken Batlle, Jane Millar and Daniel Meyer.

References

Battle, K. and Mendelson, M. (eds) (2001) *Benefits for Children: A Four Country Study*, Caledon Institute of Social Policy, Ottawa.

HMSO (1942) *Social Insurance and Allied Services*, Cmnd 6404, London, HMSO.

Organization for Economic Co-operation and Development (2000) *Purchasing Power Parities – Comparative Price Levels – Main Economic Indicators* from http://www.oecd.org//std/pppl.pdf.

Timmins, N. (1996) *The Five Giants: A Biography of the Welfare State*, Fontana Press, London.

2.2 Understanding the generosity of government financial support to families with children

James Banks and Mike Brewer[1]

I Introduction

The provision of financial support to families with children has become an important area of applied welfare policy analysis as a result of increasing interest in a number of areas. These include concerns about child poverty, the effects on expenditures of differences in the allocation of household resources across household members, and an increasing understanding of potential labour market incentive effects for those with child care responsibilities. This paper discusses methodological factors that arise when thinking about comparing the nature and generosity of government support for families with children.

A natural starting point (excluding a comparison of benefit or tax credit rules) is to plot the value of child-related payments as they vary with gross household income for some stylised family-types. A related comparison is to look at budget constraints - the relationship between gross and net income - for families with children. Recent studies have used such methods to compare the value of financial support for children (Battle and Mendelson, forthcoming; Brewer, 2001; Brewer and Gregg, 2001), and such methods typically underlie claims that policy reforms are more or less 'generous' to families with children. Such comparisons, though, leave out three potentially important differences between systems, each of which might affect the conclusions of the comparison. First, the costs of children may be different in the two regimes being compared. Second, the joint distribution of income and children may be different across the two regimes, so that unweighted comparisons across all income points need not reflect average outcomes. Finally, other factors could be differentially associated with the presence of children in the two regimes so that differences in payments labelled as child-related need not fully reflect differences in total payments to families with children. Not all of these issues are always relevant; international comparisons, or comparisons of the same country in two time periods that are separated by a number of years, though, would be affected by all three.

In this paper, we discuss ways of controlling for each of the above factors when comparing the generosity of financial support for households with children. Throughout, we take the US and the UK as an illustrative model through which to discuss the issues that arise in comparing transfer systems. We argue that the generosity of support for children should be understood with respect to a non-zero baseline transfer, thus allowing the researcher to control for payments to children made solely as part of the redistribution taking place within the system as a whole. That is, we aim to separate the components of transfers to children that arise because children are often in households who are poor, from those transfers that arise simply because the household has children. By estimating the part of the transfer system that is designed to achieve horizontal equity and subtracting this from child-related payments one is left with a measure of how much support to children within any particular system goes further than - or falls short of - this horizontal equity benchmark. Put simply, our methodology is first to calculate, for all possible values of pre-transfer income, the difference in state support for households that are identical in all dimensions other than the number of children. We then compare these differences to equivalence scales which estimate the relative costs of children at similar levels of income. This does not directly compare the generosity of the total level of support for a family with children in each country - it compares the additional support for children relative to the support given to adults to the costs of children relative to adults. Section II explains this methodology in more detail, Section III outlines the transfer programmes for families with children in the US and the UK, and Section IV evaluates the generosity. Section V concludes.

II The generosity of financial support for children

An important guiding principle in social security design issues is the pursuit of horizontal equity: households that are the same in a particular set of dimensions of interest should be treated similarly (see Musgrave, 1959; Atkinson, 1980). Our interpretation of this is that households with the same pre-transfer incomes and consumption needs should receive the same post-transfer incomes. This is not concerned with children in particular - it is about raising the incomes of poor households controlling for consumption needs. Children tend to do well out of this principle though, as families with children often have lower incomes than those without, presumably because of the limitations children place on labour supply.

There has been a formal recognition amongst economists of the differing needs of households with children for many years. A number of techniques have been developed to estimate the economic costs of children, and such costs can be summarised in an *equivalence scale*, defined as the cost (to a household) of achieving a particular standard of living, given its composition, expressed in comparison to the costs that a 'reference household' would incur in achieving the same standard of living. Such a scale can then be used to convert any given household into a household of 'equivalent adults', and this can be used to deflate household incomes or expenditures for comparison with the rest of the population. Equivalence scales are designed to capture precisely the variation in household needs that is required in order to adjust post-transfer incomes of the population to ensure horizontal equity, given the way in which we have defined it. Another way of thinking about this issue in an internationally-comparative context would be as a way of adjusting for the fact that families with children do not consume the average bundle of goods, and hence do not consume the bundle of goods implicit in PPP comparisons.

One concern is whether such costs should be expressed as a constant ratio of, or a constant difference between, the costs of the two households under comparison. The most common approach is the ratio approach, and when considering horizontal inequity in pre-transfer incomes it seems preferable. If one intends just to compensate households for the presence of children, then the minimum cost of a child can be estimated using other methods (see Parker, 1999). This analysis is also concerned only with the direct, financial, costs of children - those that arise through the necessity of spending more in order to reach the same standard of living. The true costs of children may be different, arising from loss of earnings whilst adult household members are out of the labour market, or the utility gain from the presence of children. The economist cannot measure this latter welfare gain and hence it is traditionally ignored in the computation of scales, although such omissions are shown to be important when focusing on the identification of equivalence scales, as pointed out by Pollak and Wales (1979). Ignoring the welfare gain to children is unsatisfactory, but this potential welfare gain may not be the most important issue when thinking of financial support at the bottom of the income distribution. Paternalistic governments may also care about the utility of a child independent from its parents, and this provides a further justification for not focusing on the welfare gains accruing to the household.

Many equivalence scales are used to adjust household incomes in applied social security policy or policy analysis. For illustrative purposes, we use the OECD scale, the scales most commonly used to analyse poverty and income inequality in the UK and US (the McClements and Orshansky scales respectively - see DSS, 2001, Appendix 4, and Bureau of the Census, 2000, respectively), and a set of equivalence scales estimated from directly-comparable data using a directly-comparable methodology.[2] For the last, we use a simple set of Engel equivalence scales for each country, allowing different relativities according to marital status and the number of children, but not across the age of children.[3]

In addition to redistribution there are other principles that might lead to the government directing money explicitly at families with children, as opposed to households that have low incomes relative to their needs. In recent years, the UK government has given more increasing attention to an efficiency argument - that society has an interest in the outcomes for (poor) children over and above the parents' own interest. Similarly, governments may also wish to favour explicitly certain types of families with children over those without children (possibly in supporting married as opposed to cohabiting couples), or they may want to adopt explicit pro-parenting policies (see Milligan, 2000, for example). Finally, policy-makers may also care about possible work incentives when structuring financial support for families with children, particularly with regard to child-care related payments (see Blundell and Hoynes, 2001; Brewer, 2001, who both compare the financial work incentives for low-income families with children in the US and UK). Even where governments want to help children, they cannot directly affect children's own incomes, nor do they know that increasing incomes in families with children will help children's well-being. Even if low incomes are linked with adverse outcomes, it need not be the case that increasing family income will improve these outcomes - there may be some hidden factor that is producing the apparent causation or income sharing rules in the household might mean that children see no gain from the income - and so governments may turn to public services to improve child well-being directly.

III Financial support for children in the UK and US

Both the UK and US governments support families with children in a variety of ways. The financial costs of children are recognised in both countries: in the benefit system, by in-work refundable tax credits, and by non-refundable tax credits or extra tax deductions or allowances. However, the vagaries of perception and political economy mean that these support systems are often presented from very different perspectives, and in consequence can be difficult to compare. In this paper, we consider a simplified version of the US system, ignoring: state taxes, state EITCs or Medicaid, and assuming the TANF system operating in Florida. Housing support and help with child care costs are ignored in both countries.

For a given PPP-adjusted pre-transfer income level and family composition, post-transfer PPP-adjusted incomes are higher in the UK, and the transfer system as a whole is also more redistributive among families with children in the UK than the US. Figures 2.2.1 and 2.2.2 show the financial support provided for children: the cash difference in the budget constraints of a couple with no children and a couple with a child. This way of identifying support for children is used by Ellwood and Liebman (2000), who look at the tax treatment of US families with children, in Battle and Mendelson (forthcoming), who compare systems of support in the UK, US, Australia and Canada, and in Brewer and Gregg (2001) who compare the UK with the US. It assumes full take-up of all transfer programmes, and that the distribution of gross income, the presence of children, and the structure of the transfer system are all exogenous to each other (see the Appendix for a list of the relevant programmes in each country. The full budget constraints are presented in Banks and Brewer, 2001).

In the UK, financial support for children increases at pre-transfer incomes of around £3,100, and then falls as income rises. The spike is due to the Working Families' Tax Credit as nothing comparable is available for those without children. The US system does not continuously decrease with income either.

First, complex interactions between TANF and Food Stamps, the different eligibility rules for people with and without children, and the phase-in of the EITC gives a range where support is broadly flat for those on the lowest incomes. Second, after the EITC has been phased out, the value of the child exemptions and the head of household filing status increase with income. A striking feature of the US system is the trough after the EITC has been withdrawn and before the tax allowances and deductions increase in value, discussed more in Ellwood and Liebman (2000).

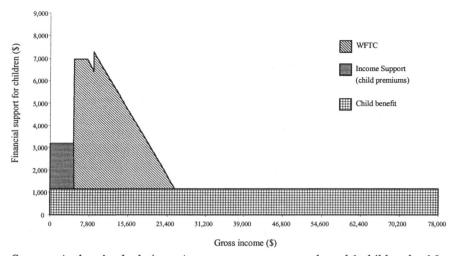

Source: Authors' calculations. Assumes one-earner couple and 1 child under 16. Ignores support for housing and child care

Figure 2.2.1   Financial support for 1 child, UK, 2000

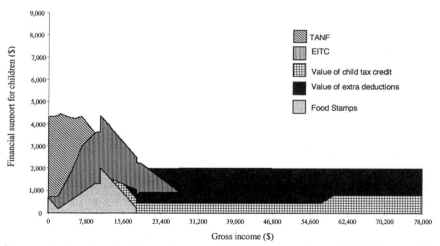

Source: Authors' calculations. Assumes one-earner couple and 1 child under 16. Ignores support for housing and child care

Figure 2.2.2   Financial support for 1 child, US, 2000

108

The figures have been drawn with PPP-comparable income levels (the 2000 OECD rate of 0.665 was used); an eyeball comparison shows that both countries are about equally generous to children at low incomes. At very high incomes (not shown), the US is more generous to children. But this provides a limited comparison of the generosity of financial support for children, as we have not controlled in any way for the costs of children, nor have we considered the distribution of income for families with children in each country (to evaluate our conclusions above more precisely, one would need to compare both absolute PPP-adjusted income levels and percentiles of the income distribution across countries, to match points in the income distributions).

Figure 2.2.3 shows the series graphed in Figures 2.2.1 and 2.2.2 expressed as a fraction of the post-transfer income received by an otherwise identical family without children. Figure 2.2.4 shows the extra payments for each child as a fraction of the payments for a family with without that child. The interpretation is, for example, that at a pre-transfer income of zero, a couple with 1 child receives 50 per cent more post-transfer income than a couple with no children, and we refer to this as the 'implicit equivalence scale' in the transfer system. The US appears to be more generous to children than the UK at very low incomes, providing over 2.5 times as much disposable income to families with children than those without. But we are measuring support for children relative to the support provided to adults alone: at low incomes, the US provides about as much in cash terms for children as the UK, but it provides far less to adults without children than the UK, so the correct conclusion is that the generosity of the US' support for children *relative to adults* is greater than the UK's. The second point is the dramatic spike in support for children in the UK at low incomes, as discussed above.

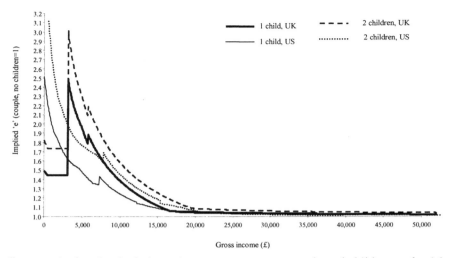

Source: Authors' calculations. Assumes one-earner couple and children under 16. Ignores support for housing and child care

Figure 2.2.3   The equivalence scale implicit for couples with children

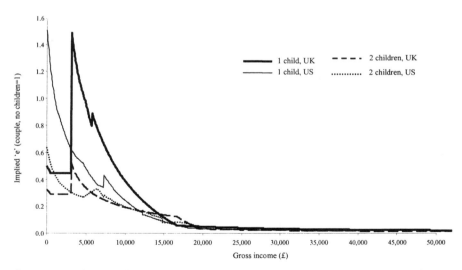

Source: Authors' calculations. Assumes one-earner couple and children under 16. Ignores support for housing and child care

Figure 2.2.4   The implicit equivalence scales for children

110

IV Comparing the generosity of the US and UK system

The analysis above showed how the US and UK systems differ in payments to children, expressed both in absolute terms and in respect to the payments given to an equivalent household without children. Two remaining possibilities need to be controlled for: either the costs of children or the distribution of incomes may differ. In this section we control for both factors.

To control for the cost of children, one can compare graphically the transfer systems with an equivalence scale (see Figure 9 in Banks and Brewer, 2001, for example; but the reader will be able to do this themselves on Figure 2.2.3 or 2.2.4, noting that the total equivalence weight for a couple with 1 child is 1.23 in McClements (child aged 8-10), 1.20 in the Orshansky scale, and 1.33 and 1.39 in our Engel scales in the UK and US). At sufficiently low incomes, implicit support will exceed all of these equivalence scales, and at high incomes, implicit support is lower than all of these scales (we refer to this as 'under-compensation' and discuss the interpretation in Section V).

The next step is to weight these comparisons by the income distribution. For each family in our dataset (households with 2 adults and up to 3 children), we assign them a calculated implicit equivalence scale, based on their pre-transfer income and the number of children.[4] In both countries, the implicit equivalence scales increase with the number of children and decrease markedly with income (see Tables 2.2.1 and 2.2.2).[5]

We then compare these implicit equivalence scales to three equivalence scales: the official scales in each country, scales calculated using the Engel methodology in each country, and the same numerical scale in both countries (for simplicity we take the scale recommended in Citro and Michael (1995), given by $E = (A + 0.7K)^{0.7}$ where A is the number of adults and K is the number of children, referred to as the CM scale hereafter). Tables 2.2.1 and 2.2.2 show the mean value of these three equivalence scales by the number of adults and the number of children, and the number of adults and income quartile. Our estimated Engel scale puts a higher weight on children relative to adults than both the official scales in each country and the CM scale.

Table 2.2.1   Evaluation of generosity by family type

Children	US				UK			
	1	2	3	any	1	2	3	any
Official equivalence scale	1.201	1.514	1.782	1.439	1.207	1.440	1.668	1.393
Engel equivalence scale	1.390	1.800	2.202	1.708	1.326	1.700	1.893	1.599
$E = (A + 0.7K)^{0.7}$	1.234	1.450	1.653	1.401	1.234	1.450	1.653	1.407
Implicit equivalence scale								
- mean	1.370	1.503	1.746	1.495	1.159	1.239	1.434	1.234
- median	1.031	1.056	1.100	1.061	1.044	1.070	1.122	1.068

Note: Authors' calculations based on FRS 1997-8 and CEX 1998-9. Families with children with incomes over £1,000/$2,000 a week have been assumed to have incomes of £1,000/$2,000. Quartiles are of gross income distribution for families with less than 4 children.

Table 2.2.2   Evaluation of generosity by family type and income quartile

Children	US				UK			
	1	2	3	any	1	2	3	any
Official equivalence scale	1.439	1.436	1.448	1.433	1.416	1.374	1.392	1.405
Engel equivalence scale	1.709	1.705	1.721	1.700	1.625	1.589	1.597	1.601
$E = (A + 0.7K)^{0.7}$	1.401	1.400	1.408	1.396	1.428	1.401	1.404	1.405
Implicit equivalence scale								
- mean	2.908	1.288	1.048	1.031	1.798	1.257	1.054	1.034
- median	3.144	1.230	1.044	1.025	1.823	1.148	1.054	1.040

Note: Authors' calculations based on FRS 1997-8 and CEX 1998-9. Families with children with incomes over £1,000/$2,000 a week have been assumed to have incomes of £1,000/$2,000. Quartiles are of gross income distribution for families with less than 4 children.

In the UK, the mean implicit equivalence scale is almost always less than all three comparison scales: only in the bottom income quartile of couple families does the mean implicit equivalence scale exceed our three comparison equivalence scales. In the US, the mean implicit equivalence scale is closer in value to the three scales when averaged across the income distribution, but over-compensation only occurs in the bottom income quartile, as in the UK. We can also look at the proportion of families in each group who are 'over-compensated': this is 100 per cent in the bottom income quartile, less than 30 per cent in the second quartile, and zero in the top half of the distribution in both countries and for all three equivalence scales. There is remarkable stability in the proportion of families 'over-compensated' by number of children: across the three scales considered, this ranges from 23-31 per cent in the US, and 16-26 per cent in the UK despite differences in the mean values by family type (see Banks and Brewer, 2001, Tables 4-7, for the full results).

This all suggests that the US system is more generous than the UK for couples in the sense in which we are interested. This is true when considering either mean implicit equivalence scales, mean differences between implicit scales and equivalence scales (of whatever form) or the proportion of households who are being over-compensated.[6]

Conclusions

We have discussed ways of evaluating the generosity of financial support for families with children. We contend that there are two reasons to give support to such families, and separating these two can enhance a comparative exercise in a dimension that closely corresponds to much of the rhetoric relating to financial support for children. On the one hand, families with children are often poor given their needs. On the other, governments may be more concerned that children are in poverty than with poverty alone. Separating these two requires one to decide how much of transfers capture pure redistribution, and we argue that this concept can be captured with an equivalence scale.

We demonstrated the issues using the US and UK systems. In structure and generosity they are superficially similar. But differences emerge when comparing the ratios of payments received by families with and without children. In the UK, couples with children receive less than the official equivalence scales imply; in the US, payments are roughly in line with the relativities in the Orshansky scale. The poorer families are over-compensated in both countries, and better-off families are under-compensated. Much of this results from the fact that, since the US gives less support to childless households than does the UK, the generosity of the US system for children relative to adults for some household types is greater. The US system redistributes less, so equal-sized dollar transfers to households with children are more 'generous' when assessed against the stance of the system as a whole.

Our analysis adds an important dimension to a comparative exercise, but is not without problems. First, we need to know the correct equivalence scales (but our broad conclusions are robust across our three scales). Second, we assume the redistributive stance of the transfer system is identified from payments to childless households, because these are the denominator of our implicit equivalence scale - we could equally have shown how support for adults relative to children compares to the cost of adults relative to children. Finally, as we pointed out earlier, children are supported in ways other than financial transfers, and we ignore these. These concerns are relevant, and important to bear in mind in international comparisons, but do not invalidate the methodology.

Notes

1   This study forms part of the research program of the ESRC Centre for the Microeconomic Analysis of Fiscal Policy at IFS. We are grateful to the Leverhulme Trust for co-funding as part of the research programme 'The changing distribution of consumption, economic resources and the welfare of households', reference number F/386/J. Material from the FES, made available by the ONS through the ESRC data archive, has been used by permission of the controller of The Stationery Office. The FRS was used with permission of the Department for Work and Pensions. None of the institutions bear responsibility for the analysis or interpretation of the data reported here. The authors are grateful to Michael Mendelson, and for helpful discussions with Tom Clark and Paul Gregg.

2   The US poverty thresholds vary by household composition and one can infer an equivalence scale from these variations (see Citro and Michael, 1995).

3   An Engel scale assumes the proportion of a household's expenditure on food proxies their welfare. By estimating the relationship between spending on food, total spending or income, and household demographic variables one can evaluate the income one would need to give to a household of a particular type in order to bring its food spending into line with the reference household. An Engel scale probably overestimates the costs of. But this means our estimates of the relative generosity will be underestimates if anything. We use data on household budgets and household demographic variables from the 1998 UK Family Expenditure Survey and 1998 US Consumer Expenditure Survey - full results are available from the authors.

4   We use the FRS and the CEX as estimates of the pre-transfer income distribution (we include earnings, investment pension income in the US; all private income in the UK). Banks and Brewer (2001) contains results for lone parents.

114

5   The first 2 rows in Tables 4-7 (Banks and Brewer, 2001) (labelled 'Implicit equivalences scales') use only information on pre-transfer income and family composition to calculate the implicit equivalence scale. In practice, net transfers to families depend upon characteristics like the age of children and adults, the distribution of earnings within a family, child care costs, tenure and housing costs, and disability: accounting for all of these gives a more accurate picture. Banks and Brewer (2001) present results from using a micro-simulation model to do just that for the UK.

6   Banks and Brewer (2001) report the results of investigating what sort of equivalence scale is implied by the transfer system (this approach has been used by Banks and Johnson, 1994, as well as Betson and Michael, 1993, cited in Citro and Michael, 1995).

References

Atkinson, A.B. (1980) 'Horizontal Equity and the Distribution of the Tax Burden', in H. Aaron and M. Boskin (eds), *The Economics of Taxation*, Brookings Institution, Washington, pp. 3-18.

Banks, J. and Brewer, M. (2001) *Understanding the Generosity of Government Financial Support to Families With Children*, WP [xx], Institute for Fiscal Studies, London.

Banks, J. and Johnson, P. (1993) *Children and Household Living Standards*, Institute for Fiscal Studies, London.

Banks, J. and Johnson, P. (1994) 'Equivalence Scale Relativities Revisited', *Economic Journal*, no. 104, pp. 883-90.

Battle, K. and Mendelson, M. (forthcoming) *Benefits for Children: A Four Country Study*, Caledon Institute, Ottawa and Joseph Rowntree Foundation, York, UK.

Blundell, R. and Hoynes, H. (2001) 'Has "In-work" Benefit Reform Helped the Labour Market?', NBER Working Paper 8546, Cambridge, MA.

Brewer, M. (2001) 'Comparing In-Work Benefits and the Reward to Work for Families with Children in the US and the UK', *Fiscal Studies*, vol. 22, no. 1, pp. 41-77.

Brewer, M. and Gregg, P. (2001) 'Eradicating Child Poverty in Britain: Welfare Reform and Children since 1997', Institute for Fiscal Studies WP 01/08, http://www.ifs.org.uk/workingpapers/wp0108.pdf.

Bureau of the Census (2000) 'Poverty Thresholds in 2000, by Size of Family and Number of Related Children Under 18 Years', http://www.census.gov/hhes/poverty/threshld/thresh00.html/.

Citro, C.F. and Michael, R.T. (eds) (1995) *Measuring Poverty: A New Approach*, National Academy Press, Washington DC.

Deaton, A. (1997) *The Analysis of Household Surveys*, Johns Hopkins University Press, Baltimore, MD.

Department of Social Security (2001), *Households Below Average Income, 1994/5 - 1999/00*, Government Statistical Service, London.

Ellwood, D. and Liebmann, J. (2000) 'The Middle Class Parent Penalty: Child Benefits in the US Tax Code', NBER WP 8031.

McClements, L. (1977) 'Equivalence Scales for Children', *Journal of Public Economics*, vol. 8, no. 2.

McClements, L. (1979) 'Muellbauer on equivalence scales', *Journal of Public Economics*, vol. 12, no. 2.

Milligan, K.S. (2000) 'Subsidizing the Stork: New Evidence on Tax Incentives and Fertility', manuscript, University of Toronto, September 2000.

Muellbauer, J. (1979a) 'McClements on equivalence scales for children', *Journal of Public Economics*, vol. 12, no. 2.

Muellbauer, J. (1979b) 'Reply to McClements', *Journal of Public Economics*, vol. 12, no. 2.

Musgrave, R.A. (1959) *The Theory of Public Finance*, McGraw-Hill, New York.

Parker, H. (ed) (1999) *Low Cost but Acceptable – A Minimum Income Standard for the UK: Families with Young Children*, Policy Press, Bristol.

Pollak, R.A. and Wales, T.J. (1979) 'Welfare Comparisons and Equivalence Scales', *American Economic Review*, vol. 69, pp. 216-21.

Appendix - Transfer programmes for families with children

This summarises the important transfer programmes for families with children in the UK and US. More detailed descriptions are in Banks and Brewer (2001) and Battle and Mendelson (forthcoming).

Families with children in the US can potentially receive financial support from Food Stamps, Temporary Assistance for Needy Families (TANF), the Earned Income Tax Credit (EITC), and through the income tax system. States have discretion over welfare policy under the TANF block grant, making it difficult to characterise for a typical low-income family. Most states provide a maximum credit varying with household composition, subject to resource limits, time limits and work requirements, tapered away as income rises. People without children cannot claim TANF. Food Stamps are available to low-income families with or without children subject to resource constraints and job-search or training or working conditions. They provide a monthly allowance depending on household composition tapered away as incomes rise. Low-income families with and without children can apply for the Earned Income Tax Credit (EITC). It is a refundable tax credit: awards in excess of tax liability are paid direct to the taxpayer. Eligibility depends upon earned income and the number of qualifying children. Families may also have to pay federal income taxes and payroll taxes, but children lower tax liabilities through allowances for dependents, a partially refundable Child Tax Credit, and a change in filing status. We do not consider state income taxes or state Earned Income Credits, federal or state child care programs, or in-kind support.

In the UK, families with children can receive financial support from means-tested and non-means-tested benefits, and through the income tax system. First, Child Benefit is a flat-rate, non-means-tested benefit for each child. Out-of-work families with or without children may be able to claim a means-tested benefit which has extra child allowances. Working low-income families with children may claim an in-work benefit, the working families tax credit, which depends upon earnings, hours worked, and the number of qualifying children. The Children's Tax Credit is a non-refundable tax credit worth up to £520 a year regardless of the number of children, withdrawn at 6.7 per cent from people paying higher-rates of income tax (over £33,935 from April 2001).

2.3 Re-orienting support for children in New Zealand

Robert Stephens

Abstract

The extensive economic and social policy reforms undertaken in New Zealand between 1984 and 1999 resulted in a widened income distribution, increased economic hardship and poorer housing and health outcomes. The impact was heaviest on families with dependent children, especially those headed by lone mothers. International comparisons on the prevalence and employment rates of lone parent families and the level of assistance to families with dependent children showed additional reasons for the high level of poverty for New Zealand children. Current solutions are based on the provision of services to 'at-risk' families, improving employment prospects for lone mothers and offsetting ethnic disadvantage, rather than addressing poverty directly through additional welfare assistance.

Introduction

A cold climate for social and economic policy among Anglo-countries dominated the 1980s and 1990s. This cold policy climate had a significant effect on outcomes in lower socio-economic groups, especially families with dependent children. New Zealand is used as a case study to analyse this impact, starting from Veit-Wilson's (2000) contention that 'New Zealand after the change of government in 1990 is a good example of a rapid move from a mature welfare state to a neo-liberal testbed'.

The change in the nature of the welfare state actually started with the comprehensive economic reforms introduced by Labour between 1984 and 1990.[1] The cumulative impact of rapid and poorly sequenced reform resulted in slow economic growth and rising unemployment (Figure 2.3.1). The majority of New Zealand families had a decline in their real disposable income, the country had the largest increase in inequality in the OECD and the number of children raised in families receiving a benefit more than doubled (St. John *et al.*, 2001).

After campaigning on the slogan of 'the decent society', the conservative National government reduced real social security benefit levels by an average of 14 per cent, with larger cuts for those with closer connections to the labour market. Child assistance was targeted, entitlement rules for benefits tightened with a mandatory work-for-welfare scheme, market rents replaced income-related rents for state-house tenants, subsidies for primary and secondary health care were targeted and tertiary education fees introduced (Stephens, 1996). Quasi-markets in health, social services and education were introduced for efficiency gains, greater consumer choice and reductions in state provision of services.

A plethora of small-scale community studies claimed that the combined impact of these policies had resulted in increasing hardship among beneficiary households. The studies showed respondents doubling-up on accommodation, forgoing doctor's visits, accepting food-parcels from charitable organizations and not replacing worn-out assets. While the government claimed that these reports were not statistically valid, and the results were either a temporary adjustment issue or the result of poor budgeting skills, the reports placed the issue of hardship in the media and political spotlight. With no official poverty line and a refusal by government to monitor the social impacts of policy change, the Poverty Measurement Project was established to provide a consistent statistical analysis of the incidence and severity of income poverty. Some of the results of this analysis are reported in the next section.

Several international comparative studies have highlighted social conditions in New Zealand - child assistance (Bradshaw *et al.*, 1993; Stephens and Bradshaw, 1995), social assistance (Eardley *et al.*, 1996), lone parents (Bradshaw *et al.*, 1996; Stephens, 2000; Bradshaw *et al.*, 2000) and child poverty (Bradbury and Jantii, 1999; Stephens, 2000). The following section uses these international studies to explain the high level and trends in poverty for New Zealand families with dependent children.

The final section analyses policy responses to improve child outcomes that emerge from the comparative evidence, statistical analysis of poverty and the election of a centre-left government in 1999. One response was the use of child-centred welfare services, rather than welfare payments, to improve life-chances of children raised in lower socio-economic households. The second response was a change from a welfare office delivering financial assistance passively according to eligibility criteria to a pro-active organization using case-management to deliver the appropriate mix of skills, services and financial assistance. The third response was an attempt to offset ethnic disparities between the indigenous Maori and immigrant Pacific peoples with the dominant white population.

Social policy development in New Zealand

Total reliance upon income-tested social assistance benefits resulted in the New Zealand social welfare system being labelled residualist or liberal (Esping-Andersen, 1990). Until 1984, the outcomes of income inequality and poverty relief were those of a social democratic regime. Castles and Mitchell (1992) used this dichotomy between entitlement rules and outcomes to argue that New Zealand and Australia should be considered 'radical or labourite' welfare states. The state only faced residual pockets of hardship as political pressure maintained living standards through full employment and a family-based minimum wage (Castles, 1985).

Large family size, as a cause of hardship, was offset by the 1926 introduction of income-tested family assistance for the third and subsequent children. Following the depression, the wage system took on more of an economic character. The social policy reaction was a universal and relatively generous family benefit. The depression led to the Social Security Act 1938, with the unemployment and sickness benefits added to the traditional 'deserving poor' categories of the elderly, widows and invalids. When lone parent numbers increased, a Domestic Purposes Benefit (DPB) was introduced in 1972, with the objective that lone mothers should be able to care for and raise their children without the prospect of poverty or expensive litigation with the non-custodial parent.

By the end of the social and economic reforms, the New Zealand welfare state was 'residualist'. Although social policy expenditure increased from 21.5 per cent of GDP in 1984 to 25.2 per cent in 1999, this was a reaction to increased need for income transfers following a doubling of unemployed and lone parent numbers. Tightening of entitlement rules, greater targeting, user charges, and a greater reliance upon private financing and provision of services increased social stratification. Flexible labour markets and cuts in benefit levels adversely affected social outcomes in terms of poverty alleviation and income inequality.

A centre-left government is unlikely to return to the generous 1970s: the larger number of beneficiaries, constraints on tax levels due to globalisation, incentive effects from high tax rates and benefit levels, plus social attitudes towards the poor will ensure that any thaw is gradual. A Social Development strategy, more in common with Blair's 'Third Way' than existing typologies of the welfare state, is being developed, giving a more holistic and integrated approach across economic and social sectors. The aim is economic development and long-term eradication of of the causes of poverty rather than financial alleviation.

Measuring poverty in New Zealand

The Poverty Measurement project used focus groups, drawn from low-income households, to develop a consensual poverty threshold based on their collective experience of living on low incomes (Stephens *et al.*, 1995). The poverty measure is time-specific, relating to current economic conditions and policy parameters. The focus groups started with a budget that would enable them to participate in society and then pared down their estimates to a minimum adequate level. On this budget the household can purchase food and clothing and go the doctor without the need for food-parcels, special benefits or go into debt, but meals out and paying for leisure activities are not permitted.

The methodological issues in going from a focus group determined poverty line to poverty measurement are set out in Stephens *et al.* (2000). The 1993 focus group poverty line was equivalent to 60 per cent of median household equivalent disposable income,[2] with a 50 per cent threshold as a sensitivity measure. The 1993 threshold has been adjusted by movements in consumer prices (an absolute poverty standard) and by movements in median equivalent household disposable income (a relative measure).

Who were the poor in 1998

Using a relative adjustment to the focus group poverty level, Table 2.3.1 shows the incidence, structure and severity of poverty, by household type. The impact of net social security benefits in reducing the incidence and severity of poverty is also shown. At the 60 per cent threshold, 15.4 per cent of the population were poor, compared to 4.1 per cent at the 50 per cent level.[3] Most social security benefit levels lie between the 50 and 60 per cent thresholds, with the old age pension just below the 60 per cent threshold.

The incidence of poverty varies between the family types. Lone parents have the highest poverty incidence, with 45 per cent below the focus group threshold, and 13.2 per cent below the 50 per cent level. The structure of poverty indicates that lone parents only account for 17.7 per cent of the total poor. Single adults, consisting of elderly and unemployed youth, have the second highest poverty incidence. The poverty rate for the elderly (both singles and couples) is 20.2 per cent, indicating that many elderly have no market income.

Table 2.3.1   The incidence, structure and severity of poverty, by household type, 1998

Household Type (A=Adult, C=Child)	Incidence		Structure	Poverty Gap		PRE* 60%	
	50%	60%	60%	$m	$ person	Incid	
1A	3.9	21.9	30.2	86.6	1710	58.2	95.2
1A + 1C	13.2	45.0	17.7	77.3	808	43.0	90.7
2A	3.1	11.7	23.9	99.4	1242	60.2	92.5
2A + 1C	4.4	10.2	4.8	26.0	1082	29.7	81.3
2A + 2C	3.9	12.4	7.8	31.0	594	27.1	79.6
2A + >3C	5.8	17.5	8.5	40.2	498	19.0	76.2
>3A	1.9	5.2	3.5	20.4	1077	63.6	86.9
3A + 1C	3.4	8.3	3.6	19.6	604	59.3	85.2
TOTAL	4.1	15.4	100.0	400.6	921	52.3	91.6

* PRE - poverty reduction effectiveness: [(market income poverty rate - disposable income poverty rate) / market income poverty rate]
Source: derived from Poverty Measurement project data base.

In couple relationships, the incidence of poverty increases with the number of dependent children. The majority of families with dependent children are in full-time work, receiving a small, targeted tax credit, with low take-up. Many larger families are Maori and Pacific people, where socio-economic disparities (Table 2.3.4) result in higher poverty rates for Maori: 22 per cent (17.9 per cent adults, 26.3 per cent children), Pacific people: 26 per cent (18.3 per cent adults, 35.1 per cent children), compared to Europeans: 12 per cent (11 per cent adults, 15.5 per cent children). The total poverty gap of $400 million is 0.4 per cent of GDP, or 13 per cent of welfare spending. The largest poverty gap and the greatest per person is for households without children. While the poverty gap per person falls with number of dependent children, the household poverty gap increases.

The last two columns of Table 2.3.1 indicate the extent to which net transfer payments (social security less personal income tax) reduce the incidence and severity of poverty, assuming no behavioural response.[4] The incidence of poverty is reduced by 52.3 per cent from the 34 per cent based on market income to 15.4 per cent using disposable income, while the poverty gap is reduced by over 90 per cent. Poverty reduction effectiveness (PRE) is very low for couples with dependent children where the high labour force participation rate gives a low pre-tax market income poverty rate - 14 per cent for couples with one child and 22 per cent for couples with three or more children. The earnings-abated tax credit is small, and the income tax rate is comparatively high. The market income poverty rate for lone parents was 79 per cent, so the high final poverty incidence for this group is a combination of low market income and a low PRE.

Trends in the incidence of poverty, 1984-1998

One objective of the poverty study was to measure the impact of the economic and social restructuring on standards of living. As Figure 2.3.1 shows, economic growth has been low or negative over much of the period, except for 1994 to 1996. Registered unemployed, and number on income-tested benefits, grew until 1993. Since then, the decrease in unemployment has not matched the rise in employment.

Trends in income inequality, using the economic distance measure [(decile 9 -decile 1) / decile 5], showed a major increase between 1988 and 1993. Between 1984 and 1993 the bottom half of the population had a fall in their standard of living of 14 per cent, and only the top 20 per cent improved their economic position. The bottom decile had the largest fall, but the next decile, consisting mainly of the elderly, had a far smaller fall. Since 1993, average standards of living have risen by 7.5 per cent, with the top decile having a larger increase. Over the full 1984-1998 period, the top decile's real disposable income rose by 42.7 per cent, the mean rose by 3.6 per cent and the median fell by 6.8 per cent. Lone parents and young couples with children had the largest falls in their income levels, while older couples with and without children were generally better off. Within each household type, income inequality increased.

The interaction between the changing rate of economic growth, the impact of the distributional changes, especially for different household types and the movement in the poverty level means that the absolute and relative poverty measures have distinct paths. The absolute poverty standard conveys the impression of increasing hardship during the period of low and negative growth from 1984 to 1993, with the poverty rate jumping from 4.8 per cent to 10.8 per cent. But the decline to 6.7 per cent in 1998, when growth has fallen to 2.1 per cent, exaggerates the improvements in living standards.

The relative poverty measure shows a decline in the incidence of poverty during the recession. This results from a combination of median income, used as the basis for relative poverty, falling faster than the bottom quintile, and the old age pension rising from slightly below to slightly above the poverty threshold. In 1998, the pension fell just below the poverty line, explaining the jump in incidence. Most non-elderly households had an increase in their poverty incidence and severity.

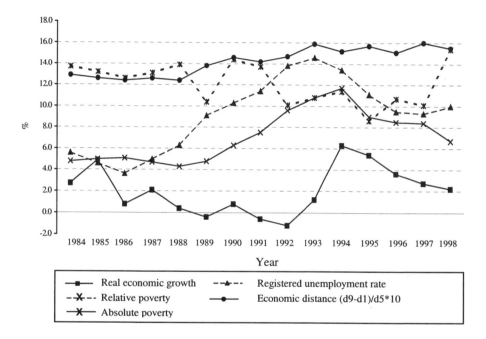

Figure 2.3.1 Trends in economic growth, unemployment in 1984-1998

Trends in the absolute incidence of poverty, by stage of lifecycle

Figure 2.3.2 looks at poverty rates for individuals, adjusting the 1993 focus group results by price movements. All age groups, bar the elderly, have a significant rise in their poverty rate until 1994, and then an equal decline. Children have the highest incidence of poverty in every year.

Children brought up in lone parent households have a very high poverty incidence. The most substantial increase occurs after the 1991 benefit cuts, but

125

from 1995 there has been a significant decrease. This trend in poverty is partly explained by an initial rise in the market poverty rate due to lower employment levels among lone parents. The market rate falls slightly as lone parents moved into the part-time work-force. After the benefit cuts, the effectiveness of social security in reducing poverty collapses from 60 per cent to 30 per cent, but rises from 1996 when part-time earnings supplement the benefit. Growth of lone parenting led to the proportion of poor children raised in lone parent households increasing from 20 per cent in the 1980s to 40 per cent by the end of the 1990s.

The lower poverty rate for two-parent children indicates greater attachment to the full-time labour force. When unemployment increased during the early 1990s, the incidence of poverty rose to 20 per cent, with the incidence greater for larger family sizes. Since then, with a decrease in unemployment, a greater proliferation of work-rich households and a rise in wage rates relative to median disposable income, a reduction in poverty has occurred for this group despite lower real levels of child assistance. The mean poverty gap also increased over this period, while the effectiveness of social security benefits in lowering the incidence of poverty decreased.

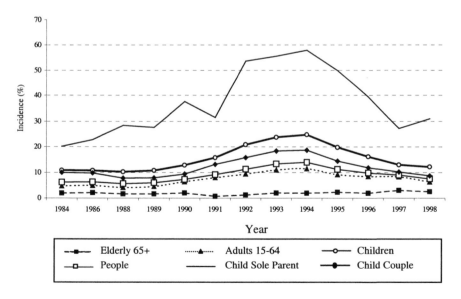

Source: derived from Poverty Measurement project database

Figure 2.3.2   Incidence of poverty, 1984-1998. People by stage of lifecycle. Absolute poverty measure

126

Intergenerational risks: A concern is that this high poverty rate for children will have long-term adverse impacts on child development, leading to cycles of dependency or inter-generational transmission of poverty. Poor children have, on average, lower health status and educational achievements, resulting in lower wages and a higher risk of being unemployed when adults. Politicians argued that this inter-generational transmission resulted from benefit dependency, especially for lone mothers, leading to pressure to make work mandatory and benefits less attractive. Reviews of the international evidence indicate that poverty during childhood was the major transmission mechanism, requiring more generous benefits and training to provide employment at adequate wage levels (Corcoran and Boggess 2000).

New Zealand data suggests that adolescent problems such as conduct disorder, early sexual activity, depression and anxiety are present prior to parental separation rather than being a consequence of separation. Thus instead of concentrating on lone parenthood, policy should place attention on parental factors that expose all children to risk of academic under-achievement and adjustment difficulties (Fergusson, 1998).

Lone parents in an international context

The conflict for lone parents between the roles as breadwinners and child rearers has resulted in a lower standard of living as well as policies to alleviate hardship through combinations of encouraging employment and cash transfers (OECD, 1993). Growth of single parenting, especially never-married mothers, was a major demographic feature of the latter half of the twentieth century. While about 15 per cent of families in the OECD are headed by lone parents, over the lifecycle a far greater proportion will face lone parenthood as a consequence of births outside marriage, separation and widowhood, with cohabitation, (re)marriage and children reaching adulthood as the source of exits from lone parenthood.

Countries offer a variety of social assistance and employment policies for lone parents, with different outcomes in terms of poverty relief, fiscal costs, employment levels, child development and trends in lone parenting, especially teenage pregnancy. Each country has placed different weights on these inter-related objectives. The growth in the number of lone parents has resulted in greater emphasis on employment, in the belief that employment provides the long-term solution to poverty and fiscal costs.

International studies on lone parents show that New Zealand is an outlier in terms of policies and outcomes for those families (Bradshaw *et al.*, 1996, 2000; Stephens, 2000). New Zealand has double the average share of lone parent families, very low employment rates, a large difference between lone and married mother employment rates, but a moderate child poverty rate (Table 2.3.2). The US is also an outlier, with a high incidence of child poverty despite a high employment rate. This contrasts with the OECD (1993) finding that employment reduces the likelihood of poverty.

Column 1 of Table 2.3.2 shows that cultural, religious and ethnic factors are important determinants of lone parenting. In 1992 the US and New Zealand had the highest proportion of lone parent families in the OECD.[5] There is a gap to the northern European and Anglo countries at about 20 per cent. In southern Europe the proportion of lone parent families is around ten per cent, and only five per cent in Japan.

The growth of single parenting has been more marked in the US and New Zealand. In 1975, the Scandinavian countries, New Zealand, Australia and UK all had ten per cent of families with children headed by lone parents, and the US 17 per cent. Twenty years later, the US had 32 per cent and New Zealand 27 per cent, with the other countries around 20 per cent. The increase results from a mix of divorce levels, ex-nuptial births, ethnicity and teenage pregnancy issues (Stephens, 2000).

In both the US and New Zealand half of lone mothers are separated or divorced, with divorce more likely in the US. The fastest growing segment is never-married, increasing from 17 per cent to 45 per cent between 1980 and 1995. This group of lone mothers are younger, have less educational qualifications, work experience and younger children, all factors associated with an increased risk of child poverty.[6]

Both countries top the charts in terms of teenage births - the US missed the decline in teen fertility after the introduction of the contraceptive pill in the 1970s, while New Zealand has had an increase in teen fertility over the last ten years (Singh and Darroch, 2000). Teen pregnancy in the US fell over the last ten years, but so did the abortion ratio, so that teen births fell only slightly. The New Zealand abortion rate is moderately high, but constant. The increase in fertility is due to a change in ethnic mix, with more Maori and Pacific people, who have substantially higher fertility and teen fertility, in this age group.

After standarising for factors resulting in high lone parenthood - age structure, income levels, unemployment and education - there is a strong ethnic dimension to lone parenthood. Two-fifths of Maori families are headed by a lone parent and 29 per cent of Pacific peoples, compared with 17 per cent for Europeans. In the US 64 per cent of African-American families are headed by a lone parent compared with 26 per cent for European and Hispanics. Maori and Pacific people make up half of all lone parent families, and this ethnic composition has grown over the last decade. Extended family structures in these ethnic groupings do not make this high incidence less of a concern as only one-fifth of lone mothers in the US share accommodation, and 13 per cent in New Zealand. Women head the majority of lone parent families. As single fathers are generally older, have higher labour force participation rates and lower poverty rates, most analysis and policy development concentrates on lone mothers.

Employment and poverty among lone parent families

In the analysis of eight countries, OECD (1993) argued that employment rates for lone and married mothers in each country would be similar, reflecting the socio-cultural environment in regard to employment of females. The 19 countries in Table 2.3.2 show a greater diversity of rates of employment for both lone mothers and between married and lone mothers.

While married mother employment rates are similar between US and New Zealand, the US has twice the proportion of lone mothers employed. New Zealand has the lowest employment rate for lone mothers bar Ireland, and the largest differential in employment rates between married and lone mothers. The structure and operation of the lone parents benefit affected employment rates. As changes in cultural norms led married women into the labour force, lone mother employment rates fell - the DPB encouraged lone mothers to raise their children without the threat of poverty or being forced into employment (Royal Commission on Social Security, 1972).

Sweden has high levels of employment for both lone and married mothers based on a system which is supportive of all women working; Germany and Ireland have relatively low employment for both groups, and an expectation that the mother will be at home to look after the children. The high level of employment for lone mothers in Japan and modest rate for married mothers represents a strong version of the male breadwinner model as well as stigma about lone motherhood and receipt of social assistance (Peng, 1997). In the US and Scandinavia, full-time work dominates. In New Zealand, lone mothers are more likely to work full-time, whereas married mothers are as likely to work part-time.

Table 2.3.2 Demographic and employment characteristics of lone parent households in 19 OECD countries, circa 1992

Country	Single parent family % all	Single mother % all singles	% single mothers employed			% married mothers	Child poverty rate 50% income	
			Part-time	Full-time	Total		Single	Two parents
USA	29	87	13	47	60	64	59.6	16.7
New Zealand	25	84	10	17	27	58	19.5*	5.1*
Norway	21	91	17	44	61	77	10.4	3.4
UK	21	91	24	17	41	62	40.3	17.5
Denmark	19	87	10	59	69	84	10.5	5.5
Germany	19	84	12	28	40	41	43.3	8.5
Sweden	18	85	29	41	70	80	4.5	3.6
Australia	18	87	20	23	43	56	38.3	14.7
Holland	16	85	24	16	40	52	29.6	6.8
Finland	16	87	4	61	65	70	6.2	3.0
Austria	15	88	15	43	58	46	33.2	2.9
Portugal	13	86	7	43	50	55	--	--
France	12	86	15	67	82	68	25.4	7.7
Ireland	11	90	--	--	23	32	--	--
Belgium	11	88	16	52	68	61	11.8	6.1
Spain	7	87	--	--	68	38	25.2	12.4
Luxembourg	7	83	13	61	74	45	30.1	4.4
Italy	6	83	11	58	69	41	20.2	20.9
Japan	5	85	34	57	87	54	--	--

* New Zealand added, data not strictly comparable: see text for details.
Source: Bradshaw *et al.* (1996), Bradbury and Jantii (1999)

The final columns look at child poverty, using LIS data and 50 per cent of median equivalent household disposable income as the poverty measure. Some doubt is thrown on the OECD claim that employment is the route out of poverty. Despite its employment rate, the US has by far the highest poverty rate for children brought up in lone or two-parent households. New Zealand, on the other hand, has a moderate poverty rate[7] despite the low labour force participation rate. As 50.9 per cent of children of lone parents are below the 60 per cent line, DPB has kept many children from serious poverty, but not from the hardships of inadequate income.

In the wider OECD context, the Scandinavian countries tend to have high employment and low poverty, while the Anglo-countries and Germany have low employment and high poverty. In the US unemployed lone mothers had a poverty rate of 85 per cent and those employed 30 per cent. The UK had poverty rate of 80 per cent for non-employed lone mothers compared to 27 per cent for employed, while in Sweden the differential was ten per cent to one per cent (Bradshaw *et al.*, 1996). The poverty rate for New Zealand lone parents in full-time work is about six per cent and over 30 per cent for those out of work.

The impact of labour market incentive effects

Lone mothers have high labour supply elasticities as they enter the labour market (Moffitt, 1992). The existence of child-care and travel-to-work costs, the level of the benefit replacement rate and abatement rate drive this result. To encourage labour force participation for the increased number of lone mothers, many countries cut real benefit levels, eased benefit abatement rates and improved access to child care while tightening entitlement rules and implementing work-for-the-dole schemes.

When the benefit replacement rate for the DPB was high from 1972 to 1990, employment rates for lone mothers fell from 60 per cent to 27 per cent. A change in attitude to child-rearing and the impact of the post-1984 recession are also important. Equally the rise in the employment rate to 44 per cent in 2001 was due to economic recovery, the imposition of work expectations for lone mothers with the youngest child over six, as well as the impact of the 1991 benefit cuts and an increase in the free zone before 100 per cent benefit abatement from $80 to $180 per week.

In the US, conservatives argue that the existence of benefits for single mothers provided an incentive to form single-mother families, locking some children into poverty. While AFDC/TANF had an impact on non-employment of lone mothers, the dedicated benefit could not explain the growth of lone parenting (Moffitt, 1999). New Zealand evidence suggests some growth in lone parenting due to the DPB as it allowed many mothers to raise their child rather than adopt out, avoid serious poverty and escape domestic violence. A police campaign against domestic violence resulted in an increased DPB case-load. If Snively's (1995) estimate of the annual cost of domestic violence of $1.2 billion NZ is correct, then the campaign would have a desirable social outcome despite the short-term fiscal cost.

International comparisons raise questions over economists' measures of labour supply elasticity. Eardley *et al.* (1996) used a model family approach to develop replacement rates that take account of both cash and in-kind benefits for beneficiary and in-work lone parents. Countries with higher replacement rates also have higher employment rates. The Scandinavian countries have high benefit levels and replacement rates, and high employment levels. Anglo-speaking countries have far lower benefit replacement rates and low employment rates. France and Germany with similar replacement rates have different employment rates. Japan and New Zealand have similar replacement rates but Japan has 87 per cent of lone parents employed while New Zealand had 27 per cent. The US has a very low benefit rate, modest replacement rate and relatively high employment.

Labour force incentive effects may be less important than cultural expectations of work force participation and entitlement rules. The most important factor influencing employment is the availability of good quality, flexible and affordable child care. In the absence of reliable child care arrangements, measures such as the state of the labour market, the level of in-work income compared to benefit levels, cultural attitudes to mothers' employment and degree of training and education are unlikely to increase the employment of lone parents.

The level of support for lone- and two-parent families

This section investigates why New Zealand has a moderate poverty rate for children and lone parent families despite the very low employment rate. In 1992, New Zealand was one of the less generous countries in the OECD for assistance to families with dependent children (Bradshaw *et al.*, 1993; Stephens and Bradshaw, 1995). The model family approach was based on comparable income levels and family types, universal and targeted child assistance, child tax credits plus additional costs for education, health care, child care and housing due to the presence of children. While the US, Australia and the UK have significantly expanded the level of targeted, in-work family assistance since then, the approach shows the different ways that countries structure assistance, the degree of targeting as well as the distribution of costs of raising the next generation of workers.

Table 2.3.3, based on a lone parent family receiving half average male earnings, shows how countries structure their child assistance. New Zealand is one of five countries without a universal family benefit, which is the main vehicle for horizontal redistribution in six countries. Income or means tested benefits are significant in six countries. In New Zealand, Family Support is reasonably generous for the first child, but far less generous for second and subsequent children. A significant number of countries provide a tax credit for children, either in the form of a tax rebate (a fixed level irrespective of income) or a tax allowance (value increases with rising marginal tax rates). The New Zealand figure relates to a targeted guaranteed minimum family income that reduces tax liability. Only 2000 households receive this tax credit due to a low take-up rate.

Health care and education costs are generally small. New Zealand's community services card provides subsidised primary and secondary health care for low income and high usage families. Under-sixes now receive free health care. Pre-school costs often offset the value of assistance given through the tax and social security system. Child care costs in New Zealand are high, partially offset by a targeted subsidy. The full child-care cost of £221 per month is a substantial disincentive to enter full-time work.

With a wider range of income levels and family types, New Zealand was just above Spain and Greece in terms of support for dependent children. For families on social assistance and at low income levels, the country was more generous, though still less than the OECD average. The objective was vertical redistribution, but the results show that fiscal savings dominate poverty relief. Small families fared better than large families. At anything above average male earnings no financial assistance was provided to families with dependent children compared to couples without children. Explanations for the moderate poverty rate given the low level, albeit targeted, nature of child assistance seem to relate to an average benefit replacement rate for beneficiaries without children being relatively generous rather than the additional assistance for children.

Table 2.3.3 Components of child support package, before housing costs. Lone parent with one child aged 3, at half average male earnings. (£Stg per month, purchasing power parity)

Country	Universal family benefit	Means-tested family benefit	Income tax credits	Health costs	Pre-school costs	Total assistance
Belgium	34	--	-29	1	--	6
Denmark	138	--	-85	--	-73	-20
France	113	89	--	--	-49	153
Germany	21	--	22	2	-30	14
Greece	4	-32	5	--	--	-23
Ireland	16	19	13	2	-155	-105
Italy	--	--	9	--	--	9
Luxembourg	33	--	--	--	--	33
Netherlands	29	--	4	--	-49	-16

Table 2.3.3 (continued)

Country	Universal family benefit	Means-tested family benefit	Income tax credits	Health costs	Pre-school costs	Total assistance
Portugal	12	--	--	1	-1	12
Spain	--	--	--	--	-142	-142
UK	67	53	--	4	-156	-32
Australia	22	158	8	8	-68	128
Norway	214	139	15	3	-125	246
USA	--	--	43	--	-36	7
Sweden	50	2	--	3	-24	-27
Japan	-40	88	-2	--	-49	-3
New Zealand	--	76	44	4	-93	31

Source: Stephens and Bradshaw (1995)

Re-orienting policy for children

Although the level of child poverty has been recognised, there has been no attempt to increase the level of financial assistance. Policy has been geared toward improving the employment opportunities and prospects for lone mothers, developing a child-centred approach to investments in children, especially those most at risk of future socio-economic disadvantage, and reducing social and economic disparities between Maori and Pacific peoples and the dominant white population. These developments are response to the ratification of the United Nations Conventions on the Rights of the Child (UNCROC) in 1993, and a reaction to local issues and needs.

Strengthening families

This is a multi-sector agency collaborative providing co-ordinated health, welfare and education services to improve the outcomes for the most at-risk children. Strengthening Families commenced in 1997 in response to two issues. First, there was a recognition that a small proportion of children were receiving a large number of separate visits and services from a plethora of agencies, often providing conflicting advice and services, whilst other children in need were missing out on services. This problem became acute following the State Sector

Act 1989 that separated policy from funding and from implementation. Departments were separated by function with Ministers responsible for the outputs of their ministries, resulting in silos with limited integration. Issues such as truancy, mental health and youth offending often fell between the cracks as they were not the direct responsibility of any one ministry or delivery agency.

Second, the Christchurch Health and Development longitudinal survey[8] showed that five per cent of families were at risk of persistent multiple and serious disadvantage, compromising family functioning, and increasing the chances that children would have poor long-term outcomes. A cycle of disadvantage due to a lack of resources, limited parenting skills and lowered aspirations was more likely following adverse shocks such as unemployment or separation. A further 40 per cent of families were at risk of poor outcomes if adverse circumstances prevail (Fergusson, 1998). The most at-risk families had a combination of low income, inadequate housing, poor health, low educational attainment, often lone-parented, in poor neighbourhoods or geographic regions, and in long-term receipt of social security benefits. Although lone parenthood was strongly associated with family risk, when the other variables were controlled for, lone parenting was found to be a small additional risk variable.

Under the Strengthening Families initiative, the social sector agencies interact to develop strategic priorities and work with local government and community organisations to provide an integrated service to families at risk. The strategy operates at the levels of policy development, programme implementation, service delivery and outcome monitoring.

A series of social indicators and target measures have been established to assess progress towards achieving the goals of better health status, improved educational attainment, the ability to form positive relationships and the prevention of persistent offending (Strengthening Families, 2000). There are a mix of output and outcome measures and risk behavioural indicators, comprising child mortality, illness and injury indicators, data on abuse and neglect, care and protection orders, participation in early education, health prevention activities and behavioural measures such as smoking, drug and alcohol abuse and criminal offending. A 1995 baseline was established, with targets for 2000 and 2010, by ethnic grouping where possible. The approach recognises that there is no direct link between the strategy and the outcome measure due to individual and socio-economic factors. While it is too early to evaluate the impact of the strategy on these outcome measures, the collaborative process has resulted in joint inter-agency programme development, more integrated service delivery, and successful feedback loops between case managers and policy advisers.

Much of the social and economic disadvantage in New Zealand is ethnically based. The difference between the dominant European and indigenous Maori level of achievement in the social and economic indicators shown in Table 2.3.4 has become known as 'the gap' (Te Puni Kokiri, 2000). For instance, in early childhood education, which plays an important role in the shaping of a child's attitude towards learning and basic socialisation skills, there is a 33.2 percentage point difference between the Maori and European participation rates Lower participation in secondary school reduces the opportunities for higher learning and training and entry into the upper echelons of the labour market. Despite improvements in school retention and tertiary education participation rates for Maori, the differential still persists. The differential explains the lower labour force participation rates, higher unemployment and lower median earnings. Lower earnings lead to lower home ownership rates, and Maori are likely to pay a greater share of their income for housing and live in overcrowded or inadequate housing. Maori apprehension rates are three times non-Maori, and conviction rates six times. This disparity in criminal justice starts at a young age. Child abuse and violence is more likely. Health statistics are adverse, with lower life expectancy, higher infant mortality and far higher teen birth rates.

Table 2.3.4   Indicators of Maori/non-Maori socio-economic disadvantage, 1998

Indicator	Maori	Non-Maori
Early childhood enrolment % 3-4 year olds	65.2	98.4
School retention rate at age 17 (%)	67.4	85.4
Labour force participation rate Males 15-64 %	69.8	75.2
Labour force participation rate Females 15-64 %	49.6	59.7
Unemployment rate %	12.2	5.0
Median weekly earnings	$485	$536
Rented Accommodation %	46.4	25.9
Criminal convictions males (per 1000)	68.4	11.6
Under 16 prosecutions, males (per 1000)	28.7	6.1
Life expectancy Males	67.2	75.3
Life expectancy Females	71.6	80.6
Infant Mortality per 1000 births	10.7	4.6
Under 18 birth rate per 1000 females	22.7	4.9
Reported child abuse per 1000 children	12.0	5.3

Source: Te Puni Kokiri (2000)

Closing the Gaps was started by the conservative National Government through the development of key performance indicators. But no strategy was developed to achieve the objective. The Labour/Alliance Government made Closing the Gaps a flagship policy, only to see a political backlash change the policy to an anaemic 'Reducing Disparities'.

The change was the product of political pressure from Europeans and government research. Chapple (2000) concentrated on income (the indicator with the least disparity), and while confirming the gap in average earnings, argued that the overall distributions were similar.[9] There were more Maori on low incomes and less on high incomes, but this was due to the younger Maori age structure, and that Maori are concentrated in less developed regions. The disparity was one of socio-economic class and geographic location, not ethnicity. While the incidence of poverty for Maori is double that of European, supporting a policy of targeting by ethnicity, 64 per cent of the poor are Europeans (Stephens *et al.*, 2000).

There are several reasons for maintaining Closing the Gaps. First, social justice and equality of opportunity arguments indicate that additional resources should flow to Maori to offset current and future disadvantage. Second, Article of the Treaty of Waitangi[10] guarantees Maori equal citizenship rights enjoyed by other subjects. Maori interpret this article as a right to equality of social and economic outcome.

Third, population dynamics indicate that future economic growth requires this intergenerational disadvantage to be addressed. Maori and Pacific people have both a younger population age structure and a higher fertility rate. At present, Maori constitute 14.7 per cent of the population and Pacific people eight per cent. These proportions will rise to 22 per cent and 13 per cent by 2051. The change in the ethnic distribution of children will be even more marked: by 2016 European children will be a minority.

If the existing socio-economic disadvantage continues, the lower educational attainments and labour force skills of Maori and Pacific peoples will reduce overall productivity and growth. The lower tax base will make social service delivery harder, and make it difficult to support, politically and economically, the increasing European ageing population.

137

Conclusions

The New Zealand case study has shown that residual income-tested social assistance systems are not robust against changes in political ideology, demographic effects or economic restructuring. Those most adversely affected by the concentration on economic efficiency to the detriment of social justice were the most vulnerable: children in lone and two parent households with low skill levels and limited resources, in ethnic minority families and poor geographic regions. The result was rising levels of poverty among families with dependent children, and increasing concerns over the development of inter-generational cycles of disadvantage.

But in a country that was once proud of its social policy initiatives and policy towards children, humanitarian concerns cannot remain submerged, especially when the economic gains have been elusive. The new millennium has witnessed a revival of social justice concerns, but fiscal constraints and the magnitude of the social problems has resulted in limited additional financial assistance. Policy towards children has concentrated on issues which potentially result in poor outcomes for children when they become adults. Targeting of integrated social services to at-risk families should help offset the possibility of cycles of disadvantage, but in the absence of greater financial assistance, the all-constraining problem of poverty will persist and probably dominate the effect of co-ordinated social services.

By international standards, New Zealand children escape the worst strictures of severe poverty, but a large number face lengthy periods of hardship from inadequate income. The large number of lone parent families, the low employment rate of lone mothers and the relative lack of generosity of social assistance to offset the cost of children contribute to the hardship. Children in ethnic minorities have the greatest probability of disadvantage, and this social disparity needs to be closed both for reasons of social justice and for future economic development.

Notes

1   The aim of the economic reform was that market forces, rather than level of government assistance, determined resource allocation. Among the policies introduced were the elimination of all industry and agricultural assistance, the removal of import protection, the corporatisation and privatization of government trading departments, deregulation of the financial sector and tax reform (Silverstone *et al.*, 1996).
2   Using the formula-based Jensen (1988) equivalence scale.

3   After adjusting for housing costs, the poverty incidence rose to 19.3 per cent at the 60 per cent level, with the increase largest for those in state housing and among Maori and Pacific families. To avoid after-housing cost poverty, there was an increase in overcrowding and a move to cheap rural housing with little prospect of employment.

4   An absence of behavioural response is unlikely if the programme has operated for some time and its presence included in planning future income needs (e.g. pensions). The response for income-tested working age benefits is smaller (Moffitt 1992).

5   Thirteen per cent of lone mothers cohabit and share income with non-biological parents in the US. These are excluded from the normal OECD definition and give the US the same share of lone parent families as New Zealand.

6   Norway and Sweden both have a higher proportion of never-married mothers, but they tend to be older and have better education and considerable work experience.

7   The New Zealand data is not strictly comparable. The LIS equivalence scale is more generous for single people and per additional child than the Jensen (1988) scale, and the omission of 'outliers' has lowered the poverty rate by several percentage points. The different equivalence scale makes little difference to the aggregate poverty level, but may affect the composition of the poor.

8   The Christchurch Health and Development Study is a longitudinal study of 1265 children based on a cohort of births in 1977, concentrating mainly on psychological and health variables and analysis, with limited income and economic data.

9   Chapple (2000) also queried the definition of ethnicity. There is considerable ethnic inter-marriage, but all children of such unions are listed as Maori, overstating the Maori share of the population.

10   The Treaty of Waitangi is the founding constitutional document of post-colonial New Zealand, signed by the Crown and the paramount Maori chiefs. Since 1980, the Treaty has been used as a vehicle to correct past grievances such as the illegal acquisition of land, with significant monetary and land settlement compensation being paid by the state to iwi (tribes). The restoration of the asset base for Maori should improve the cultural, social and economic position of the recipient iwis.

References

Bradbury, B. and Jantii, M. (1999) 'Child Poverty Across Industrialised Countries', *Innocenti Occasional Papers*, No. 71, Florence.

Bradshaw, J., Ditch, J., Holmes, H. and Whiteford, P. (1993) *Support for Children: A Comparison of Arrangements in Fifteen Countries*, Department of Social Security Research Report, No. 21, HMSO, London.

Bradshaw, J., Kennedy, S., Kilkey, M., Hutton, S., Corden, A., Eardley, T., Holmes, H. and Neale, J. (1996) *Policy and Employment of Lone Parents in 20 Countries*, European Commission, York.

Bradshaw, J., Terum, L-I. and Skevik, A. (2000) 'Lone Parenthood in the 1990s: New Challenges, New Responses?', Paper presented to the ISSA Conference, Social Security in a Global Village, Helsinki, September.

Castles, F. (1985) *The Working Class and Welfare: Reflections on the political development of the welfare state in Australia and New Zealand, 1890-1980*, Allen and Unwin, Wellington.

Castles, F. and Mitchell, D. (1992) 'Identifying Welfare State Regimes: The links between politics, instruments and outcomes', *Governance*, vol. 5, no. 1.

Chapple, S. (2000) 'Maori socio-economic disparity', Paper presented to the July 2000 New Zealand Association of Economists Conference, Wellington.

Corcoran, M. and Boggess, S. (2000) *The Intergenerational Transmission of Poverty and Inequality: A Review of the Literature*, Institute of Policy Studies, Wellington.

Eardley, T., Bradshaw, J., Ditch, J., Gough, I. and Whiteford, P. (1996) *Social Assistance Schemes in OECD Countries: The synthesis report*, DSS Research Report No. 46, HMSO, London.

Esping-Andersen, G. (1990) *The Three Worlds of Welfare Capitalism*, Polity Press, Cambridge.

Fergusson, D. (1998) 'The Christchurch Health and Development Study: An Overview and Key Findings', *Social Policy Journal of New Zealand*, Issue 10, June, pp. 154-76.

Jensen, J. (1988) 'Income Equivalences and the Estimation of Family Expenditures on Children', unpublished paper, Department of Social Welfare, Wellington.

Moffitt, R. (1992) 'Incentive Effects of the US Welfare System', *Journal of Economic Literature*, vol. 30, pp.1-61.

Moffitt, R. (1999) 'Explaining Welfare Reform: Public Choice and the Labour Market', *International Tax and Public Finance*, no. 6.

OECD (1993) *Breadwinners or Childrearers: The Dilemma for Lone Mothers*, Paris, OECD Occasional Paper, Labour Market and Social Policy, No. 12.

Peng, I. (1997) 'Single Mothers in Japan: Unsupported Mothers Who Work', in Duncan, S. and Edwards, R. (eds), *Single Mothers in an International Context: Mothers or Workers?*, UCL Press, London.

Royal Commission on Social Security (1972) *Social Security in New Zealand*, Government Printer, Wellington.

Silverstone, B., Bollard, A. and Lattimore, R. (eds) (1996) *A Study of Economic Reform: The Case of New Zealand*, North-Holland, Amsterdam.

Singh, S. and Darroch, D. (2000) 'Adolescent Pregnancy and Childbearing: Levels and Trends in Developed Countries', *Family Planning Perspectives*, vol. 32, no. 1, pp. 14-23.

Snively, S. (1995) 'The New Zealand Economic Cost of Family Violence', *Social Policy Journal of New Zealand*, vol. 4, pp. 98-110.

St. John, S., Dale, C., O'Brien, M. and Milne, S. (2001) *Our Children: The priority of policy*, Child Poverty Action Group, Auckland.

Stephens, R. (1996) 'Social Services', in Silverstone, B., Bollard, A. and Lattimore, R. (eds), *A Study of Economic Reform: The Case of New Zealand*, North-Holland, Amsterdam.

Stephens, R. (2000) 'Poverty and Employment: A Comparison of Policy and Outcomes for Single Mothers between the US and New Zealand', Institute for Policy Studies, Johns Hopkins University, Baltimore.

Stephens, R. and Bradshaw, J. (1995) 'The Generosity of New Zealand's Assistance to Families with Dependent Children', *Social Policy Journal of New Zealand*, issue 4, pp. 53-75.

Stephens, R., Frater, P. and Waldegrave, C. (2000) 'Below the Line: An analysis of income poverty in New Zealand 1984-1998', *Graduate School of Business and Government Management Research Paper*, Victoria University of Wellington, Wellington.

Stephens, R., Waldegrave, C. and Frater, P. (1995) 'Measuring Poverty in New Zealand', *Social Policy Journal of New Zealand*, issue 5, pp. 88-112.

Strengthening Families (2000) *Report on Cross-Sectoral Outcome Measures and Targets*, Ministry of Social Policy, Wellington.

Te Puni Kokiri (2000) *Progress Towards Closing Social and Economic Gaps Between Maori and non-Maori*, Te Puni Kokiri, Wellington.

Veit-Wilson, J. (2000) 'States of Welfare: A Conceptual Challenge', *Social Policy and Administration*, vol. 34, no. 1, March, pp.1-26.

140

2.4 Child expenditure and public pensions: policy issues
Martin Werding

1 Introduction

Families are like the *Homo neanderthalensis* or the Red Indians: they have been around when modern civilisation arrived. But unlike many other cultures, they embraced the challenge of modernisation. They have down-sized from extended family networks to the core family of the twentieth century, they have out-sourced many activities that can be provided more efficiently by the market, and they have invested in new technologies. It appears that the institution of the family has adapted to the competitive environment of contemporaneous market economies. Yet, a new threat that arrived some 50 years ago is the rise of the Western-style welfare state. If state intervention that interferes with family decisions remains as it is, the role of the family in modern society may shrink even further, while a few traditional families will take refuge to some remote reservations.

A major source of these problems is given by the heavy involvement of public authorities in the area of old age provision. All over the world, there is a pervasive type of public 'first-pillar' pension scheme that is unfunded and therefore rests on both the existence and productivity of future workers. At the same time, these systems cut through essential links across generations, thus removing important incentives to engage in rearing and educating children. As a result, public pensions may crowd out private child-related expenditure and depress human capital investment on a social level.

In many cases, old-age pensions are supplemented by further interventions into the overall system of inter-generational transactions. Prominent examples are given by public education and a host of other child-related benefits, the latter being mainly located in the distribution branch of public policies. At a first glance, these measures could be regarded a potential cure for the problems involved in conventional public pension schemes. Closer inspection reveals, however, that this need not be true as long as the natural link between child expenditure and unfunded pensions is not fully re-established.

141

In Section 2, I will try to spell out in more detail how public pensions interact with private child expenditure and how the introduction of public education etc. affects the aggregate level of expenditure on children. In Section 3, I will use the results derived from a simple model of parental decisions to simulate the effects based on a modified version of 'generational accounting'. Section 4 is devoted to an empirical illustration of the findings, showing that there are striking similarities between theoretical predictions and actual behaviour in the case of Germany (and potentially in many other industrialised countries). Section 5 concludes, turning to the policy issues that arise.

2 Inter-generational transactions: Theory

Abstracting from quite a number of institutional arrangements - both public and private - that are in existence today, the fundamental pattern of inter-generational transactions can easily be understood based on the following, stylised description (cf. Figure 2.4.1). Each generation is largely self-reliant in their period of economic activity. Individuals of working age in period t ('generation t') engage in production of various kinds, employing the stock of capital, if any, and therefore being entitled to receive a major fraction of total income Y_t from which they can nourish their current consumption. At the same time, they know that one period ahead they will be out of activity and thus should now make arrangements to provide for their old age. One way of doing so is to spend part of period t earnings on raising and educating a new generation who will be productive in period $t+1$, but has no means to spend on themselves when young. In return, the next generation will nourish old-age consumption of generation t, just as the latter supports generation $t-1$ for similar reasons.

In pre-modern times, this set of inter-generational transactions mostly took place within an (extended) family network, where there were always members of at least three generations present. The system was backed by informal rules - a 'family constitution' (Cigno, 1993) - that governed both the responsibilities for expenditure on children and the obligations towards the elderly. At the same time, it may have been stabilised by the lack of feasible alternatives with regard to shifting resources over time. Nonetheless, the system sketched here is a straightforward arrangement which looks like a simultaneous pay-as-you-go financing of child expenditure and retirement income, but effectively is a funded pension scheme which is based on human capital investment (Werding, 1999).

An important innovation arrives when broad access to capital markets enters the picture. (In Figure 2.4.1, the dashed lines represent savings and investment which exceed the low-level stock of capital that is present even in a pre-industrial economy.) As financial markets develop, some agents may switch their strategy of investing for old age entirely, now choosing to have no children (Cigno, 1993). Others prefer to make both investment in children *and* precautionary savings because there are additional motives for having children (Becker, 1960; Becker and Barro, 1988); because it is a strategy of risk diversification (Rosati, 1996); or simply because the marginal rate of return to having children is declining fast, falling short of the market rate of interest before a sufficient level of old-age provision is reached. In any case, the family may well be able to stand competition with other types of investment.

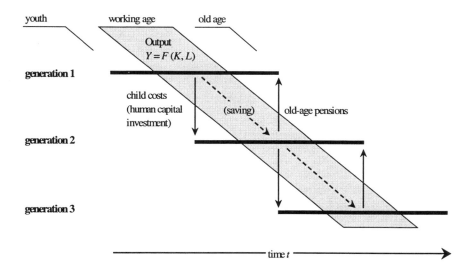

Figure 2.4.1 Inter-generational transactions - the basic structure

Unfortunately, our stylised description does not end here. Whatever the precise reasons, at some point in time public institutions for old-age provision were introduced, affecting the pattern of inter-generational exchange more deeply than the expansion of the market. The trouble with this type of solution is that, if compared to Figure 2.4.1, public pensions do not really mimic the 'family constitution' model of pay-as-you-go financing. Instead, individual pension claims accruing to generation t are mostly contingent on having

143

contributed to paying pensions to generation $t-1$. Half (or more) of the system of inter-generational transactions is therefore ignored.

In order to highlight the problems involved in both public pensions and supplementary interventions in the field of public education, I will employ a stylised 'overlapping generations' model of family behaviour. (Most of the technical details involved are dealt with in the annex.) Throughout the following, potential parents are assumed to maximise life-time utility

$$u_t = c_t^\alpha z_{t+1}^\beta (1 + n_{t+1})^\gamma, \quad \alpha + \beta + \gamma = 1. \tag{1}$$

Here, c_t and z_{t+1} denote current consumption and old-age consumption, respectively; $1 + n_{t+1}$ measures the number of children per parent and, hence, the growth rate of the active population. In the objective function, children are taken to be consumption goods for their parents. Through the budget constraint, they may also exhibit the characteristics of investment goods, depending on the institutional framework for family decisions.

The 'family constitution'

In a 'family constitution' model, elderly parents are entitled to receive some fraction a of their children's wages w_{t+1}, given that they complied with the same rule in period t. At the same time, they can increase the productivity of their children by making investment $1 + e_t$ in 'child quality', in a sense lending resources to their children. The cost of raising one child of 'zero quality' is p_t, while the price of each unit of $1 + e_t$ is q_t. Alternatively, parents may save an amount of s_t for old age, thus increasing their period $t+1$ consumption by $(1 + r_{t+1})s_t$.

In a 'small open economy' framework, where current wages w_t and interest rates r_t are determined exogenously, budget constraints that are relevant for periods t and $t+1$ are:

$$
\begin{aligned}
c_t &\equiv (1-a)w_t - s_t - \left(p_t + q_t(1 + e_t)\right)(1 + n_{t+1}) \\
z_{t+1} &\equiv a(1 + e_t)^{1/\delta} w_t (1 + n_{t+1}) + (1 + r_{t+1})s_t
\end{aligned}
\tag{2}
$$

It is easy to see that investment per child is optimal if the marginal rate of return, $aw_{t+1}/q_t - 1$, equals the market rate of interest, r_{t+1}. Solving the model leads to restrictions to be imposed on p_t, q_t, δ and e_t in order to make sure that, in spite of their return, children involve a net cost. Further restrictions, making sure that s_t (and e_t) are positive in an interior optimum, can be, but need not be, imposed. The case where $s_t < 0$ can run into potential credit-rationing, thus conflicting with optimal investment in children. With

144

plausible parameter values applying to representative agents, however, all of these restrictions can be met.

By virtue of the Cobb-Douglas specification of u_t, demand for c_t, z_{t+1} and $1 + n_{t+1}$ is linear in life-time income w_t. In particular,

$$1 + n_{t+1}^* = \frac{\gamma(1-a)}{p_t + q_t(1-\delta)(1+e_t)} w_t \tag{3}$$

can be determined where, given optimal investment per child, parents will spend a constant fraction of period t wages on raising children.

Capital markets

It has been shown that a 'family constitution' can be self-enforcing (see Hammond, 1975; Cigno, 1993 or, for a survey, Rangel, 1999), as I implicitly assumed before. Given the alternative of providing for old age through capital markets, however, there may as well be a strong incentive to avoid the 'entrance fee' involved in the family-based model (through paying aw_t to generation $t-1$) and to rely exclusively on saving and market investment instead. Note that in the very first instant when this option dominates that of making intra-family loans, the family constitution will break down. Based on $u_t(\cdot, 1+n_{t+1})$, generation t will still have children. But they will refrain from making voluntary investment in child quality. (For simplicity, I assume that e_t is now bound to be non-negative, at least.) If compared to successive age cohorts, generation t is left with an extra-benefit, having received $1+e_{t-1} > 1$ from their parents. At the same time, generation $t-1$ faces a serious disappointment because they forgo an important fraction of what they invested for old age.

Formally, starting from period t, parental decisions are based on a model of pure consumption motives for fertility. The relevant budget constraints now are:

$$c_t \equiv w_t - s_t - (p_t + q_t)(1 + n_{t+1})$$
$$z_{t+1} \equiv (1 + r_{t+1})s_t \tag{4}$$

If (negative) substitution effects are stronger than (positive) income effects, optimum fertility turns out to be

$$(1 + n_{t+1}^*)_{CM} = \frac{\gamma}{p_t + q_t} w_t < (1 + n_{t+1}^*)_{FC}. \tag{5}$$

(Indices *FC* and *CM* refer to the 'family constitution' and to the 'capital markets' scenario, respectively.)

Two major problems are involved in this new solution. First, in the present case the reduction in fertility is mainly a sub-optimal outcome of strategic interactions between generations. As a result, there is some degree of inter-generational redistribution going along with the switch in strategies for old-age provision: generation t increases their life-time income at the expense of the preceding generation. Second, the amount of human capital investment per child is clearly reduced: all subsequent generations forego higher earnings based on $1+e_t$, and aggregate production growth decreases.

Public pensions

In order to solve the first of these problems, public authorities may consider the introduction of compulsory pay-as-you-go pensions in period t, thus replacing the family constitution by external enforcement. Basically, schemes of this type collect some fraction b_t of current wages and distribute it to current pensioners either as a uniform lump sum or contingent on their period $t-1$ earnings.

If compared to the pure capital market scenario, this solution smooths the inter-generational pattern of burdens and benefits. But since old age pensions are independent of individual child expenditure, the investment motive for having children is again removed. The periodic budget constraints associated with the public pensions (*PP*) model are:

$$c_t \equiv (1-b_t)w_t - s_t - (p_t + q_t)(1+n_{t+1})$$
$$z_{t+1} \equiv b_{t+1}w_t(1+\bar{n}_{t+1}) + (1+r_{t+1})s_t, \tag{6}$$

where aggregate fertility is now denoted by $1+\bar{n}_{t+1}$.

Assuming for simplicity that $b_t = b_{t+1} = a$, fertility is given by

$$(1+n_{t+1}^*)_{PP} = \frac{\gamma(1-b_t)}{p_t + q_t - \gamma b_{t+1}w_t/(1+r_{t+1})} w_t < (1+n_{t+1}^*)_{FC}. \tag{7}$$

For conventional public pension schemes, both a lower number of children and lower productivity of future workers constitute a problem because, on an aggregate level, the rate of payroll growth determines the amount of old age income to be derived from pay-as-you-go financing (Aaron, 1966). If public pensions are meant to provide a constant benefit level (with respect to current wages w_t), then contribution rates have to be increased in period $t+1$. By equation (7), this implies that the reduction in fertility in period t will be mitigated, while future fertility will decrease even further.

In order to solve the second problem mentioned before, the state may combine public pensions with the introduction of public education, thus increasing e_t (or, rather, average investment per child $\bar{e}_t$) again to its optimum level. In order to do so, an additional tax $d_t w_t$ has to be collected which will be partly off-set by higher pensions later on because generation $t+1$ is more productive. In addition, there may be other types of child-related benefits that are meant to increase total expenditure per child. For simplicity, they are taken to be subsumed here under $\bar{e}_t > 0$ that is publicly provided.

The budget set for the 'public pensions *cum* public education' (*PE*) scenario is given by:

$$c_t \equiv (1 - b_t - d_t)w_t - s_t - (p_t + q_t)(1 + n_{t+1})$$
$$z_{t+1} \equiv b_{t+1}(1 + \bar{e}_t)^{1/\delta} w_t (1 + \bar{n}_{t+1}) + (1 + r_{t+1})s_t$$

(8)

The solution is

$$(1 + \overset{*}{n}_{t+1})_{PE} = \frac{\gamma(1 - b_t - d_t)w_t}{p_t + q_t - \gamma b_{t+1}(1 + \bar{e}_t)^{1/\delta} w_t /(1 + r_{t+1})} < (1 + \overset{*}{n}_{t+1})_{FC},$$ (9)

where the inequality result clearly holds for $b_t = b_{t+1} = a$, but also for any other reasonable constellation of parameters. While the state may restore optimum investment per child - abstracting from a host of potential problems regarding information and motivation involved in public education - there is still a strong incentive to free-ride on other people's efforts with respect to the value of children as an investment for old age. Again, this is due to the fact that pensions received in period $t+1$ are conditioned on contributions $b_t w_t$, but not on individual child expenditure.

A 'social compact' between subsequent generations

From a social point of view, pay-as-you-go pensions are effectively funded by the next generation's human capital, to be measured both by the number and qualification of future workers. As long as this is not fully reflected within the design of pay-as-you-go institutions, a particular type of 'fiscal externality' is created which distorts parental decisions (Willis, 1987; Sinn, 1997; Werding, 1998, ch. 5). The only way to avoid the problem of differing private and social returns to raising children is to condition individual pension benefits on individual investment in children, thus mimicking the incentives created by the old family constitution.

What is needed is a 'social compact' enjoining any pair of successive generations to co-operate in the full system of inter-generational exchange. In our model, this can be achieved by making public pension claims contingent on the number of children raised, since public education takes care of optimum investment per child. An important alternative is to let people choose their contribution to educating generation $t+1$, but to define their pension claims in such a way that investment in children is treated 'as if' it were made in own offspring. Technically, the fact that *ex post* $1+\bar{n}_{t+1}$ will always equal $1+n_{t+1}$ for the average agent (and that $\bar{e}_t$ can be set to equal e_t) must be reflected within the pension formula (*i.e.*, $b_{t+1} = d_t$). Given that, the budget constraints for a 'social compact' (*SC*) scenario turn out to be:

$$c_t \equiv (1-d_t)w_t - s_t - \left(p_t + q_t(1+e_t)\right)(1+n_{t+1})$$
$$z_{t+1} \equiv d_t(1+e_t)^{1/\delta} w_t(1+n_{t+1}) + (1+r_{t+1})s_t \tag{10}$$

This takes us back to the original 'family constitution' model, such that:

$$(1+n_{t+1}^*)_{SC} = (1+n_{t+1}^*)_{FC}, \tag{11}$$

provided that $d_t = a$. (Note that d_t need not be totally time-invariant, but that the rates applying to each pair of mutual transactions should be systematically linked.)

From these theoretical considerations to clear-cut policy recommendations it is certainly some way to go. An immediate implication is that current policies that interfere with inter-generational transactions may be built on a fundamental misconception, the major source of disturbance being public pension schemes. Another important finding is that placing further interventions - like child- related transfers or public education - on top of these schemes is not an ideal solution. But in any case, the view developed here implies that, in the public debate on demographic change, attention should shift from old age pensions to private and public expenditure on children.

3 Generational accounts: Child expenditure and old-age pensions

Nailing down an assessment of the different arrangements for inter-genera-tional transactions which have been sketched before is a hard task. What can be done, however, is this: based on the model of individual decisions employed before, I will now simulate the effects in terms of stylised generational accounts and then compare the results to empirical observations, thus illustrating the impact of different types of public interventions in some more detail.

In their seminal contribution, Auerbach *et al.* (1991) established 'generational accounting' as a measure for the inter-generational distribution of burdens and benefits that are associated with many activities of public policy. Here, the concept will be modified regarding several aspects. First, generational accounting usually comprises as many budget items as possible in order to obtain a broad picture of the relevant effects. Instead, I will confine my attention to public pensions and child-related expenditure only. Second, generational accounts are exclusively concerned with interactions between private households and the public sector. Here, I will include a specific class of purely private transactions - private child expenditure - that are intimately linked to (public) old age pensions. Finally, it should be stressed from the very beginning that, based on the model developed in Section 2, one can do more than just look at inter-generational (re-)distribution.

The stylised generational accounts I am going to set up are based on two major components: payments to the elderly and expenditure on children. What is important, then, is the timing of these transactions over a typical life cycle, where each individual will first receive (make) and then make (receive) payments related to child-rearing (old age provision). If discounted at period t values, the net present value of child-related payments that are relevant for generation t is

$$\underbrace{-\chi_{t-1}(1+r_t)w_{t-1}}_{\text{payments received}} + \underbrace{\chi_t w_t}_{\text{payments made}} = \left(\chi_t - \chi_{t-1}\frac{1+r_t}{(1+g_t)(1+n_t)}\right)w_t. \quad (12)$$

Here, χ measures the fraction of current wages (i.e. of life-time income if there are no bequests) that each generation spends on their children. Similarly, the period t net present value of old-age provision is

$$\underbrace{\pi_t w_t}_{\text{payments made}} - \underbrace{\frac{\pi_{t+1}w_{t+1}}{1+r_{t+1}}}_{\text{payments received}} = \left(\pi_t - \pi_{t+1}\frac{(1+g_{t+1})(1+n_{t+1})}{1+r_{t+1}}\right)w_t, \quad (13)$$

where π is the fraction of income devoted to the elderly. Combining these two types of transactions to obtain the net life-time tax rate τ_t leads to:

$$\tau_t w_t = \underbrace{\left(\pi\left(1-\frac{(1+g_{t+1})(1+n_{t+1})}{1+r_{t+1}}\right)\right.}_{\substack{\text{net tax involved in} \\ \text{public pensions}}} \underbrace{\left. - \chi\left(\frac{1+r_t}{(1+g_t)(1+n_t)}-1\right)\right)w_t,}_{\text{net child expenditure}} \quad (14)$$

$\underbrace{}_{\substack{\text{life-time} \\ \text{net tax}}}$

if the relevant 'transfer' rates π and χ are kept constant over time.

149

The definition of net life-time taxes introduced here is easily applied to the results obtained from our model in Section 2. As long as the 'family constitution' is in place, child-expenditure is determined by optimal decisions regarding $1+e$ and $1+n$, while the fraction of income spent on old age provision is determined by a. Assuming that prices p and q grow in line with wages, net life-time tax rates are constant across all the generations who comply with the current rules. If, starting from period t, one of the alternative arrangements is introduced, individual responses taken by generations $t+x$, $x \in \{0, 1, 2 \ldots\}$, determine the pattern of τ_{t+x} over the sequence of successive generations (eventually also affecting τ_{t-1}).

If we calibrate the model using plausible parameter values, it thus yields alternative simulations for the development of τ_t across generations, given the different institutional settings that have been analysed before. The results of this exercise are displayed in Figure 2.4.2. Figure 2.4.3 gives a breakdown of the results by expenditure on children (χ_t) and the net tax involved in old-age pensions (based on π_t and π_{t+1}). For the calibration, I assume that $\alpha = 0.58$, $\beta = 0.22$, $\gamma = 0.2$, $\delta = 2$, $w_t = 1,000$, $p_t = 200$, $q_t = 20$, and $1 + r_{t+1} = 1,04^{25} \approx 2.67$. Initial values for the 'contribution rates' a and b_t are set to 0.15, while b_{t+1} etc. have to be adjusted to meet the periodic pay-as-you-go constraint with constant levels of pension benefits. In each of the scenarios, the 'family constitution' is assumed to be operative for all generations prior to generation t, implying a steady-state level of τ_t which is close to zero.[1] Generation t is the first to adopt another strategy, based on a switch in the institutional framework: the move is from informal rules that govern intra-family behaviour to using the 'capital market' only for old age provision or to different types of public interventions such as 'public pensions' or 'public pensions *cum* public education'.

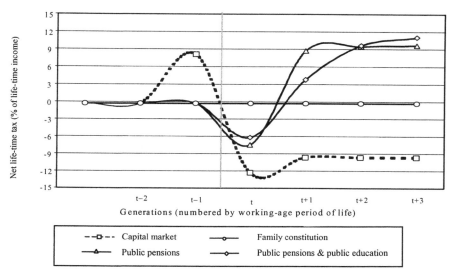

Figure 2.4.2   Stylised generational accounts - simulations

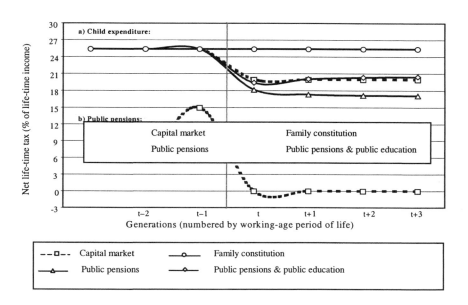

Figure 2.4.3   Stylised generational accounts - components

151

The market-based strategy for old age provision involves a strong shift in net life-time burdens across generations. The net life-time tax falling on generation $t-1$ increases substantially, while all subsequent generations are better off. The reason is that the latter spend nothing on old-age provision of their parents and expend less on their children than earlier generations. The fact that, due to the non-anticipated change in institutions, generation t still receives some amount of investment in their human capital gives them an extra-benefit if compared to generations $t+1$ etc. Also, it should be noted that the unexpected loss falling on generation $t-1$ has a very unfortunate timing, urging them to reduce their old-age consumption by a considerable margin.

The pattern of inter-generational distribution implied by the alternative models of public intervention is different. Since the family constitution is immediately replaced by public old-age provision, the extra burden falling on generation $t-1$ is avoided. Nonetheless, generation t faces an advantage over all other generations due to the fact that they are the first to spend less on (fewer) children. In the public education model, the advantage is somewhat smaller because, given the reduced number of children, generation t is at least liable for educational expenses through tax financed public investment. For subsequent generations, the total burden involved in the public pension scenario exceeds all earlier levels. The reason is that contribution rates for public pensions have to be increased to a new level (of around 0.20) in order to keep the replacement rate of the system a constant.[2] As mentioned before, this reduces the number of children even further, but convergence to a new steady state appears to be rapid. In the case of public pensions plus public education, the story is a little more complicated. Additional taxes that are needed to finance for public education depress fertility even more than in the pure public pension model. At the same time, those children who enter the stage are more productive than in the alternative case such that increases in contribution rates are slower. In the final steady state, however, net life-time taxes placed on future generations will be even more pressing than with just the public pension scheme.

From the composition of changes in net life-time burdens that go along with the different scenarios we have considered (Figure 2.4.3), it is possible to conclude that all these effects are not just a matter of redistribution across generations (of a given size). Our results indicate that, through their design, conventional pay-as-you-go pensions crowd out human capital investment by which they are actually funded. Curing these problems requires more sophistication than installing public education as an auxiliary intervention. Again, the only way to obtain a constant flow of investment in children and, hence, a constant net life-time tax across all generations is given by replacing the family constitution by a 'social compact' scheme as soon as the option of defaulting on one's obligations towards earlier generations becomes effective.

4 Empirical illustration

I will now try to show that the predictions derived from our model largely conform with empirical observations if real-world data are plugged into the stylised generational accounts sketched before. Accounting for the net tax involved in public pension schemes is not much of a problem (Fenge and Werding, 2001).[3] Calculating the net burden involved in child expenditure in a similar fashion turns out to be more complicated. On a conceptual level, one has to be careful to account for those kinds of child-related expenditure only that can be compared with the mandatory burden involved in public pensions. In other words, parental expenditure that are mainly motivated by the consumption of 'child quality' should not be included. This can be done by concentrating on expenditure that conforms with some notion of a minimum standard of living of children which parents are legally obliged to cover in virtually all industrialised countries. In addition, private expenditure on raising and educating children has to be corrected for all kinds of public 'transfers' that are relevant for the case of an average family. One country for which I have gone all the way of doing calculations of this kind is Germany (see Sinn and Werding, 2000).[4]

In the following, I will look at the net life-time burden involved in public pensions *plus* parental child expenditure[5] for the case of a typical one-earner couple with average earnings, where the 'head of the household' is born between 1940 and 2000. The family life cycle is stylised in such a way that individuals born at date t are assumed to enter the labour market in period $t + 20$; to marry and have children, if any, during the following years, depending on observable behaviour of average agents; to spend some legal minimum amount of money and time on their children until they are aged 18; to leave the work-force for disability pensions or early retirement at $t + 54$ with some positive probability; to retire fully at $t + 65$; and to receive old-age pensions and survivor benefits for some 10 to 20 more years, depending on conditional life-expectancy at age 65 (60) for males (females).

Figure 2.4.4 shows the results of an intermediate step of our calculations. Here, the life-time burden incurred through public pensions plus the net cost of raising children has been estimated for couples with different numbers of children, the latter ranging from zero to two. It turns out that there is a general upward trend in total burdens which is mostly due to higher net taxes involved in the pension system. In addition, if considered against the background of a model with endogenous fertility, the effective burden of inter-generational transactions appears to be mainly a matter of individual choices regarding the number of children. Multiplying average costs per child with completed cohort fertility of those born between 1940 and 1960 - with total fertility rates going down from 2.2 to 1.6 - and forecasting completed fertility of subsequent age cohorts to settle to around 1.5, yields the result for a 'married couple with an average number of children' displayed in Figure 2.4.5.

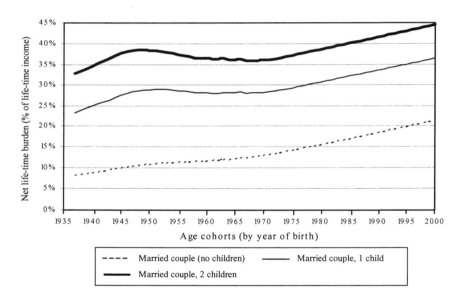

**Figure 2.4.4 Child cost and public pensions in Germany - the total
burden**

As a matter of fact, the final results look very much like the stylised generational accounts which have been simulated for the case of 'public pensions' or 'public pensions *cum* public education' in Section 3. Following the peak burden falling on the parents of the 'baby boomers' (which is not explained by our theoretical considerations), net life-time burdens are lower for individuals born 1955 through 1975 than for those born around 1940. The main reason is that these middle-aged cohorts are relatively large in size so that the contribution rates they are facing in the public pension scheme still are moderate. At the same time, these are the age cohorts who have reduced the average number of their children by a considerable margin, thus causing the demographic problems of public pensions that will become effective starting from 2020. Age cohorts born in 1975 and later will have to bear a larger total burden, due to a rapid increase in net taxes related to public pensions, even if they stick to the low-fertility behaviour invented by their parents.

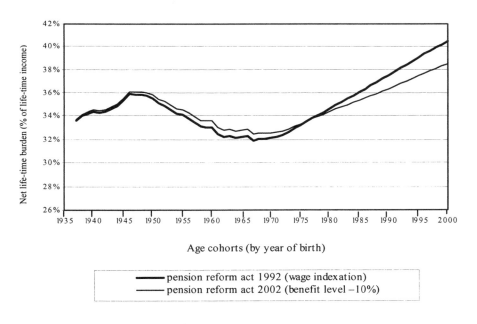

Figure 2.4.5 Stylised generational accounts - the case of Germany (married couple, average no. of children)

It is easy to understand that pension reform can contribute to some extent to smoothing net life-time burdens across generations. As an example, Figure 2.4.5 also displays the effects of the most recent reform of the German pension scheme. The reform will become effective starting from 2002 and is expected to reduce the overall level of pension benefits by about ten per cent over a period of 30 years, also moderating the rise in contribution rates. As a result, the burden falling on those who are currently young will be lower than in the status-quo scenario, while those who are currently middle-aged have to take a higher burden. However, the impact of the reform is small if measured by the overall pattern of net life-time burdens. Also, it should be noted that the correction only takes place at an aggregate level, being relevant for average individuals, and does not affect individual incentives to have more (or less) children than before.

It should be stressed that very similar results could be obtained for virtually all industrialised countries. Calculations of the net taxes involved in public pensions show that they are likely to go up by a considerable margin in many other industrialised countries, like the US, Japan or France.[6] Assuming that the structure of total child cost is basically the same as in the German example (corrected for different levels and trends in public expenditure on children) and taking into account the similar pattern of total fertility rates (declining from 3.4 to 2.0 in the case of the US, from 2.8 to 1.7 in the UK, from 2.7 to 1.8 in France, and from 2.0 to 1.3 in Japan in the period between 1960 and 2000) the time paths of total net life-time burdens will be U-shaped all around the world. To some extent, current reforms that have been designed to buffer public pensions against the impact of demographic ageing may contribute to splitting the total burden of inter-generational transactions more evenly across generations. Nonetheless, the fundamental trends remain roughly unchanged. In other words, the role of individual expenditure on children for the long-term viability of unfunded pensions is not reflected by appropriate adjustments inside the public pension systems.

5 Policy implications

The major concern of this paper lies with policy issues that are involved in the overall system of inter-generational transactions, with a particular focus on the role of child-related expenditure. It turns out that the main problems arising in this area are linked to fundamental questions of institutional design. Throughout the world, the process of modernisation may have weakened the old family constitution - where old age provision was granted in return for prior investment in children - thus establishing an important rationale for the introduction of public pension schemes. Through the design of these systems, however, the state has done the rest of the job, effectively removing the incentive for potential parents to invest in the human capital of their children.

The consequences that show up in terms of lower birth rates and a smaller stock of human capital are mainly seen as constituting a problem for old age provision in an ageing society. It appears that more human capital is needed in order to stabilise public pay-as-you-go pensions. In fact, things may as well be the other way round. If properly designed, some variant of pay-as-you-go institutions may be needed precisely in order to maintain the incentive to invest in human capital. Current systems of public child support do not fully cure the problems that have been discussed here. Instead, they create a number of loose ends on both sides. On the one hand, the growing number of people who have no children do not quite see why they should be liable for financing public education and other transfers to families. On the other hand, parents are complaining that through their expenditure on children, they are effectively funding for old-age protection, nursing care, etc. of those who remain childless. Some of the intransparencies involved in current policies, along with the imbalances and disincentives they establish,[7] will disappear if these loose ends can be tied together.

In a revised system, child expenditure is the key variable. Public old-age provision should be made contingent on private and public spending on children - for each generation as well as on an individual level. If, on average, one generations chooses to spend less on human capital investment, there are good reasons why, for these people, the level of unfunded public pensions should be reduced. Instead, they can be expected to take the resources they do not spend on raising children in order to use them for alternative strategies of old-age provision, e.g. by placing them on the capital market. Obviously, one cannot stop here. Within each generation, there is considerable variation across individuals regarding fertility and the actual amount of child expenditure (Figure 2.4.4). In order to treat all individuals equitably and to re-establish meaningful incentives with respect to child-related expenditure, pension benefits should be linked to individual human capital investment. Again, those who have no, or fewer, children can be referred to the capital market regarding their own old age provision.

Against this background, the problem of how the state should intervene in the area of inter-generational transactions effectively changes its nature. First of all, one should ask for the precise role for public intervention with respect to expenditure on children. Presuming there is one, one may then introduce co-payments by those who are childless and, hence, entitle them to receive public pensions, thus establishing a uniform framework allowing for efficient investment in human capital and for broad-based access to public old age protection.[8] One aspect is particularly important here. Actual parents can be credit-constrained regarding optimal investment in their children. In contrast, even the childless may be interested in including human capital in their investment portfolios. To the extent that actual parents are not the ideal investors, other individuals may thus step in.

The final step towards completing the 'social compact' between subsequent generations is therefore given by linking public pensions to public education, assigning a primary role to the latter. Based on a careful review of the scope for public policy within this area, the 'social compact' will just have to define the mutual obligations of parents, children and 'outside investors', thus putting into perspective all other types of public intervention in the overall system of inter-generational transactions.

Notes

1 Effectively, τ is $- 0.28\%$, thus indicating a small net benefit for all the generations involved. Note that this is perfectly possible since all spending on childrearing (old-age pensions) is off-set by reverse flows one period before (later). (For a broader discussion, see Werding, 2000.)

2 Clearly, this is just one strategy of running public pay-as-you-go systems in the presence of demographic change. The alternative is to keep contribution rates constant, so that the level of benefits adjusts automatically. The assumption made for our simulations conforms to what can be observed around the world, unless contribution rates exceed certain limits.

3 For the case of Germany, this exercise has been pioneered by Thum and Weizsäcker (2000). Using an up-dated version of their model, Fenge and Warding (2001) extended the scope of these calculations to an international level, now comprising the US, Japan, Germany, France, the UK, and some other European countries. The CESifo Pension Model offers a simple accounting framework, neglecting individual responses that could be considered in a general equilibrium context only. It can be used to forecast the long-term financial prospects for running pay-as-you-go public pension schemes.

4 For more details on the way child-related expenditure is taken into account, see Sinn and Warding (2000). The results reported here build on an up-date of their earlier version.

5 Child expenditure received by representative agents when they were young ("χ_{t-1}") is excluded here. Historical data of this kind are not available. Since each individual must be expected to have been a child at some point in time, this omission mainly leads to a shift in levels of net life-time taxes, but does not affect their structure over time.

6 The UK appears to be an outlier. Given current policies, the trend is a decline in net pension taxes for age cohorts born 1960 and later on. This is due to the implicit phase-out of National Insurance effected by a constant policy of CPI indexation of all relevant parameters over the next 50 years. If instead, the British pension scheme would switch to wage indexation, the time-path of net burdens would follow the common pattern of other industrialised countries.

7   Next to the problems involved in public pensions which have been discussed here at length, current systems of child-related transfers may distort educational choices (on behalf) of the children and decisions regarding labour force participation of parents (in particular, mothers). Many of these features might disappear if the full set of policy interventions in inter-generational transactions is reconsidered.

8   A solution of this kind was clearly envisaged by Schreiber (1955), a German economist who drafted the blueprint for the German public pension scheme of the post-war period. For a revival of his ideas, see Lüdeke (1988), Warding (1998, 1999), or Ott (2001).

References

Aaron, H.J. (1996) 'The Social Insurance Paradox', *The Canadian Journal of Economics and Political Science*, vol. 32, pp. 371-74.

Auerbach, A.J., Gokhale, J. and Kotlikoff, L.J. (1991) 'Generational Accounts: A meaningful alternative to deficit accounting', in D. Bradford (ed), *Tax Policy and the Economy*5, MIT Press, Cambridge, pp. 55-110.

Becker, G.S. (1960) 'An Economic Analysis of Fertility', in NBER (ed), *Demographic and Economic Change in Developed Countries*, Columbia University Press, New York, London, pp. 209-31.

Becker, G.S. and Barro, R.J. (1988) 'A Reformulation of the Economic Theory of Fertility', *Quarterly Journal of Economics*, vol. 103, pp. 1-25.

Becker, G.S. and Murphy, K.M. (1988) 'The Family and the State', *The Journal of Law and Economics*, vol. 31, pp. 1-18.

Ben-Porath, Y. (1980) 'The F-Connection: Families, Friends and Firms, and the Organization of Exchange', *Population and Development Review*, vol. 6, pp. 1-30.

Cigno, A. (1993) 'Intergenerational Transfers Without Altruism. Family, Market and State', *European Journal of Political Economy*, vol. 9, pp. 505-18.

Cigno, A., Casolaro, L. and Rosati, F.C. (2000) 'The Role of Social Security in Household Decisions: VAR Estimates of Saving and Fertility Behaviour in Germany', CESifo Working Paper No. 934.

Cigno, A. and Rosati, F.C. (1996) 'Jointly Determined Saving and Fertility Behaviour: Theory and Estimates for Germany, Italy, UK and USA', *European Economic Review*, vol. 40, pp. 1561-89.

Ehrlich, I. and Lui, F.T. (1998) 'Social Security, the Family, and Economic Growth', *Economic Inquiry*, vol. 36, pp. 390-409.

Ehrlich, I. and Zhong, J-G. (1998) 'Social Security and the Real Economy: An Inquiry into Some Neglected Issues', *American Economic Review PP,* vol. 88, pp. 151-57.

Fenge, R. and Warding, M. (2001) *Old-age Provision in Ageing Societies. Equity, Efficiency, and Sustainability*, Interim Report (mimeo), CESifo, Munich.

Hammond, P.J. (1975) 'Cahrity: Altruism or Cooperative Egoism', in Phelps, E.S. (ed), *Altruism, Morality and Economic Theory*, Russell Sage, New York, pp. 115-31.

Lḥdeke, R. (1988) 'Staatsverschuldung, Intergenerative Redistribution und Umlagefinanzierte Rentenversicherung', in Klaus, J. and Klemmer, P. (eds), *Wirtschaftliche Strukturprobleme und Soziale Fragen*, Duncker & Humblot, Berlin, pp. 167-81.

Mulligan, C.B. and Martin, X.S. (1999) 'Social Security in Theory and Practice (parts I + II)', *NBER Working Papers* Nos. 7118 and 7119.

Ott, N. (1992) *Intrafamily Bargaining and Household Decisions*, Springer, Berlin.

Ott, N. (2001) 'Die Sicherstellung Familialer Funktionen als Ordnungspolitische Aufgabe', forthcoming in Mhckl, W. (ed), *Familienpolitik*, Sch`ningh, Paderborn.

Pollak, R.A. (1985) 'A Transaction Cost Approach to Families and Households', *Journal of Economic Literature*, pp. 23, 581-608.

Prinz, A. (1990) 'Endogenous fertility, altruistic behaviour across generations, and social security systems', *Journal of Population Economics*, pp. 3, 179-92.

Rangel, A. (1999) 'Forward and Backward Intergenerational Goods: A Theory of Intergenerational Exchange', Working paper (mimeo), Stanford University.

Rosati, F.C. (1996) 'Social Security in a Non-altruistic Model with Uncertainty and Endogenous Fertility', *Journal of Public Economics*, vol. 60, pp. 283-94.

Samuelson, P.A. (1958) 'An Exact Consumption-Loan Model of Interest with or Without the Social Contrivance of Money', *Journal of Political Economy*, vol. 66, pp. 467-82.

Schreiber, W. (1955) *Existenzsicherheit in der Industriellen Gesellschaft*, Bachem, K`ln.

Sen, A. (1990) 'Cooperation, Inequality and the Family', in McNicoll, G. and Cain, M. (eds), *Rural Development and Population: Institutions and Policy*, Oxford University Press, New York, Oxford, pp. 61-76.

Sinn, H-W. (1997) 'The Value of Children and Immigrants in a Pay-as-you-go Pension System', *NBER Working Paper* No. 6229.

Sinn, H-W. and Warding, M. (2000) 'Rentenniveausenkung und Teilkapitaldeckung: ifo Empfehlungen zur Konsolidierung des Umlageverfahrens', *ifo Schnelldienst*, vol. 53, pp. 12-25.

Thum, M. and von Weizs@cker, J. (2000) 'Implizite Einkommensteuer als Messlatte fhr die aktuellen Rentenreformvorschl@ge', *Perspektiven der Wirtschaftspolitik*, vol. 1, pp. 453-68.

Werding, M. (1998) *Zur Rekonstruktion des Generationenvertrages*, Mohr-Siebeck, Thbingen.

Werding, M. (1999) 'Umlagefinanzierung als Humankapitaldeckung: Grundrisse eines erneuerten "Generationenvertrages"', *Jahrbhcher fhr National`konomie und Statistik*, vol. 218, pp. 491-511.

Warding, M. (2000) 'Is there a new "Social Insurance Paradox"? An alternative of pay-as-you-go institutions', Working paper (mimeo), Ifo Institute, Munich.

Willis, R.J. (1987) 'Externalities and Population', in Johnson, D.G. and Lee, R. (eds), *Population Growth and Economic Development*, University of Wisconsin, Madison, pp. 661-702.

Annex   Inter-generational transactions - a simple model

The model employed in Section 2 has the following generic form:

$$\max u_t = c_t^\alpha z_{t+1}^\beta (1 + n_{t+1})^\gamma$$

$$\text{s.t.} \quad (1 - T_t) w_t \equiv c_t + \frac{z_{t+1}}{1 + r_{t+1}} + P_t (1 + n_{t+1}) \qquad \text{(A.1)}$$

Utility is assumed to be Cobb-Douglas, with $\alpha + \beta + \gamma = 1$. In each case, inter-temporal budget constraints can be derived from the periodic constraints reported in the main text. $0 \le T_t \le 1$ is a levy imposed on period t wages through the family constitution or public compulsion. $P_t > 0$ is the effective cost of raising children, taking into account potential returns that accrue in the different systems of inter-generational transactions.

In principle, parents can increase the productivity of their children by maing investment $1 + e_t$ in 'child quality', such that

$$w_{t+1} = (1 + e_t)^{1/\delta} w_t, \quad \delta > 1 \qquad \text{(A.2)}$$

Taking logs, the utility function can be transformed into a utility index

$$v_t = \alpha \ln c_t + \beta \ln z_{t+1} + \gamma \ln(1 + n_{t+1})$$

which can be handled much easier following analyses. Note that for all effects discussed below, closed-form solutions can be derived. Since they are dependent on complicated sets of assumptions regarding quite a number of parameters, I will restrict my attention to highlighting the main results.

The 'family constitution'

In the pure intra-family model of inter-generalisation transactions, $T_t = a$ and

$$P_t = p_t + (q_t - \frac{a(1 + e_t^*)^{1/\delta - 1} w_t}{1 + r_{t+1}})(1 + e_t^*) = p_t + q_t (\delta - 1)(1 + e_t^*)$$

The latter result is obtained by minimising effective child costs (or, maximising life-time income) with respect to e_t, taking into account the 'human capital production function' given in eq. (A.2). This yields

$$\frac{a(1+e_t^*)^{1/\delta-1} w_t}{\delta q_t} = 1 + r_{t+1}$$

The first-order conditions are

$$\alpha / c_t \equiv \lambda, \tag{A.3}$$

$$\beta / z_{t+1} \equiv \lambda /(1 + r_{t+1}), \tag{A.4}$$

$$\gamma /(1 + n_{t+1}) \equiv \lambda(p_t + q_t(1-\delta)(1+e_t)) \tag{A.5}$$

where λ is a Lagrange multiplier. This leads to a number of familiar results, like $v_z = v_c /(1 + r_{t+1})$, etc. Marshallian demand is given by

$$c_t^* = \alpha(1-a)w_t, \tag{A.6}$$

$$z_{t+1}^* = \beta(1 + r_{t+1})(1-a)w_t' \tag{A.7}$$

$$1 + n_{t+1}^* = \frac{\gamma(1-a)}{p_t + q_t(1-\delta)(1+e_t)} w_t, \tag{A.8}$$

Note that, in optimum

$$1 + e_t^* = ((1 + r_{t+1})\frac{\delta q_t}{aw_t})^{\delta/(1-\delta)}, \tag{A.9}$$

$$s_t^* = (\beta - \frac{\gamma \delta q_t(1+e_t)}{p_t + q_t(1-\delta)(1+e_t)})(1-a)w_t \tag{A.10}$$

Depending on the relevant parameters, saving s_t as well as human capital investment (per child) e_t can turn out to be negative in an interior solution. None of these cases necessarily constitutes a problem - given that individuals are not credit-constraint. The only restriction which really has to be imposed for the overall problem to be well-behaved is

$$1 + e_t < \frac{p_t}{q_t(\delta - 1)} \Leftrightarrow P_t > 0$$

Capital markets

In this case $T_t = 0$, $P_t = p_t + q_t$, while e_t automatically drops to zero. Hence, Marshallian demand is given by

$$c_t^* = \alpha w_t, \qquad (A.11)$$

$$z_{t+1}^* = \beta(1 + r_{t+1})w_t, \qquad (A.12)$$

$$1 + n_{t+1}^* = \frac{\gamma}{p_t + q_t} w_t \qquad (A.13)$$

Optimum savings is $s_t^* = z_{t+1}^*/(1 + r_{t+1}) = \beta w_t$. Optimum fertility is lower than in the family constitution model since, with reasonable assumptions on a, the increase in child cost P_t more than off-sets the increase in net income.

Public pensions

Now,

$$T_t = b_t(1 - \frac{b_{t+1}}{b_t} \frac{1 + \overline{n}_{t+1}}{1 + r_{t+1}})$$

And $P_t = p_t + q_t$. Again e_t will be zero.

As a consequence, Marshallian demand functions are

$$c_t^* = \alpha(1 - b_t(1 - \frac{b_{t+1}}{b_t} \frac{1 + \overline{n}_{t+1}}{1 + r_{t+1}}))w_t \qquad (A.14)$$

$$z_{t+1}^* = \beta(1 + r_{t+1})(1 - b_t(1 - \frac{b_{t+1}}{b_t} \frac{1 + \overline{n}_{t+1}}{1 + r_{t+1}}))w_t \qquad (A.15)$$

$$1 + n_{t+1}^* = \gamma(1 - b_b(1 - \frac{b_{t+1}}{b_t} \frac{1 + \overline{n}_{t+1}}{1 + r_{t+1}})) \frac{w_t}{p_t + q_t} \qquad (A.16)$$

Ex post, $\overline{n}_{t+1}$ will of course equal n_{t+1}^*. Assuming that $b_t = b_{t+1} = a$, fertility will be strictly lower than in the baseline case since $(1 + e_t)^{1/\delta} > \gamma$. Allowing for variations in b that are needed in order to keep the level of pension benefits constant will not alter this result substantially.

Another result which may be less intuitive is that, for $b_t = a$, saving

$$s_t^* = (\beta(1 - b_t) - (1 - \beta)b_{t+1} \frac{1 + \overline{n}_{t+1}}{1 + r_{t+1}})w_t \qquad (A.17)$$

can be higher than in the 'family constitution' case, although public pensions are generally assumed to displace private savings. The reason is that, with endogenous fertility and due to lower numbers of children and lower returns per child, the representative individual will have to rely more heavily on the capital market with regard to optimal provisions for old age.

Public pensions and public education

In this case, investment in children is financed through an additional tax

$$d_t + \frac{q_t \overline{e}_t (1 + \overline{n}_{t+1})}{w_t}$$

As a consequence, investment in children in financed through an additional tax

$$T_t = b_t (1 - \frac{b_{t+1}}{b_t} \frac{(1 + \overline{e}_t)^{1/\delta}(1 + \overline{n}_{t+1})}{1 + r_{t+1}}) + d_t,$$

while P_t still equals $p_t + q_t$.
   Marshallian demand is

$$c_t^* = \alpha (1 - b_t (1 - \frac{b_{t+1}}{b_t} \frac{(1 + \overline{e}_t)^{1/\delta}(1 + \overline{n}_{t+1})}{1 + r_{t+1}}) - d_t) w_t, \qquad (A.18)$$

$$z_{t+1}^* = \beta (1 + r_{t+1})(1 - b_t (1 - \frac{b_{t+1}}{b_t} \frac{(1 + \overline{e}_t)^{1/\delta}(1 + \overline{n}_{t+1})}{1 + r_{t+1}}) - d_t) w_t, \quad (A.19)$$

$$1 + n_{t+1}^* = \gamma (1 - b_t (1 - \frac{b_{t+1}}{b_t} \frac{(1 + \overline{e}_t)^{1/\delta}(1 + \overline{n}_{t+1})}{1 + r_{t+1}}) - d_t) \frac{w_t}{p_t + q_t}, \quad (A.20)$$

Again, $\overline{n}_{t+1}$ will equal n_{t+1}^* *ex post*. The comparison between eqs. (A.20) and (A.8) is a little more complicated here. For cases where $b_t = b_{t+1} = a$ or even $b_t + d_t = a$ etc. fertility will be strictly lower than in the intra-family model. Only if b_{t+1} is much larger than a, fertility *can* be higher, because the returns to having children may over-compensate for lower net wages.

Now, d_t is relevant for both investment in children and old-age pensions that have to be paid to the parent generation - like a in the case of the 'family constitution'. If the returns to human capital are attributed according to individual investment, $T_t = d_t$ (not $2d_t$) and

$$P_t = p_t + (q_t - \frac{d_t(1+e_t)^{1/\delta-1}w_t}{1+r_{t+1}})(1+e_t) = p_t + q_t(\delta - 1)(1 + e_t^*).$$

This implies that e_t is adjusted (or chosen) to be at the original optimum level. For $d_t = a$, the maximisation problem therefore boils down to that of the baseline intra-family model. The only difference is that, absent the old system of social norms and family cohesion, some public compulsion may be needed in order to make the system operative.

PART 3

OTHER ASPECTS OF SOCIAL SECURITY PROVISION FOR CHILDREN

3.1 Formalising the informal: family obligations in modern Asia

Peter Scherer[*]

Introduction

This article explores some aspects of the nature of the family relationships which underlie Asian social policies, and raises some questions about the strains they are likely to face. It argues that the distinction that is sometimes drawn between 'informal' family based systems in Asia and 'formal' systems in Western countries confuses cause and effect. The reason that Asian systems appear 'informal' is because of the living arrangements on which they are based. Where these have changed due to economic change, formal institutions have started to appear. While there is still a difference with Western arrangements, it is less stark than many Asian and Western analysts often assume.

The discussion centres on responsibility for support of elderly people by their children. After a review of residential patterns for the elderly in Asia, the relation between formal and informal obligations is discussed. This is followed by an account of how Singapore has 'formalised the informal' by establishing a tribunal to settle disputes between elderly parents and their children about the level of support, including a description of the way the tribunal functions. The final section addresses broader issues about how to reconcile the preservation of family solidarity with the needs of a dynamic economy and falling family size.

Living arrangements for the elderly

In Thailand, the Philippines, Taiwan and Singapore, only five per cent of the elderly have no living child. Amongst those with an adult child, at least 70 per cent are co-resident with an adult child: in Singapore, this figure is 90 per cent for Chinese and Malay families (Ofstedal *et al.*, 1999, Table 1).

Additionally, many children are quasi co-resident: they live next door or near enough to be in daily contact. Overall, in Thailand and Philippines about 90 per cent of elderly parents are co-resident or quasi co-resident (Ofstedal *et al.*, 1999, p. 5). In both these countries, children who are not co-resident provide resources to their parents, and monetary transfers are greatest on the part of those living furthest away (Ofstedal *et al.*, 1999, Table 6).

Similar patterns apply in Indonesia: in a 1986 ASEAN survey of almost 4,000 elderly Javanese, three-quarters of the respondents lived with family members other than or in addition to their spouse. An analysis of the (separate) 1993 Indonesian family life survey shows that 55 per cent of them received money from non co-resident children. However, the pattern of transfers is complex, and due to transfers from elderly parents to younger children still at school, the transfers from and to parents were, on average, equal. Since these transfers are, in aggregate, equal to three per cent of the household incomes of the elderly, they are clearly of minor importance, *on average,* compared with income shared with those who are co-resident. Patterns of transfers are similar in Malaysia amongst Malays, although per capita GDP is three times as high as in Indonesia. In both countries, transfers between households are very heterogeneous: some families have extremely close knit transfer networks, while others do not engage in transfers much at all. Hence the low average amount of transfers per household is only a crude indicator of their importance (Frankenberg *et al.*, 2001).

The percentage living with one child or at least one married child has been falling in Japan, Korea and Taiwan over the past decades, though it remains high by European standards (Hermalin, 2000, Table 7). The decline has been greatest in Korea and Japan. In Korea, the proportion of elderly people not living with a child more than doubled (to 47 per cent) between 1984 and 1998 (OECD, 2000, p. 123). In Japan, the figure was also approximately 45 per cent in the mid-1990's (OECD, 2001, p. 33). It is likely that averages now represent a combination of cohorts with growing tendencies to live separately: in Japan, the proportion of individuals in a household of three (or more) increases after age 60. This suggests that the cohorts of retired people who were born more recently are more likely to live separately.[1] Older parents living without their children may signify a greater preference for privacy and independence, as well as the economic means to achieve this. (Hermalin, 2000, p. 11).

Survey data from 1995 for Thailand suggest a similar mild tendency for those able to afford it to remain in separate households. The proportion of the elderly who lived only with a spouse almost doubled (from 7 to 12 per cent) between 1986 and 1995 (Knodel and Chayovan, 1997, Table 3). In urban areas, such couples were particularly likely to live in households rated by interviewers as 'well built', and in rural areas they were likely to have a toilet (Knodel and Chayovan, 1997, Table 5). However, they were less likely to have access to other household possessions (such as a colour TV or refrigerator) than those living with their children (though the causal relationships here are not definite: some children may well prefer to live with parents with extensive possessions!). Those living alone (without a spouse or children) had access to substantially fewer possessions and had poorer living conditions. This latter group had not grown in importance, remaining less than five per cent of the elderly in 1986 and 1995.

The tendency for increasing affluence to lead to separate households is not universal, however. In 1995, amongst elderly Singaporeans with at least one child, only ten per cent of those with a spouse lived alone. Amongst those without a spouse the figure was five per cent (Chan and Cheung, 1997, Table 1b).

It is important to emphasise that such separate housing arrangements are quite consistent with continuing family ties. 'Quasi co-residence' means that even elderly couples living alone are likely to have daily visits and support from their children.

Formal and informal obligations

Since it is in practice impossible to prescribe support obligations within a co-resident household, support for the elderly is, in these countries, not usually a matter for formal or legal rules. These can only come into play for relations between family members who are not co-resident. Such rules are to be found in many Western societies. However, in societies where co-residence is the rule, basing obligations on rules will generally be felt to be inappropriate, even for family members who do not live in the same dwelling. In addition, countries with a strong Confucian influence on public affairs will not be comfortable with the strong emphasis on formal legal processes found in both Romano-Germanic law and in the English common law. For example, the Encyclopædia Britannica article on Japanese law asserts:

> ... In many areas of Japanese life, it is still difficult to predict whether a dispute will be settled under legal standards, and it is often impossible to know whether a person will enforce those rights that are legally available to him. The concepts pervasive in Western law - that the legal consequences of a particular

conduct should be predictable before the conduct has occurred, that in any dispute the courts should give full effect to claims (a plaintiff receiving all or nothing), and that individual disputes should be settled without considering the parties social and economic background - have not penetrated deeply into Japanese law. ... Compromise based on legally irrelevant considerations is encouraged, and disputes are often resolved by techniques which fall outside formal law.

Perhaps for this reason, formal support systems in such societies do not mandate support by those who are not residing together, but they do assume that it is available. For example, in Korea there is no legal requirement to support elderly parents, but public policy both encourages it through tax concessions and assumes that such support is available. Korea has just revised its social assistance legislation to make the granting of assistance an entitlement (in cases of established need) rather than discretionary. But these entitlements to social assistance in case of need are conditional on an assessment of the capacity of all family members to assist: public assistance can be refused if an able-bodied relative could provide it (even if that relative is not in employment and therefore does not have the resources to provide help) (OECD, 2000, p. 129).

Similar practices apply in Japan (Goodman, 1998). Goodman describes how, in Japan, the *minseiiin* network of social mentors undertakes responsibility for safeguarding the welfare of their communities. He describes a system in which moral persuasion, rather than the assessment of legal entitlements, is the main form of intervention. He points out that while those eligible for assistance now have (in principle) the right to appeal against a failure to recommend it on the part of *minseiiin*, few of them exercise this. Hence many of those who are formally eligible for benefits do not apply for them: he cites a study which estimated a take-up rate of 25 per cent (Goodman, 1998, p. 148). Goodman argues that one reason for this is that the assumption that the *minseiiin* will have sufficient knowledge of each household to intervene to prevent extreme distress is not always justified in urban areas, where individuals can become socially isolated and invisible to their neighbours.

In other countries with a colonial past, such as Indonesia, formal law is distrusted as a foreign imposition. Customary and religious law have standing, but are not in general enforced through formal courts. Customary law, in particular, is interpreted by community leaders. The uncertainty which results from the lack of clear rules - particularly when inheritance rights to property are concerned - is an important reason for co-residence in many instances. Possession (the saying goes) is nine-tenths of the law. If this is the case even in countries where property rights are clearly delineated, it is even more the case where they are fluid.

The sense of obligation and gratitude towards parents by children, which is a an underlying feature of the family relations in many societies, can have perverted consequences, particularly when fast economic development is driving aspirations to rapid increases in wealth. In Thailand, for example, concepts of obligation and gratitude towards parents can lead young people to leave school and their home villages in order to provide remittances to their parents: sometimes by entering harmful occupations, including prostitution.[2]

Formalising the informal: The Singapore maintenance of Parents Act

In the light of the difficulties of introducing formal legal obligations into these relationships, and the cultural resistance to doing so in Asian societies, it is interesting to examine an important break with this tradition of relying on informal community sanctions to ensure elderly people are cared for. Singapore has been particularly successful at maintaining a high rate of co-habitation between elderly people and their adult children. It provides both tax incentives and housing priority for children co-residing with or caring for elderly parents, and in spite of its high level of economic development has a rate of co-residence similar to or even above that found in its less affluent neighbours. This would suggest, on the surface, that there was no need for formal obligations. This is confirmed by survey data: in a survey carried out in 1995, only 11 per cent of elderly Singaporeans stated that they had inadequate financial security for old age. Of this 11 per cent, only six per cent (that is, less than one per cent of all the elderly) said that the main reason for inadequacy was that their children were not giving enough (Chan and Cheung, 1997, Table 2).

Nonetheless, in 1996 Singapore passed a *Maintenance of Parents Act*, which introduced a legal obligation for children to support their aged parents, and established a special tribunal, the *Tribunal for the Maintenance of Parents*, to mediate and, if necessary, adjudicate such claims. In a speech delivered prior to the passage of the Act, a Singapore Minister summarised the need for such a measure by contrasting it with the 'negative experiences' of other countries 'to warn ourselves that their experiences can be ours too, if we are not too careful':

The key question behind the proposed Parents Maintenance bill is who should support vulnerable old people who cannot maintain themselves adequately. The option is clear - should each family continue to take care of its elderly dependents, as families have done throughout history before the advent of the socialist welfare state? Or alternatively, should looking after the aged be the collective responsibility of all taxpayers? Is it better for children to contribute something to support their parents each month or for them to pay higher taxes so that the state will distribute maintenance to the elderly in society? Over the last four decades, the people in Europe, North America and Australia have chosen the welfare state with high taxes and high social security transfers (Lim, 1994).

The Act he was describing, the *Maintenance of Parents Act*, was passed in 1995 (Act 35 of 1995, Republic of Singapore). It originated with a proposal from Associate Professor Cheong Ming Woon, who was a nominated MP from 1994 to 1996.[3] The original proposal appears to have been for parents to have recourse to the District Court to seek an order to provide support. In the words of a description provided by the Tribunal:

> He (Associate Professor Woon) felt that 'a parent's right to support from his children should be seen as a corollary of a parent's obligation to support his children'. Hence he was of the view that is the latter could be legislated, there should be no objection to legislate the former. The intent of this bill was to provide legal recourse for securing financial maintenance from children and not to legislate filial piety. Besides providing this safety net for aged parents, the Act also serves as a deterrent to children neglecting their parents.

After lengthy hearings,[4] he bill was amended to establish a Tribunal, modelled after an Industrial Tribunal with an initial conciliation procedure and then arbitration if conciliation fails.[5] The only clear opposition to the proposal in the submissions printed by the Select Committee which considered the Bill came from representatives of the Singapore National Front, who were from the Malay community. Their submission includes the statements:

> To look after parent is a moral obligation of every child. To enforce court order upon the child to pay maintenance to their parent is to enforce moral obligation upon the child. Do we need legislation to enforce moral obligation? The answer is NO, we do not need any legislation to enforce moral obligation.

> Legal action between parent and child do not conform to our Asian values and norm. It encourages:

i)   families washing their dirty linen in public
ii)   animosity among the family members, relative and even friend; and
iii)   parent separating from each other or end up in divorce.

Such action is left unchecked will result in the Woon epidemic spreading throughout our societies tearing apart the very fabric that has all this while knitted our family tightly together.[6]

In the subsequent hearings, these spokesmen argued that:

It is possible that parents may disregard their own duties to save for their own future. That is why we disagree with having such a law.[7]

When pressed, they stated that in cases where children have failed to provide for their parents, those parents should be maintained by the State.[8]

This latter point of view was rejected and the bill was enacted. However, several submissions did propose that evidence be heard in private and that orders not be published. In spite of some advocacy of 'naming and shaming' ungrateful children, the fears of the consequence of public disputes won out. In speaking to the issue, the member of the Committee who moved the (agreed) amendments, Mrs. Yu-Foo Yee Shan, said:

There were varying responses as to whether children should be shamed for not maintaining their parents. The general reaction was that is would be best to keep such proceedings private as they involve family relationships. To do otherwise may damage an already fragile familial relationship and hinder further efforts at mediation ... [9]

Functioning of the tribunal for the maintenance of parents[10]

The tribunal has now been in operation since 1 June 1996. In spite of initial predictions (in the parliamentary hearings) that it would hear few cases, it has had a steady caseload (see Table 3.1.1) although there is a slight downward trend over the years.

Table 3.1.1   Number of applications for maintenance and variation of maintenance orders from June 1999 to October 2000

Year	Applications for maintenance	Variations of maintenance orders
1996 (*1 June – Dec 96*)	152	-
1997	138	39
1998	134	63
1999	127	89
2000 (*1 Jan 00 – 31 Oct 00*)	90	82
Total	641	273

Source: Office of the Secretary; Tribunal for the Maintenance of Parents - 1 November 2000

Table 3.1.2   Outcome of applications as at 31 May 2000

Outcome of applications	Number	%
Maintenance order made	452	77.1
Dismissed/withdrawn/no maintenance order etc.	123	21.0
Applications pending	11	1.9
Total	586	100.0

Source: Office of the Secretary; Tribunal for the Maintenance of Parents - 11 July 2000

The Act also provides for the Minister to appoint a Commissioner for the Maintenance of Parents. Currently, the Director of Social Welfare (Deputy Secretary of the Ministry for Community Development) is also the Commissioner for the Maintenance of Parents. He or she represents parents who cannot do so themselves, and will if necessary bring cases on their behalf.

Only Singapore residents can lodge a claim, and only children resident in Singapore can be cited. When a claim is lodged, there is initially an attempt to arrive at a consent agreement through conciliation: these proceedings cannot be used in evidence if the matter does have to be determined. If an agreement is made, it still goes before the Tribunal for mention, for the Tribunal to satisfy itself that it is in fact just and equitable to be converted into a maintenance order. Between 1996-1999, 68 per cent of applications where the Tribunal had ordered maintenance achieved full or partial settlement at mediation. About 60 per cent of applications are settled by such an agreement, although parties occasionally withdraw their consent. If no agreement is reached, a hearing is held. There is a permanent President and 11 lay members; each case is heard by the President and two other members. The composition of each bench is influenced by the ethnic composition of the family in question.

The proceedings are non-adversarial and private: no legal representation is allowed. Orders are supposed to be on the basis of what is 'just and equitable'. The Act specifies:

> ... a parent is unable to maintain himself if his total or expected income and other financial resources are inadequate to provide him with basic amenities and basic physical needs including (but not limited to) shelter, food and clothing.

The circumstances of the children, including their own family responsibilities, are taken into account: they are not required to pay more than they can afford. The tribunal will examine both the needs of the applicant and the circumstances of the respondent children. If it is not 'just and equitable' that an order be made because of the children cannot afford to provide support, no order will be made.

The amount payable per child can vary: one may be ordered to pay $50 per month, another $300. On average, for the 1996-1999 period, the total awarded per parent was about $350 for those children named as respondents. However, it can be higher if the children consent to pay more in the conciliation hearing. Nursing home costs will be taken into account in determining need. An order can include care arrangements: one child may be ordered to provide board and/or lodging as his maintenance contribution, and another cash.

Orders are enforced in the family court by the same enforcement proceedings as are used for maintenance orders for children. In order to guide the public, grounds for decision with the names omitted are occasionally released by the Tribunal for publication. Orders can be (and are) varied over time by the Tribunal as family circumstances and needs change, and can be extended to previously uncited children (if, for example, children return from abroad and resume their residence in Singapore). Appeals on 'law, mixed law or fact' can be made to the High Court, but only one such case has ever been brought, and the maintenance order concerned was annulled by consent.

For the future, it is hoped that the need for such claims will decline as more retired people are able to support themselves from their Provident Fund savings. Survey data indicate that this hope is well founded: in 1995, those amongst the elderly who had Provident Fund accounts were significantly less likely to cite their children as their main source of financial support (Chan and Cheung, 1997). If this happens, it is possible that the tribunal may be ease to be a separate jurisdiction, and be merged with another body.

The limits of family networks

The decision to pass the Maintenance of Parents Act, and the significant number of cases brought before the tribunal established under the Act, shows that securing a high rate of co-residence was in itself not sufficient to ensure all families provided the support they could afford. Ironically, in introducing such legislation Singapore was not introducing a uniquely Asian approach. In European countries with a civil law tradition, the obligation to provide support to parents and grandparents has long been a feature of the civil law, and remains to this day enforceable in the law courts. In fact, some features of welfare state developments in these countries can be interpreted as insurance against the risk of being required to provide such support. This is, for example, clearly the case for the 'fourth branch' of the German system of social insurance, which was introduced in 1994 to provide coverage against long term care costs. In such cases, taxpayers have become liable to help not because of the *absence* of family support obligations, but because of their *presence*.

Well-financed formal social insurance systems can clearly contribute to security for those in the formal economy. However, in any society with a large informal sector, they cannot be the basis of the safety net. Those who are most in need of assistance will often not be covered by formal institutions, or will quickly exhaust their entitlements. In a country in which the formal sector incomes are in general higher than the informal sector, the subsidy itself will be regressive in its overall impact[11] and will still not address the most urgent needs. Edwards and Manning (2000) discuss how a system of income security for employees in the formal sector might best be designed in a way that avoids this problem.

But this does not mean that the safety net issue can then be just left to family support obligations, formal or informal. The informal networks which tie families together are, of course, the basis for both economic development and mutual protection. It is well understood by economists that economic development does not come about by the actions of disconnected individuals. Business networks and arrangements - within families and communities - are an essential part of a successful competitive economy, and understanding the nature of their contribution is at the core of the current interest in 'social capital' as a component of the growth process. However, recent experience in South East Asia has suggested that these traditional obligations have become less effective as traditional ties have become more distant. Urban dwellers who lost their jobs in the crisis often found they were not welcome in the rural villages where their relatives still lived.

Also, social networks can be used to block change as well as to promote it. Families work together to build up businesses and pool investment funds, but also work together to exclude outsiders and protect established ways. Ethnic groups draw on common understandings to launch new ventures, but also close ranks to exclude outsiders and prevent them competing with local groups.

It is in times of crisis that such defensive uses of family and community ties are particularly likely to come to the fore. Competition from outside the group which was tolerated, even if resented, during periods of economic growth can come to be feared and attacked when times are hard. When there is no safety net to limit the distress resulting from failure, such tensions can become violent and destructive. Such tensions were a major cause of the rise of fascist regimes in Europe, and the generalisation of social insurance after the second world war was in large part a response to this tragedy.

In a country with a very low per capita income, policies that promote economic growth are clearly the primary condition for durably reducing the rate of absolute poverty. Any safety net programme which impedes growth is therefore likely to be potentially counter-productive, as it risks at best protecting a part of the population from sharing the endemic poverty of the rest of the population. For example, formal sector safety nets can easily fall into this defensive role in countries in which that sector employs a minority of the population.

However, it is important here not to confuse a necessity with a sufficient condition. Economic growth that leaves significant portions of the population feeling insecure, with only community and family resources to rely on in times of crisis, is vulnerable to social unrest. Social unrest will be a continuing threat even if, as long as growth continues, the disposable income of the majority of the population does grow. The stock of physical capital and economic relationships, which constitute the fruits of growth, are always under threat of destruction and deterioration through civil

179

unrest. Developing an approach which builds on but also extends beyond family solidarity is therefore a necessity for sustainable economic development.

Notes

* Head, Social Policy Division, OECD. The views expressed in this article are the author's and do not necessarily represent the views of the OECD or its member countries.

1 Though it could also mean that old people who formerly lived separately move in with their children as they grow older. Longitudinal data would be needed to distinguish between these two hypotheses.

2 I am grateful to Ms Chongcharen Sornkaew (Country Director for Thailand, Global Alliance for Workers and Communities) for this observation.

3 Associate Professor Woon (LLb Hons Singapore, LLM Hons Cambridge) has published on company and business law, and was Singapore ambassador to Germany in 2000. He was the first non-Cabinet member ever to table a bill. *Who's Who in Singapore, 2000*, Singapore: Who's who publishing, 2000.

4 Eighth Parliament of Singapore. *Report of the Select Committee on the Maintenance of Parents Bill* [Parl.2 of 1995] Singapore: Singapore National Press (SNP), 1995.

5 On this point, the evidence of a former court interpreter, Joshua Lim, who emphasised the ill feeling that formal court proceedings can generate, appears to have been influential. *op cit* p. B8, C18-C19.

6 Singapore's system of Industrial Tribunals was originally modelled on those in Australia

7 *Op cit* B31, B33.

8 Mr. Ibrahim Arif: *op cit*, p. C31.

9 Ibid.

10 *Op Cit* p. E17.

11 I am grateful for the assistance in compiling this account that was generously provided by Mrs Belen Tan, Secretary to the Tribunal, and for the corrections she provided to an earlier draft. However, she is not responsible for any opinions - or errors - it contains.

References

Chan, A. and Cheung, P. (1997) *The Interrelationship between Public and Private Support of the Elderly: What can we learn from the Singapore Case?*, Elderly in Asia Research Report No. 97-41, Ann Arbor: Population Studies Centre, University of Michigan.

Edwards, A.C. and Manning, C. (2001) 'The Economics of Employment Protection and Unemployment Insurance Schemes: Reflections on policy options for Thailand, Malaysia, the Philippines and Indonesia', in Betcherman, G. and Islam, R. (eds), *East Asian Labour Markets and the Economic Crisis: Impacts and Policy Responses*, World Bank and ILO, Washington DC, pp. 345-78.

Frankenberg, E. *et al.* (2001) *Money for Nothing? Altruism, Exchange and Old Age Security in Southeast Asia*, Unpublished Working Paper, RAND, Santa Monica.

Goodman, R. (1998) 'The "Japanese-style Welfare State" and the Delivery of Personal Social Services', in Goodman, R., White, G. and Kwon, H. (eds), *The East Asian Welfare Model: Welfare Orientalism and the State*, Routledge, London, pp. 139-58.

Hermalin, A.I. (2000) *Ageing in Asia: Facing the Crossroads*, Comparative Study of the Elderly in Asia, Research Report No. 00-55, Ann Arbor, Population Studies Centre, Institute of Social Research, University of Michigan.

Knodel, J. and Chayovan, N. (1997) *Persistence and Change in the Living Arrangements and Support of the Thai Elderly*, Elderly in Asia Research Report No. 97-42, Ann Arbor, Population Studies Centre, University of Michigan.

Lim, Boon Heng (1994) *Family Values*, (Speech at the Opening of the NTUC Seminar on Family Values, Singapore), www.gov.sg/mita/speech/speeches/v18n6011.htr.

OECD (2000) *Labour Market And Social Safety Net Policies In Korea*, OECD, Paris.

OECD (2001) *Ageing and Income: Financial Resources and Retirement in 9 OECD Countries*, OECD, Paris.

Ofstedal, M.B. *et al.* (1999) *Intergenerational Support and Gender: A Comparison of Four Asian Countries*, Comparative Study of the Elderly in Asia, Research Report No. 00-54, Ann Arbor, Population Studies Centre, Institute of Social Research, University of Michigan.

3.2 Child support reforms in the United Kingdom and the United States

Anne Benson

The UK and the US have undertaken significant reforms in their child support enforcement programs to ensure that noncustodial parents provide financial support for their children. This paper compares the themes and policies of the child support reforms passed in 2000 in the UK and in 1996 in the US, focusing on contextual issues preceding reform, performance, and policy choices. The purpose of the analysis is to focus on the key drivers for the reforms and to examine the similarities and differences in policy themes and decisions. During the creation of the UK Child Support Agency (CSA) in the early 1990s and again in the late 1990s, the UK government examined and adopted policies from the older and more established US child support program. The decisions made by the UK in 2000 represent a growing convergence in child support policies between the UK and the US, albeit with some significant and notable differences.

The first part of the paper describes the UK and the US child support programs, setting their general policy aims within the context of the public assistance programs that provide financial support to the poorest families. The second part of the paper describes the historical development of the national child support programs in both countries, while the third part describes the themes and policies adopted by both countries in the recent child support reforms.

Part I: Current UK and US child support programs - rationale, description and context

The purpose of government child support programs is to facilitate the transfer of financial resources from noncustodial parents to custodial parents and children.[1] In the UK and US, parents who are divorced or separated are obligated to provide financial support for their children. For parents who are not married, paternity must be established before a child support order can be established on behalf of a child. Countries hold different values regarding the balance between private obligations and public responsibility and the role that government should play in intervening in family matters (Millar and Warman, 1996). In the UK and US, traditional two-parent families are accorded a high degree of family privacy and autonomy. If the parental relationship breaks down, however, the State intervenes to ensure that parents meet their legal responsibilities to provide for their children.

In comparing child support systems, Millar (1996) places the UK and US within an 'Anglo-Saxon' model, where the State intervenes to enforce private family obligations, as opposed to a 'Scandinavian model', where the State guarantees advanced child support payment if the noncustodial parent cannot or does not pay. Within the Anglo-Saxon model, the UK and US face an inherent public policy tension: they aim to enforce the moral responsibility of private family obligations, while respecting traditional public resistance to State intervention in private family matters. The primary reasons that led the UK and US to create government child support programs, in 1991 and 1975 respectively, were concerns over the economic deprivation of single parent families and children, the corresponding increases in welfare dependency and expenditures, and a moralistic desire to crack down on noncustodial parents, mostly fathers, who abandoned their children.

The UK and US have experienced similar demographic trends regarding high divorce and teen birth rates, rising rates of cohabitation and non-marital births, and high numbers of single parents with children who live in poverty. In the US the number of single parent families grew from 13 per cent of all families in 1970 to 32 per cent in 1998 (House Ways and Means Committee, 2000). In the UK the number of single parent families with dependent children increased from nine to 16 per cent of all families between 1986 and 1998 (Haskey, 2001). These single parent families have a much higher likelihood of living in poverty than married families (House Ways and Means Committee, 2000; McRae, 1999). Of particular concern for child support programs is the increase in non-marital births. During the early 1990s both the UK and US experienced non-marital birth rates in excess of 30 per cent of all live births (Coleman and Chandola, 1999; House Ways and Means Committee, 2000). These demographic factors have enormous implications for the child support program and portend continued caseload growth in both countries.

The UK and US invest considerable resources in large-scale government administrative programs to establish and enforce child support obligations. The following section provides a basic description of the UK and US programs.

In the UK the Child Support Agency (CSA) has responsibility for establishing and enforcing child support obligations for families who are in receipt of welfare benefits, Income Support or Jobseeker's Allowance. Welfare recipients are subject to a benefit sanction (reduction in benefit) unless they cooperate with the CSA in establishing paternity and obtaining support. Families who are not receiving benefits have the option of whether or not to use the CSA's services at no cost.

The CSA provides child support services via seven Business Units across the UK. In addition, each Business Unit has a network of Satellite Processing Centres and Local Service Bases to provide services to customers. The CSA is located within the Department of Social Security.

The CSA calculates child support assessment amounts using a complicated formula that takes into account the circumstances and income of both parents, costs of caring for children and number of children. The formula is complex because it takes into account the many and varied financial circumstances of families. The result is that the majority of the CSA's resources are devoted to the assessment process. 'CSA staff spend on average 90 per cent of their time making assessments, keeping them up to date and making initial payment arrangements' (Department of Social Security, 1999, p. 3). Once an assessment has been made, parents can choose to use the CSA collection service or to make their own payment arrangements. The CSA applies the assessment formula administratively to determine the child support amount and works with the courts to impose enforcement measures against non-compliant parents.

As in the US system, the CSA administers the government child support program, while the courts process private child support agreements. Under UK law, the CSA must work closely with the court system to enforce and collect child support debt. The one exception to this rule is that if the noncustodial parent falls one month behind in child support payments, the CSA can administratively issue a Deduction of Earnings order (income withholding) to the noncustodial parent's employer. Otherwise, the CSA cannot take any enforcement actions, such as seizing property or bank accounts, without first going to a Magistrates Court to obtain a liability order. The liability order legally establishes the amount of the debt. Further enforcement options are described as follows:

...[the CSA will seek to] recover the debt by distress action (using bailiffs to seize and sell goods). Where this is not successful we will have the option of seeking a Garnishee Order (on bank or building society funds) or a Charging Order through the County Court (on property so that if it is sold, the proceeds offset the debt). Where all else fails there will be a power to commit to prison any non-resident parent who continues to default on his payments.
(Department of Social Security, 1999)

The UK caseload in 1999/2000 included 1,030,100 cases. Of these cases, child support payments were due to be paid through the CSA's collection service in 353,780 cases.[2] In 1999/2000, the CSA collected £439 million of the £648 million of child support payments that were due to be paid through the CSA's collection service (Department of Social Security, 2001).[3] In November 2000, 65 per cent of custodial parents with full maintenance assessments were receiving welfare benefits (Department of Social Security, 2001).

General description of the US child support program

The US Federal Office of Child Support Enforcement (OCSE) has responsibility for overseeing and monitoring the US child support enforcement program. In return for federal funding, States are required to establish State child support offices and to comply with Federal laws, regulations and policies. OCSE is located within the Department of Health and Human Services.

State child support programs provide the following services: locating parents, establishing paternity, establishing and modifying child support orders, collecting and disbursing support, and enforcing child support orders. States are required to provide child support services to welfare recipients. Welfare applicants are required to assign their rights to receive child support to the State and cooperate in establishing paternity for the children and in obtaining child support. As in the UK, those that do not cooperate are subject to benefit sanctions. Individuals not receiving welfare may apply for child support services from the State for a fee of $25 or less.

The intergovernmental nature of the US child support program is quite complex. Although Federal authority has increased considerably over State programs in recent years, there is variation among States in how child support services are delivered and in how their programs are structured. As long as States comply with Federal standards, they have flexibility in the design and delivery of child support services. For example, in some States courts remain heavily involved in the child support program, while other States use a combination of judicial and administrative processes or predominantly use administrative processes to deliver child support services.

Federal law requires States to use numeric guidelines to establish child support obligations and gives States flexibility in deciding which factors to take into account in constructing their guidelines, such as child care, transportation, and health care costs. Thirty-three States use an income-shares model, which considers the income of both parents and ensures that children receive the same proportion of income from each parent that they would have done had the parents remained together. Thirteen States use a percentage-of-income model. This approach considers the noncustodial parent's income and determines the child support amount based on selected percentages, depending on the number of children. The first two approaches utilise estimates of child-rearing costs from consumer expenditure surveys (Rothe and Meyer, 2000). Three States use the Melson formula, a more complicated formula that incorporates a primary support allowance for each parent. This allowance ensures that each parent retains a subsistence level of income before the child support amount is calculated (House Ways and Means Committee, 2000).

US law requires child support orders to include provisions for immediate income withholding and for notices to be issued to employers to deduct and forward child support payments to the child support agency. Exceptions apply for non-welfare parents if a written agreement for an alternative payment arrangement can be reached or if there is good cause not to require immediate income withholding. The US program possesses a large variety of enforcement techniques to collect child support from non-compliant parents. Examples include: delinquency notices, interception of State and Federal tax refunds, seizure of financial and property assets, civil and criminal contempt of court, attachment of lottery winnings, and imprisonment.

The caseload composition in the US child support program has changed dramatically since 1975. Initially, families receiving welfare benefits were the primary recipients of child support services. In 1984, Federal law required all States to guarantee equal services for welfare and non-welfare families. The arguments in favor of this policy focused on the importance of deterrence. Specifically, by assisting in the collection of child support for non-welfare families and former welfare families, the government prevented future welfare receipt and recidivism (Kahn and Kamerman, 1988). By 1998 approximately half of all US families needing child support services utilised the public child support program (House Ways and Means Committee, 2000).

: OCSE FY 1999 Preliminary Data Report notes that in 1999, 'there
almost 3.6 million current assistance (welfare) cases, 6.8 million former
ance cases and 6 million never assistance cases'. In 1999 the US program
___ :ted over $15.8 billion dollars in child support payments. Of these
collections, $14.3 billion dollars were for non-welfare families, while $1.5
billion dollars were for welfare families. The program serviced over 16.4
million cases (OCSE, 1999).

Part II: History of the UK and US child support programs

United Kingdom

Background: The UK CSA opened its doors in 1993 following the passage of
the Child Support Act in 1991. Prior to 1993 the courts were responsible for
child support arrangements. The Department of Social Security also
administered a 'liable relatives' scheme to collect child and spousal support
from noncustodial parents whose children were receiving Income Support
benefits. Bradshaw and Millar (1991) reported that in 1989 only 30 per cent of
single parents were receiving child support payments. In putting forth its
proposals, the government was critical of the courts' handling of child support
for being fragmented and unreliable (Department of Social Security, 1990).
There were two other key factors influencing Prime Minister Thatcher's
decision to push for the creation of a new child support program: the increase
in numbers of single parent families who were dependent on welfare benefits;
and fears of a growing moral crisis regarding fatherless families (Garnham and
Knights, 1994). The numbers of single parents receiving Income Support
benefits more than doubled between 1980 and 1989. Towards the late 1980s,
70 per cent of all single parents were receiving Income Support (Ford *et al.*,
1995). Politicians expressed alarm that 'feckless fathers' were relinquishing
their provider role to the State and abandoning their parental responsibilities.
Concerns were also raised about the negative impacts of father absence on
children (Dennis and Erdos, 1993). In a speech in 1990, Prime Minister
Thatcher said:

> When one of the parents not only walks away from marriage but neither maintains
> nor shows any interest in the child, an enormous unfair burden is placed on the
> other. ... No father should be able to escape from his responsibility and that is why
> the Government is looking at ways of strengthening the system for tracing absent
> fathers and making the arrangements for recovering maintenance more effective
> (Garnham and Knights, 1994, p. 1).

Barnes *et al.* (1998) provide a thorough and comprehensive examination of the development of the child support proposals in the early 1990s. The new child support proposals were developed quickly and passed through Parliament with relatively little scrutiny or debate (Davis *et al.*, 1998). During the consultation period, pressure groups raised concerns about various features of the legislation that were not addressed, including objections that the assessment formula was complicated and inflexible. There was an overwhelming consensus in Parliament for pushing forward a new child support program based on the moral principle that parents should contribute to the support of their children. The new child support program represented a dramatic shift in the balance between private obligations and public responsibility, a change in the government's expectation of how children would be cared for financially after family break-up.

The UK child support program 1993-1997: Almost immediately after opening its doors in 1993, the UK CSA experienced an inability to manage the caseload and backlogs developed. (For a detailed and thorough overview of UK child support policy, see McDowell and Blackwell, 2000.) Within months pressure groups mounted high profile public protests opposing the child support scheme. Over the next few years, vitriolic complaints, especially from fathers' groups, were levied against the CSA for several reasons, including the complexity of the assessment formula, retrospective application of the assessment formula, poor performance and customer service. With difficult performance targets to meet, the CSA was vilified when it became evident that caseworkers were focusing more on reassessing and enforcing easier paying cases, instead of aggressively pursuing the more difficult, non-compliant cases (ITV, 1999). External criticism from researchers and advocacy groups was also ubiquitous during the mid-late 1990s with complaints regarding management deficiencies, inadequate staff training, inaccurate assessments, and malfunctioning computer systems (Bradshaw and Skinner, 2000).

The UK program received extensive scrutiny by the media with numerous stories focused on the plight of fathers aggrieved by poor service and maladministration ('Fleecing the Fathers', *The Times,* 27 October 1994; 'Cruel Sadistic Agency', *The Daily Star*, 4 April 1994; 'I am accused of fatherhood. My trial has lasted for two years. Yet I can't conceivably be guilty', *The Observer*, 27 July 1997). In addition, the Independent Television network (ITV, 1999) presented a critical three hour television documentary presenting meticulous and candid interviews of politicians and civil servants who were involved in the creation and administration of the CSA.

The UK child support reforms 1997-2000: The landmark election win by the Labour party in 1997 provided significant momentum for far-reaching social policy changes throughout government. In fashioning social welfare policy reforms, Prime Minister Blair and the Chancellor of the Exchequer, Gordon Brown, are driven by a deep commitment to combat 'social exclusion' in Britain and to eliminate child poverty in twenty years. Labour social welfare policy is also heavily premised on two key themes: the view that citizens receive 'rights in return for responsibilities and obligations', and that welfare reform should provide 'work for those who can, security for those who cannot' (Walker, 2000; Walker and Wiseman, 2001). These values underscore the government's belief that parents should provide care and financial support for their children and that, in return, 'the government can help parents who live apart from their children meet their responsibilities' (Department of Social Security, 1999).

In its Green Paper, *Children First: A New Approach for Child Support*, the government acknowledged the CSA's past failures and pledged to reform the entire child support service process with the following principles (Department of Social Security, 1998, p. 2). Child support should:

- Be simple, straightforward and easy to use.
- Provide a good service for children and their parents.
- Be properly integrated with the benefit system.
- Provide for the quick and straightforward resolution of disputes about assessments.

The proposals put forth in the Green Paper responded directly to the numerous criticisms that the CSA endured from 1993 to 1997. DSS officials also traveled to Wisconsin to look for ideas on an effective child support program and were especially interested in the State's use of a simple percentage of income assessment formula.

After receiving extensive feedback on the Green Paper, the Government produced its final proposals in a White Paper, *A New Contract for Welfare: Children's Rights and Parents' Responsibilities* (Department of Social Security, 1999). These proposals were included in the Child Support, Pensions and Social Security Bill, which, following debate and minimal changes, received Royal Assent on July 25, 2001.

Background: In 1975 President Ford signed legislation creating a new national child support program, which would be administered by the Federal Office of Child Support Enforcement (OCSE). The purposes of the child support enforcement program were to stem the rise in welfare expenditures, to improve interstate child support enforcement, and to reduce child poverty (Krueger, 1998). When the Aid for Dependent Children's program was passed in 1935 (renamed twice as the Aid to Families with Dependent Children (AFDC), and in 1996 as the Temporary Assistance for Needy Families program (TANF)), the program's purpose was to provide welfare benefits to widows and their children. Over time the AFDC caseload composition changed with a growing majority of women seeking benefits as a circumstance of non-marital childbearing and/or desertion of a husband or cohabiting partner. States operated primarily court-based child support enforcement programs between the 1940s and 1970s that were increasingly viewed as ineffective in ensuring fair and equitable child support payments for children. Throughout the 1950s and 1960s, US politicians introduced child support bills in Congress and voiced grave concerns about the drain on the Treasury due to dramatic AFDC caseload growth and the difficulty of enforcing child support in interstate cases (Krueger, 1998).

Historically, jurisdiction for family law has rested with State and local governments. When a noncustodial parent moved to another State, the initial State had no jurisdiction to apply enforcement remedies in the noncustodial parent's new State of residence. To counter this problem, State agreements were established to improve the enforcement of child support orders. Despite these State-initiated efforts, enormous problems remained and noncustodial parents often were able to evade child support payments by moving across State lines. For these reasons, the debates over a new Federal child support program in the early 1970s discussed the need to establish Federal oversight and standards to address the problems in interstate child support enforcement.

The US child support program 1975-1991: After OCSE opened for business in 1976, the program experienced numerous legislative changes and substantial program growth. The overriding themes of the legislative changes in 1984, 1988 and 1993 were: 1) increased Federal oversight and requirements for State child support programs; 2) enhancement of Federal enforcement tools to assist States in the collection of support, such as the Federal parent locator service and Federal tax refund offset program; and 3) increased use of computer systems at the State and Federal levels.

Despite the legislative activity throughout the 1980s and early 1990s, the US child support program was criticised for not keeping pace with caseload growth and ensuring the financial needs of the majority of America's children relying on child support (Krueger, 1998). The Family Support Act of 1988 called for the creation of a Commission on Interstate Child Support to make recommendations on the establishment and enforcement of interstate child support awards. The Commission (1992) produced a seminal report, *Supporting our Children: A Blueprint for Reform* that included a comprehensive set of 120 recommendations for improving the national child support program. According to top US policymakers, the Commission's work represented the beginning of the process that led to the passage of the 1996 child support reforms (Krueger, 1998).

The Census Bureau periodically produces child support survey results of the population at large. These figures include families being served by the government child support program *and* families that have made private arrangements through family courts for child support. The Census reported that, of the custodial parents awarded child support in 1991, 49 per cent received full payments, while 24 per cent received partial payments and 25 per cent received no payments (US Census Bureau, 1995).

The US child support reforms 1992-1996: During the Presidential campaign in 1992, Governor Clinton pledged to reform the widely-disliked AFDC program and promised to 'end welfare as we know it'. He also pledged to strengthen the child support program and to punish 'deadbeat dads' who abandoned responsibility for their children. The Clinton Administration's first welfare reform bill included broad-based child support reforms that incorporated many of the Interstate Commission's child support recommendations. Although the bill did not pass, these same child support provisions were included almost verbatim in successive welfare reform bills in 1995 and 1996.

In 1996 Congressional attention was focused primarily on proposals for revolutionary new State welfare block grants and time-limited welfare benefits, which effectively ended a citizen's entitlement to welfare. While welfare reform emphasised devolution of powers to the States, the child support reform proposals increased Federal mandates to strengthen State-based child support programs, and required the development of large-scale Federal databases to facilitate enforcement against child support debtors in cases that transcend State lines.

Because welfare benefits would be time limited under the welfare reform proposals, many legislators viewed the child support provisions as an

increasingly critical part of the income package available to families. The tough new enforcement measures in the child support reform bill were viewed as a potential 'safety net' for children. In a study that received widespread attention during legislative debates, Sorenson (1994) reported that a $34 billion collections gap existed in the child support program. This figure represented the difference between the theoretical amount of child support that would be owed if all eligible children had child support awards in place and the amount that was actually collected in 1990. Advocacy groups representing custodial parents and children played a significant role in lobbying Congress to pass the child support reforms (Krueger, 1998). On 22 August 1996, the President signed the Personal Responsibility and Work Opportunity Reconciliation Act (PRWORA) and set in motion the most far-reaching changes to the child support program since its inception in 1975.

Part III: Child support reform themes

In the years preceding legislative activity in the UK and US, external commissions, inquiries and hearings were used to gather input about the problems and to make recommendations for reforms. Given that one of the key complaints about the original UK scheme was that it had been developed too hastily and without enough constructive review, the government's consultative exercises were critical for garnering support for its reform proposals. This section compares and contrasts the policy themes and choices made by each government.

In the White Paper, the UK government indicated that the key components of the new child support proposals were: simplification of the assessment rates; a child maintenance premium; a tougher sanctions regime; and a new child support service (Department of Social Security, 1999). Despite the new tougher sanctions, the UK's emphasis was on simplifying and speeding up case processing, ensuring that families on welfare benefits received more child support payments directly, and making the system more transparent to its customers.

Legler (1996), a top Clinton Administration official involved in the development of the child support reforms, described the main components of the new US legislation as follows: access to information; mass case processing; pro-active and tougher enforcement; uniformity in interstate cases; and 'family first' distribution. Both the UK and the US approached child support reform with the assumption that case processing needed to be improved dramatically by enhancing the efficiency, speed, and reliability of the child support process.

Improving service delivery was viewed as the best mechanism for helping children and increasing compliance rates. Despite this common theme, there are interesting differences in the policies that were adopted by the UK and the US. Broadly speaking, the UK policy approach focused on serving children by improving parents' interactions with the CSA. Through improvements in parents' experience with the agency, it was hoped that benefits to children would accrue because parents would be more willing to comply with their child support obligations. The US approach focused on serving children by expanding the tools necessary to access large amounts of data, to process cases in high volume and to enforce against non-payers.

In analysing specific UK and US policy decisions, four overlapping themes prevail: simplification of policy and process; improved service delivery; tougher enforcement measures; and payments for children on welfare benefits. Table 3.2.1 categorises the key policies adopted by the UK and US according to these themes.

Table 3.2.1   Themes and policies of the UK and US child support reforms

THEMES	UK REFORMS	US REFORMS
Simplification of Policy and Process	Assessment Formula - New formula based on percentage of non-resident parent's income	Expedited procedures -Taking various case processing and enforcement actions automatically, without the necessity of obtaining an order from any other judicial or administrative tribunals
	Paternity Establishment - Defining circumstances where parentage may be presumed	Paternity Establishment - Defining procedures for voluntary acknowledgment of paternity; streamlined procedures for paternity establishment
Improved Service Delivery	Case Processing – Contact with parents will be mainly by phone, with opportunities for face-to-face interviews	Case Processing in Large Volumes • Access to Data: Numerous automated data sources available to aid in finding noncustodial parents and case processing
	Phase-in Period for assessment formula to apply to new and existing cases	• Information Technology: Numerous new large-scale government databases
	New Computer System to handle assessment formula and phase-in period	• Mass Case Processing: Handling of cases in volume using advanced technology

194

Table 3.2.1 (continued)

Tougher Enforcement	Drivers' Licenses Revocation	Drivers, Professional, Occupational, and Recreational License Revocation
	New Criminal Sanctions	Passport Denial for delinquent NRPs
	Streamlined use of inspectors powers to gather information	Authority for courts to impose work requirements
	Late payment penalty of up to 25% of money due	Uniform Interstate Family Support Act (UIFSA) - Uniform State law establishing ` tandardized procedures for interstate cases
		Tribal child support programs
		International Child Support Enforcement - Federal authority to negotiate reciprocal agreements with foreign nations
		Enhanced enforcement against government employees
Child Support Payment Incentives for Families on Welfare	Child Maintenance Premium	Family First distribution Policy
		Abolition of the $50 per month disregard and pass-through

Simplification of policy and process

The UK is replacing its heavily criticised assessment formula with a simple percentage-of-income formula that will be based on the noncustodial parent's income (15 per cent of net weekly income for one child; 20 per cent for two children, and 25 per cent for three or more children). There will be reduced rates for low-income noncustodial parents, although all noncustodial parents, even those receiving Income Support and Jobseeker's Allowance benefits, will be required to make a minimum child support payment of £5 per week. Variations from the formula will be permitted in exceptional circumstances as specified in the regulations - for example, if the noncustodial parent

195

experiences high travel costs in seeing the child or experiences high care costs for a disabled child in a new family. For noncustodial parents supporting new families, deductions from net income will be made, depending on the number of children in the new family, before the percentage rates apply. The CSA will also modify the child support rates under the new assessment formula in proportion to the amount of overnight visits that a child has with a noncustodial parent.

This new simple formula for calculating the child support assessment is the hallmark of the new UK reforms. The goal is to make the child support assessment process as transparent as possible to parents. The White Paper notes that, 'parents will be able to see clearly how much maintenance will be due for their children…; and children will see maintenance more quickly and regularly' (Department of Social Security, 1999, p. 3). By using the new formula, the CSA anticipates that child support payments will be flowing within four to six weeks instead of the six months (or more) that it takes under the current formula.

The UK also adopted new procedures to simplify and speed up the process for paternity establishment. The UK's paternity establishment provisions focus on policies that define when the CSA can presume parentage. Before the reforms, some men in the UK were contesting paternity merely to slow down the child support process (Department of Social Security, 1999). To combat this delaying technique, the UK adopted a Scottish provision that parentage is presumed if a man was married to the child's mother at any time between the date of conception and the child's birth. Other grounds for the presumption of parentage include: 1) if the parents are unmarried and the man's name is registered on the birth certificate; and 2) if the alleged noncustodial parent refuses to take a DNA test or to accept its positive result.

The main US policy shift regarding simplification centres on case processing and the expansion of expedited procedures. The US adopted several new procedures to simplify and clarify the process for parents to establish paternity. The new reforms also require States to have the authority to take specified case processing and enforcement actions without the necessity of obtaining an order from any other judicial or administrative tribunal. Examples include ordering a genetic test for paternity establishment purposes, accessing data, intercepting or seizing periodic or lump-sum payments (including unemployment compensation, state benefits, lottery winnings, judgments), and attaching and seizing assets held in financial institutions. Legler (1996, p. 552) provides the following rationale for this extensive expansion of expedited procedures in the US program:

Child support agencies will have sufficient administrative authority to process the vast majority of cases without requiring prior court intervention, yet States can maintain limited court-based processes for the collection of support to the extent that they are necessary for the exceptional cases.

For the UK, simplifying the assessment formula is paramount for creating a child support program that serves children efficiently and reliably. Ensuring that the assessment amounts are accurate and flow to children quickly is critical for regaining public confidence in the legitimacy of the child support program. Because assessment amounts are determined under State guidelines, the US did not face this fundamental challenge regarding the assessment formula in 1996. In the US context, simplification was primarily a matter of instituting policies to improve the efficiency in establishing paternity and in processing child support cases.

Improved service delivery

The UK and the US focused heavily on improving the effectiveness of child support service delivery during the reform process. In order to avoid the massive backlogs that developed shortly after the child support program's inception, the UK will phase in the reform provisions. New cases will begin using the new formula in April 2002. Once the government is satisfied that new cases are being processed efficiently, existing cases will be re-assessed under the new formula and transferred to the new scheme. The government also adopted provisions to ensure that noncustodial parents do not experience large and potentially controversial changes in their child support assessments. The new rates will be phased in gradually over five years for noncustodial parents whose assessments increase by more than £10 per week under the new formula (less for low-income noncustodial parents). The UK is developing a new information technology system to handle the demands of the new scheme and the phase-in process. The UK is also restructuring its customer service strategies to ensure that all customers receive regular statements of accounts, can access case information via phone, and can have face-to-face interviews with child support staff.

A substantial portion of the US reforms centered on improved service delivery. Attention focused primarily on economies of scale and new automated mechanisms for processing child support cases in mass volume. A key goal was to make optimal use of automation to handle routine cases in a routine manner while conserving staff resources to provide services to cases requiring highly individualised attention. Many of the US reforms regarding service delivery and enforcement were modeled after successful initiatives adopted and implemented in various States.

To assist staff in getting information to find parents (and their assets), the US reforms expanded and facilitated access to various State and Federal databases - for example, motor vehicles, welfare, military service and social security. The reforms also granted new unprecedented access to other data sources, such as records of public utilities, cable television and financial institutions, and records concerning ownership of corporations, partnerships and other business entities. Privacy provisions were adopted to protect the information and to ensure that access to these data sources must be granted to the State child support agency.

The second strand of improved service delivery in the US included the development of large-scale databases to improve child support case processing, especially for interstate cases. These included State and Federal case registries of child support orders and State and National new hire reporting databases.

The third strand under improved service delivery included provisions for handling child support cases in mass volume. In testimony before the Subcommittee on Human Resources, House Committee on Ways and Means, Assistant Secretary David Ellwood said

> Child support enforcement needs to be run like modern businesses that use computers, automation, and information technology. With 17 million cases and a growing caseload, we cannot simply improve collections simply by adding more caseworkers. Routine cases have to be handled in volume.
> (Legler, 1996, p. 544)

The most visible change for customers involved the creation of State Disbursement Units (SDU), central locations in every State used for the processing of all child support payments.

Another mechanism to encourage mass case processing involved new provisions for processing liens and levies (the freezing and seizing of assets). In the US, overdue child support becomes a judgment by operation of law (automatically). This means that the child support agency does not have to go to a judicial tribunal to register the child support debt as a judgment, as in Britain. The 1996 US reforms go even farther by providing that States have procedures under which liens arise by operation of law against property for the amount of past-due support. This authority is especially powerful when combined with the new financial institution data match provisions. Once the State child support agency locates a financial account held by a child support debtor, the new provisions permit a State to seize the account automatically without the necessity of obtaining a judicial or administrative order.

198

By examining the new service delivery provisions adopted by the UK and the US, the contrast in reform approaches is most evident. In building a new computer system and implementing a new simpler formula for assessing child support obligations, the UK stresses a steady, phased-in approach to ensure that the new system does not unduly burden parents and that the transfer of existing cases will not occur until the new system is ready. Service delivery is approached as the experience and interactions that parents will have in dealing with the CSA. The language in the White Paper stresses that parents will be served fairly and with courtesy and respect. This approach is not surprising given the UK program's history and the need to rebuild trust and public support in the CSA.

In comparison, the US reform approach to improved service delivery centres on technology and new, large-scale, automated methods to enhance the collection of child support in an era of expanding caseloads. In addition, the tone and substance of the US reform provisions are about compliance and enforcement to ensure that children receive the money they deserve. Service delivery is approached from the perspective that a more efficient program with business-like processes will get more money to children faster.

Tougher enforcement

While the UK and US programs both adopted tough new enforcement measures to pursue delinquent child support obligors, the US definitely possesses a much broader range of enforcement tools. Under the 2000 reforms, the UK can impose criminal sanctions with fines up to £1,000 against anyone who lies or refuses to provide information to the CSA. Procedures have been streamlined for inspectors to gather child support information. When other enforcement measures have failed, a magistrate has the authority to confiscate the driver's license of a delinquent noncustodial parent as an alternative to committal to prison. The CSA also has the authority to impose a late payment penalty of up to 25 per cent of the amount due in child support.

The US reforms adopted several new enforcement measures: State child support agencies can revoke several types of licenses of delinquent child support obligors, including driver's, professional, occupational and recreational (hunting and fishing) licenses; noncustodial parents who owe $5,000 or more in child support debt can have their passport applications or renewals denied; and delinquent noncustodial parents can be ordered to participate in employment programs.

A very important new provision required States to adopt the Uniform Interstate Family Support Act (UIFSA), drafted by the National Conference of

Commissioners on Uniform State Laws between 1988 and 1992. This uniform State law includes new procedures and evidentiary rules that should improve dramatically the enforcement of interstate child support cases. The new reforms also included improvements in processing tribal and international child support cases.

The enforcement measures that the UK and US possess certainly send the message that the government is serious about imposing punitive measures on child support debtors. In interviews with UK CSA staff and in reviewing the child support literature, the author has observed a difference between the two programs, however, in the rhetorical and philosophical approach towards enforcement. In the UK, enforcement measures are described in terms of 'punishment' against debtors who have evaded their responsibilities. Driver's license revocation is an example, a provision that has been fairly controversial in the UK and subject to criticism. In procedural terms, the confiscation of a driver's license is carried out when all other enforcement measures have failed and as a final alternative to committal to prison. In the US program, enforcement measures are discussed more in terms of both deterrence and punishment, and with an emphasis that the ultimate beneficiaries of such measures are children. Much of the US program language focuses on measures that must be taken *to get money to children*. For example, when discussing license revocation programs, officials will indicate that the goal of this enforcement threat is to get noncustodial parents either to establish a repayment agreement or to make a lump sum payment. Certainly, the threat to revoke a license will be taken if the noncustodial parent does not respond, but the hope is that the threat will deter the noncustodial parent from future non-compliance.

There is another subtle difference regarding the language of enforcement in the two programs. In the US, tough enforcement measures are viewed as a necessity for ensuring that *children get the money they deserve*. It is common in the US program literature to read passages about children and their rights to financial support from both parents. Even in the title of the US agency, the Office of Child Support Enforcement, children and enforcement go hand in hand. There is a highly visible cultural and programmatic ethos in the US child support program that children are the beneficiaries of our efforts, resources, and services. Indeed, in the OCSE Strategic Plan for 2000–2004, 'the primary *customers* and beneficiaries of the Child Support Enforcement Program are children in need of support. Secondary customers are the parents or custodians of these children' (OCSE, 2000). The former Commissioner of the Office of Child Support Enforcement, David Gray Ross, frequently told staff that, 'when you go home at night, I want you to think about what you did today to make the lives of America's children better'. The author contends that the emphasis on the child support program as a 'children's' program serves to strengthen and solidify public support and to motivate staff.

In the UK program literature, there are many more references to parents as customers than there are to children. Although the White Paper is titled, *A New Contract for Welfare: Children's Rights and Parents' Responsibilities*, the vast majority of commentary focuses on providing better customer service to parents (Department of Social Security, 1999). In discussions with UK CSA staff, the author has discovered a prevalent view that parents are considered the primary customers of the agency. In an enforcement context, this means that the CSA is pursuing delinquent noncustodial parents who have not complied with government rules.

Child support payment incentives for families on welfare

The UK and US made different policy decisions regarding the treatment of child support payments for families on welfare. The UK adopted a policy referred to as the child maintenance premium. If a non-resident parent makes a child support payment on behalf of a child who is receiving welfare benefits in the Income Support program, the family will receive £10 per week of the child support payment and this amount will not be taken into account when determining eligibility for the Income Support benefit. The government will retain the remainder of the child support payment (over and above £10 per week) to reimburse the Treasury for the Income Support expenditure. For families receiving the Working Families' Tax Credit, a wage subsidy for low-income working families that is similar to the US Earned Income Credit, the full amount of the child support payment will be disregarded. The White Paper provides the following rationale for the child maintenance premium policy:

> ... for the first time all children will see an immediate financial advantage from any maintenance paid by the non-resident parents; non-resident parents whose children are on Income Support will still see a direct advantage to their children from the maintenance that they pay.
> (Department of Social Security, 1999, p. 4)

During the 1990s, advocates and academic researchers criticised the government vociferously for its pre-reform policy of retaining the entire child support payment for families receiving welfare benefits. Currently, there is widespread support for the child maintenance premium and a belief that this policy will increase compliance and encourage custodial parents to cooperate with the CSA.

The US took a different approach to this issue. The US reforms abolished the $50 per month disregard and pass-through of child support payments to families receiving welfare benefits. States now have the option of whether to disregard or pass through all or a portion of the child support payment. One State, Wisconsin, is disregarding and passing through the entire child support amount to most welfare recipients, while 28 States retain the entire child support amount. In the remaining States that pass through a portion of the child support payment, on average families only receive 14 per cent of the child support payment (Reichert, 2000; Cassetty, Cancian and Meyer, 2000). Thus, in the majority of American States, families on welfare are receiving little or no child support payments, in contrast to those in the UK, who will be entitled to a child maintenance premium.

The US also adopted a 'family first' distribution policy that promoted self-sufficiency. With a few exceptions, former welfare recipients receive all the child support that they are owed before the Federal and State governments are reimbursed for arrears that accrued while the family was on welfare. The government recoups child support payments made while a family is on welfare.

The US would be well-served to monitor lessons from the UK experience as it implements the child maintenance premium and to gauge its long-term impact on child support compliance and cooperation. An important consideration will be whether the child maintenance premium changes public and parental attitudes towards the CSA, as well as agency culture. As mentioned previously, many CSA staff view parents as the primary customers of the CSA. Adoption of the child support maintenance premium now means that children whose families are on welfare will see a direct financial benefit from a child support payment.

Conclusion

There were many similar drivers influencing the development of child support legislation in the UK and US. Both countries created national child support programs in order to ensure greater uniformity, certainty and fairness of child support obligations than had existed under the previous court-based child support systems. Three key factors motivated each government: the rising levels of single parent families and their economic deprivation; the growth in public expenditures on welfare programs; and an underlying moral view that some fathers were abdicating their responsibilities and needed to be held accountable to support their children. Another key driver in the US for a national program was the need for greater coordination and oversight in interstate child support cases.

Each country also confronted similar complaints during the years preceding the major child support reforms efforts. Changing demographics regarding the growth in single parent families resulted in expanding caseloads and challenged each program to keep pace with the rising demand for child support services. To cope with the rising caseload, critics and government officials called for extensive changes in the way in which child support services were delivered in the UK and US. Moreover, the UK received sharp condemnation of its complex assessment formula and the amount of agency resources dedicated to the assessment process. Both child support programs were also criticised for the policies regarding the retention of child support payments to families on welfare.

The policies adopted in response to these similar problems in the UK and the US demonstrate a combination of similar and divergent policies. By adopting a new simpler assessment formula, along with computer and customer service strategies, the UK focused sharply on improving the experience that parents have in interacting with the CSA and in understanding child support policies. The UK's new child maintenance premium also ensured that child support payments would be more visible to parents and children. The US reforms also focused heavily on service delivery by stressing the need to move away from individual child support case processing and towards expedited procedures and large-scale, mass case processing. Where possible, the goal was to limit staff intervention in taking actions on child support cases and instead use automated mechanisms to initiate enforcement measures. The US reforms also stressed expansive new access to various public and private data sources. In terms of new enforcement methods, both the UK and US governments granted new powers to the child support agencies to collect unpaid child support, although the US program adopted a much broader range of enforcement measures.

When the US child support reforms were passed in 1996, US politicians and policymakers indicated that they believed the child support program was still relatively young. With a 20 year history, the US child support program was considered still to be in its developmental stage and policymakers were still working to find the best policies for a complicated government program (Krueger, 1998). As the UK and the US child support programs carry forward the implementation of the monumental policy reforms, each country would be well advised to observe and learn from each other's experiences. When comparing child support programs, however, it is important to remain cognizant of the cultural and philosophical factors that drive policy decisions regarding the appropriate extent of the government's role in enforcing private family obligations. It is also incumbent on policymakers to appreciate the complexity and challenge of delivering child support services in such a contentious area of social policy.

Notes

1   For the sake of consistency, US child support terminology is used in the paper as follows: child maintenance is referred to as child support; lone parents are single parents; parents with care are custodial parents; non-resident parents are noncustodial parents. In the US context, a child support order represents a legal obligation for the support and maintenance of a child and includes the amount of child support that must be paid on behalf of the child.
In the UK child support program, an assessment represents the legal obligation and amount of child support due. Unless otherwise specified, 'welfare' in the UK context comprises the Income Support and Jobseeker's Allowance programs. In the US context, 'welfare' refers to the Temporary Assistance for Needy Families (TANF) program (or its predecessor, Aid to Families with Dependent Children).

2   The difference in case counts represents those cases where child support was not charged through the CSA's collection service. Some examples include: 'direct pays' - cases where payment is made directly from the noncustodial parent to the custodial parent; 'nil liability' - cases where the noncustodial parent's circumstances necessitate a nil child support assessment.

3   This collections' figure is primarily for cases that have 'full maintenance assessments' (FMA). An FMA is an 'assessment of the non-resident parent's liability to pay maintenance based on full facts having been provided by both the parent/person with care and the non-resident parent'. An 'interim maintenance assessment' (IMA) is an 'assessment of the non-resident parent's liability to pay maintenance based on incomplete facts relating to the parent with care and/or the non-resident parent' (Department of Social Security, 2001, p. 8).

References

Barnes, H., Daly, P. and Cronin, N. (1998) *Trial and Error: A review of UK child support policy*, Family Policy Studies Centre, London.

Bradshaw, J. and Millar, J. (1991) *Lone-parent Families in the UK*, Department of Social Security, Research Report 6, HMSO, London.

Bradshaw, J. and Skinner, C. (2000) 'Child Support: The British Fiasco', *Focus*, vol. 21, no. 1, Spring, pp. 80-84.

Cassetty, J., Cancian, M. and Meyer, D. (2000) 'Child Support Disregard and Pass-through Policies', *Focus*, vol. 21, no. 1, Spring, pp. 64-66.

Coleman, D. and Chandola, T. (1999) 'Britain's Place in Europe's Population', in S. McRae (ed), *Changing Britain: Families and Households in the 1990s*, Oxford University Press, Oxford.

Commission on Interstate Child Support (1992) *Supporting our Children: A Blueprint for Reform*, Government Printing Office, Washington DC.

Davis, G., Wikeley, N. and Young, R. (1998) *Child Support in Action*, Hart Publishing, Oxford.

Dennis, N. and Erdos, G. (1993) *Families Without Fatherhood*, Institute of Economic Affairs, London.

Department of Social Security (1990) *Children Come First: The Government's Proposals on the Maintenance of Children*, Cm 1264, HMSO, London.

Department of Social Security (1998) *Children First: A New Approach to Child Support*, Cm 3992, The Stationery Office, London.

Department of Social Security (1999) *A New Contract for Welfare: Children's Rights and Parents' Responsibilities*, Cm 4349, The Stationery Office, London.

Department of Social Security (2001) *Child Support Agency Quarterly Summary of Statistics, November 2000*, Department of Social Security, Analytical Services Division, London.

Ford, R., Marsh, A. and McKay, S. (1995) *Changes in Lone Parenthood 1989-93*, HMSO, London.

Garnham, A. and Knights, E. (1994) *Putting the Treasury First: The Truth About Child Support*, Child Poverty Action Group, London.

Haskey, J. (2001) 'Cohabitation in Great Britain: Past, Present and Future Trends and Attitudes', *Population Trends*, vol. 103, Spring, pp. 4-19.

House Ways and Means Committee (2000) *Overview of Entitlement Programs: 2000 Green book*, Government Printing Office, Washington DC.

ITV, Independent Television Network (1999) *Can't Pay, Won't Pay: Child Support Agency*, Television documentary.

Kahn, A. and Kamerman, S. (1988) *Child Support: From Debt Collection to Social Policy*, Sage Publications, Newbury Park.

Krueger, R. (1998) 'Analysing American Social Policy: A Study of the Development of the Child Support Provisions of PRWORA', Unpublished dissertation, University of Southern California.

Legler, P. (1996) 'The Coming Revolution in Child Support Policy: Implications of the 1996 Welfare Act', *Family Law Quarterly*, vol. 30, no. 3, pp. 519-63.

McDowell, J. and Blackwell, J. (2000) *Child Support Handbook*, Child Poverty Action Group, London.

McRae, S. (1999) 'Introduction: Family and Household Change in Britain', in S. McRae (ed), *Changing Britain: Families and Households in the 1990s*, Oxford University Press, Oxford.

Millar, J. (1996) 'Mothers, Workers and Wives: Comparing Policy Approaches to Supporting Lone Mothers', in B. Silva (ed), *Good Enough Mothering? Feminist Perspectives on Lone Motherhood*, Routledge, London.

Millar, J. and Warman, A. (1996) *Family Obligations in Europe*, Family Policy Studies Centre, London.

OCSE (1999) *Child Support Enforcement FY 1999 Preliminary Data Report*, Department of Health and Human Services, Administration for Children and Families, Washington DC.

OCSE (2000) *Child Support Enforcement Strategic Plan with Outcome Measures for FY 2000-2004*, Department of Health and Human Services, Administration for Children and Families, Washington DC.

Reichert, D. (2001) 'How Does the Child Support System Affect Low-income Families?' in *Connecting Low-income Families and Fathers: A Guide to Practical Policies*, National Conference of State Legislatures, Denver.

Rothe, I. and Meyer, D. (2000) 'Setting Child Support Orders: Historical Approaches and Ongoing Struggles', *Focus*, vol. 21, no. 1, pp. 58-63.

Sorenson, E. (1994) 'Non-custodial Fathers: Can they Afford to Pay More Child Support', Urban Institute, Washington DC.

US Census Bureau (1995) *Child Support for Custodial Mothers and Fathers: 1991* (Current Population Reports, Series P60-187), Government Printing Office, Washington DC.

US Census Bureau (2000) *Child Support for Custodial Mothers and Fathers: 1997* (Current Population Reports, Series P-60, No. 212), Government Printing Office, Washington DC.

US Congress (1996) *Personal Responsibility and Work Opportunity Reconciliation Act of 1996: Conference Report to Accompany H.R. 3734*, H. Rep. pp. 104-725. 104th Congress, 2nd session. Government Printing Office, Washington DC.

Walker, R. (2000) 'Thinking Blair's Thoughts', *Centre for Research on Social Policy Briefings*, vol. 15, Spring, pp. 1-2.

Walker, R. and Wiseman, M. (2001) *Britain's New Deal and the Next Round of US Welfare Reform*, Discussion paper no. 1223-01, Institute for Research on Poverty, Madison.

3.3 Extending cash social assistance to children and their caregivers: a South African case study

Jan Vorster and Hester Rossouw[1]

1. Introduction

The needs of children and their caregivers are protected by the Constitution of South Africa. However, no holistic integrated system exists to address children's needs. Currently their needs must be addressed through a diversity of largely segregated and uncoordinated channels and services, including those provided by the state, NGOs, communities and households/families.

Many children in South Africa face harsh socio-economic circumstances, with an estimated three out of five children living in poor households (May *et al.*, 2000, p. 32). Although not limited to poor households, many poor children are also infected or affected by HIV/AIDS and there are many AIDS orphans. Some children are even living in child-headed households and some are living on the streets.

There is a variety of ways in which the state can provide relief to the poor. Social assistance is one such policy option for the support of poor children and their caregivers. Compared to other government programmes aimed at providing household and food security in South Africa, it seems that state pensions are performing quite well. Contrary to the situation in most other developing countries, state cash transfers and grants are playing a crucial role in addressing and alleviating poverty in South Africa. The relatively advanced level of the grant system is a direct result of its apartheid past. Research indicates that cash social assistance, mainly in the form of old age and disability grants, reaches some of the most vulnerable groups - including households with children (Lund Committee, 1996, pp. 7-8). Partly based on this positive experience, the South African government introduced three years ago the Child Support Grant for poor children younger than seven years.

The aim of the paper is to examine the transformation of the system of social assistance to children and their caregivers. The first section of the paper examines the nature of poverty and the HIV/AIDS pandemic in South Africa. These realities are two main factors challenging the realisation of children's rights in South Africa. This is followed by a brief overview of the constitutional and economic frameworks providing the context for addressing social exclusion in South Africa. The paradigm switch to developmental social welfare made by the state department responsible for grant administration, the Department of Social Development, is also discussed. The next sections provide an overview and discussion of the system of cash assistance in South Africa, focusing on reforms to the system of cash assistance to poor children and their caregivers. The paper attempts to use these reforms to provide some insight into the complexities of welfare reform in the context of constitutional rights, economic constraints, the HIV/AIDS pandemic and the operationalisation of a new welfare paradigm. The paper is based on research conducted during 1999-2000 for the Department of Social Development (Vorster, Rossouw and Muller, 2000).

2. Realities facing South Africa's children

Two main factors inhibiting the realisation of children's rights in South Africa are poverty and the HIV/AIDS pandemic.

Poverty

South Africa is a highly unequal society. The richest ten per cent of South African households earn 42 per cent of the national income, whilst the poorest 20 per cent earn a mere 3.8 per cent (Nattrass and Seekings, 1996, p. 66). More than 60 per cent of children in South Africa live in poverty and this equates to 10.2 million children 18 years or younger (May *et al.*, 2000).

The distribution of poverty in South Africa has a strong racial gender as well as geographic dimension. Sixty-one per cent of Africans (the majority of the total population) are classified as poor, compared to only 38 per cent of coloureds, five per cent of Indians and one per cent of whites (May *et al.*, 2000, p. 31). In the past the latter three groups also enjoyed better social assistance benefits than Africans. In terms of the rural/urban divide, most of the poor live in rural areas. Women are also more likely to be poor. The poverty rate amongst female-headed households is 60 per cent compared to 31 per cent for male-headed households (Poverty and Inequality Report, 1998). Given that female-headed households tend to be more heavily reliant on remittance and state transfer income than male-headed households, they form households comprising of several adult women and their children, grouping around those in receipt of state grants. Research also indicates that rural children who live with a female old age pensioner are measurably heavier and healthier than those who do not.

Poor households in South Africa share characteristics similar to poor households worldwide, although the effects of apartheid exacerbated some characteristics. These characteristics include amongst others that poor households particularly are black, consist of three or often four generations, many are headed by women, in many there is an incomplete or missing generation, many pregnancies are resulting from temporary relationships, a relatively high rate of teenage pregnancies, high levels of domestic violence, discontinuous parenting and fluid boundaries of households (Lund Committee, 1996). Many children are not in the care of their biological parents and the number of children without adult supervision is growing rapidly, especially AIDS orphans.

HIV/AIDS

South Africa, with a population 20 times less than that of India, is after India the country in the world with the largest number of people who are HIV positive. It is estimated that more than 4.2 million people are HIV positive (UNAIDS, 2000) and by early 2000 there were an estimated 150,000 AIDS deaths, with 2,500 new infections occurring per day. Within eight years South Africa will reach the figure of six million AIDS related deaths (Department of Social Development, 2000).[2] It is estimated that 75 per cent of children who are currently 15 years old would not survive to the age of 60 due to AIDS. The child mortality rate increased from 67 in 1990 to 91 per 1,000 in 2000 mainly due to the HIV/AIDS pandemic (Department of Social Development, 2000). Older children are also particularly vulnerable to this pandemic, with 65 per cent of all HIV people being 15 to 19 years old (ACESS, 2001, p. 5).

The impact of HIV/AIDS on South Africa's population structure will be dramatic, with a decline in the number of people in the age groups 0-4 years and 25-34 years (Department of Social Development, 2000, p. 65). One of the major economic implications will be an increase in the number of dependants in relation to the economic active proportion of the population, with fewer people to care for children and the elderly. In cases where infected persons are earning an income, their illness and possible death will contribute to a loss of income as well as other expenses for the household. Children will grow up without much of the care many would normally have had (Department of Social Development, 2000, p. 67). According to lower estimates there were already more than 100,000 AIDS orphans in South Africa in 1999, while it is estimated that in four years time a million children younger than 15 years will have lost their mothers to AIDS (Department of Social Development, 2000, p. 65). Communities, grandparents, etc. may not be able to care for so many orphaned children. The Department of Social Development (2000, p. 68) warns that '(t)he welfare and social development implications of resultant child-headed households will be unprecedented'.

Although it is generally accepted that the growth of the HIV/AIDS pandemic in South Africa can be curbed, analysts do not foresee a levelling off in terms of HIV infections in the immediate future. It seems that in the meantime the Department of Social Development will face the challenge of dealing with those debilitated by AIDS, the numbers of AIDS orphans and the increase in elderly whose adult children die prematurely.

3. Policy frameworks for addressing social exclusion

Following political democratisation in 1994, the South African government devised new policies and frameworks to address, with limited resources, the exclusion and marginalisation of the past with a specific focus on poverty and inequity. The rights of children are being addressed within the broader framework of social exclusion and a developmental approach. Two frameworks appear to be guiding the present government's efforts in this regard, that is, the South African Constitution (including a Bill of Rights) and a macro-economic framework embodied in the RDP (Reconstruction and Development Programme) and GEAR (Growth, Employment and Redistribution). These frameworks are determining the context in which all government departments concerned with parity and equity within South Africa must act.

The following discussion provides a brief overview of these policy frameworks and the implications of a developmental approach for social welfare.

The constitutional framework

The Constitution of South Africa (Act 108 of 1996) was adopted as the supreme law of the Republic of South Africa to ensure, amongst others, that the divisions of the past are healed and a society is established based on democratic values, social justice and fundamental human rights. The constitutional embodiment in the Bill of Rights of social and economic rights is of particular importance in the context of poverty alleviation and children's rights. Of central concern to social security and the rights of children are sections 27 and 28 respectively.

Section 27 of the Constitution entrenches the right to social security and it obliges the state to take reasonable legislative and other measures, within its available resources, to achieve the progressive realisation of the right. Section 28 of the Constitution provides that every child has the right to basic nutrition, shelter, basic health care services and social services.

South Africa has also signed and ratified the Convention on the Rights of the Child and formulated the National Programme of Action (NAP) for Children in South Africa to outline the steps the country will take to realise its commitments to children. According to UNICEF's State of the World's Children Report, the country rates among those with the best intentions for young citizens (UNICEF, 1999). The key question according to this report is whether the country has adequate resources to realise its commitments and whether those are being allocated to making a difference in children's lives.

The economic policy framework

After the April 1994 elections the government adopted, in an amended form, the African National Congress's (ANC) key election manifesto as the White Paper on Reconstruction and Development (RDP). This programme would form an integrated, coherent socio-economic policy framework for redressing the poverty and deprivation of apartheid, developing human resources, building and restructuring the economy and democratising the state. The programme sets out to integrate growth, development and reconstruction and redistribution into a unified programme. The RDP promised 'the attainment of basic social welfare rights for all South Africans' (RDP, 1994 s. 2.1.3.4).

The RDP White Paper introduced an emphasis on the facilitation of economic growth by implementing a programme of saving on state consumption expenditure through fiscal discipline, the promotion of investment and a review of exchange controls (Marais, 1999, p. 181). It is this emphasis contained in the RDP White Paper that laid the foundation for the government's adoption of its policy on Growth, Employment and Redistribution (GEAR) during June 1996. The key elements of GEAR are to promote economic growth through job creation and redistribution and to impose fiscal discipline by cutting on government's expenditure.[3] The main aim is to boost economic growth and to create jobs in order to alleviate poverty.

The new policy documents had significant implications for the Department of Social Development. The White Paper for Social Welfare was adopted in August 1997 and needs to be viewed against the backdrop of government's attempts to promote economic development in terms of GEAR and constitutional obligations.

A policy shift from a rehabilitative and institutional approach to a developmental approach to social welfare (DSW) is set out in the White Paper for Social Welfare. Key principles of this new approach are to promote equal opportunities and access to resources for the poor to address their needs; to raise the standard of living for the disadvantaged, those who are vulnerable and those who have special needs by providing choices and alternatives; and to motivate people to be less dependent on state assistance and nurture their human potential.

The focus is on how social and economic interventions can be harmonised to have a positive impact on people's welfare without hampering economic growth. One of the aims of developmental social welfare is to reduce the number of South Africans relying on social security as a main source of support. At present, approximately 90 per cent of the welfare budget is directed towards social security, while social welfare services receive approximately eight per cent. In line with the Department of Social Development's emphasis on promoting social welfare, it is working towards gradually reducing social security spending to 80 per cent of its budget and increasing social welfare spending to 20 per cent (Robinson and Sadan, 1999, p. 22).

The developmental social welfare approach is appreciated by many role players in the welfare community, but many warn that unemployment and destitution in South Africa take on such high proportions that development initiatives underway will probably only reach a few of those in need. Furthermore, the White Paper for Social Welfare has been criticised for being 'strong on rhetoric and principle, but weak on concrete targets for restructuring and delivery' (Lund, 1998, p. 12). A comprehensive and rational plan for implementing the new approach is yet to be devised.

4. The South African social security system: the role of state grants

Although the Department of Social Development made a paradigm shift from remedial to developmental social welfare, social security is still recognised as an important aspect of this new paradigm. This recognition is quite significant given the fact that many other countries are scaling down on, or withdrawing from, social security spending. However, the important role assigned to social security is not surprising, as leading academics have indicated through their research on poverty in South Africa that grants are effective in terms of poverty alleviation, also reaching women and rural areas (see for example Lund, 1999, p. 2; Ardington and Lund, 1995; Case and Deaton, 1996).

Social insurance and social assistance

The South African social security system is characterised by a rigid distinction between social insurance and social assistance. Social insurance[4] affects only a small percentage of poor South Africans due to high levels of unemployment and participation in survivalist activities in the informal sector. Social insurance is based on contributions from workers and their employers and is often privately funded. It is estimated that it covers less than 40 per cent of the labour force and provides at any given stage benefits to less than six per cent of the unemployed (Department of Welfare, 1999).

Contrary to the situation in most other middle-income countries, South Africa possesses a substantial system of cash social assistance. However, there is no universal coverage, as the grants are means-tested and a categorical approach is followed. Social assistance is mainly in the form of old age and disability grants. Old age and disability grants take up close to 85 per cent of the social assistance budget, while only 15 per cent go to children and families (see Table 3.3.1 for detail).

Table 3.3.1 Overview of grants in South Africa

Grant	Grant amount July 2001 (ZAR)*	Number of beneficiaries in payment April 2001	Total amount
Old Age	570	1,906,162	1,045,293,566
Disability	570	636,144	360,925,914
War veterans	590	6,078	3,360,907
Total adult grants		**2,548,384**	**1,048,654,473**
Foster Child	410	54,130	37,674,190
Care Dependency	570	31,814	18,539,898
Child Support	110	**833,602	122,933,444
Total family & child		***919,546	**179,147,532**
		(children =1,164,828)	

* USD 1 = ZAR 8.23 (August 2001).
** Number refers to primary caregivers, 1,078,884 children are reached by the CSG.
*** Excluding 3,761 receiving a combination of child and family grants and grants-in-aid.
Source: Department of Social Development 2001a & b

Only a relatively small proportion of those with child care responsibilities are covered by social insurance and assistance. Those households with no members receiving state pensions are the poorest. Just more than ten per cent of poor children receive a child or family grant. Many children seven years or older with unemployed caregivers too young to qualify for an OAG are especially vulnerable. The present social security system in South Africa does not provide a true safety net for poor households and it operates within a context where a consistent model and plan for the alleviation of extreme poverty still has to develop.

Social assistance benefits were for many years for white people only, but since 1972 steps were taken to gradually remove discrimination. These steps to deracialise access to state grants culminated in the Social Assistance Act of 1992 which provided for the extension of all social assistance measures to all South Africans on an equal scale.[5] At the time, the Old Age Grant already covered the vast majority of poor people eligible for the grant, including those in deep rural areas (Case and Deaton, 1996, p. 10). In referring to the increases in pensions for black people in order to reach parity, Van der Berg (quoted in Ardington and Lund, 1995, p. 5) observes that it 'has reduced poverty far more and more directly than most of the other developmental efforts that have been going on for decades'.

5. Reforms to the system of social assistance for children and their caregivers

Prior to 1992, the main grant for children and their parents (until 1998), the State Maintenance Grant, did not cover all racial groups. The State Maintenance Grant (SMG) was awarded to custodian parents/caregivers in the following circumstances: if the parent was single, widowed or separated; had been deserted by her/his spouse for more than six months; her/his spouse received a social grant or had been declared unfit to work for more than six months; her/his spouse was in prison or state institution or drug treatment centre for more than six months. Parents have been eligible for this means tested grant if they have applied for financial support (private maintenance) from the fathers/mothers of their children through a magistrate's court and have been unable to get it.

The majority of impoverished Africans were excluded from this grant. Economists warned at the time that improved coverage may put the fiscal viability of the social assistance system in jeopardy (Van der Berg, 1994, p. 4).

Based on cost projections of reaching racial equity, the government decided in 1996 to terminate the SMG. The Lund Committee on Child and Family Support was appointed to undertake a critical appraisal of the existing system of state support to children and families. This task was to be fulfilled within the context of the new developmental model of social welfare, binding fiscal constraints specified in the GEAR strategy and constitutional obligations.

Recommendations of Lund Committee and new policy

Based on the Lund Committee's recommendations (with some amendments), the government decided to phase out the SMG over a three year period and to introduce a new child grant (the Child Support Grant - CSG) from April 1998. The CSG was to be financed by the phasing out of the SMG. Because of the broader coverage envisaged and the limited budget, the CSG is less than a fifth of the value of the SMG and is only awarded to children younger than seven years, while the SMG was awarded to children until the age sixteen (or even longer if they were studying).[6] The CSG is being paid via the primary caregiver to all children who qualify in terms of a (simple) means test and their age. This policy deviates from the (nuclear) family preservation policy of welfare in the past. Since many, if not the majority, poor households in South Africa are not nuclear families, this model was no longer appropriate. Within this context the Lund Committee shifted the focus from the family model to a plan modelled around a central theme 'follow the child' (Lund Committee, 1996, p. 84).

A comprehensive intersectoral collaboration was proposed on programmes aimed at poverty relief and eradication, particularly with the health and early childhood development sectors (Lund Committee, 1996, pp. 55-96). The forging of practical links between welfare, social security, poverty alleviation and other development programmes on provincial and national levels was recommended 'in order to divert as many applicants from social security as possible to opportunities which could increase their independence' (Lund Committee, 1996, p. 86). Furthermore, reform of the judicial maintenance system was advocated as one way of promoting the responsibility of individual parents towards their children.

The Lund Committee recognised that the CSG would reach only a small proportion of South Africa's needy children (those seven years or older will be excluded), and that the proposals would have severe implications, particularly for households (especially households with a single adult) where the SMG represents the only source of income. In order to minimise the impact of the termination of the State Maintenance Grant, the then minister of welfare announced that the affected beneficiaries would be provided with information on existing community development projects which would enhance the individual's capacity through skills training, job creation, education and income generation.

6. The termination the SMG and beneficiaries' experiences

During April 1999 the Department of Social Development commissioned research on the phasing out of the SMG. The SMG was cut by more than half when the study commenced in June 1999. The main purpose of the research was to establish beneficiaries' social and economic responses to the phased reduction in the grant and the realisation of developmental social welfare.

Economic and social responses to the phase-out

Even after the second reduction in the SMG it still played an important role in keeping the majority of households above the poorest of the poor. Like the Old Age Grant, it reached much wider than its intended target. The majority of beneficiaries stayed in three generational households and pool their grant income with other sources of household income. In many instances non-beneficiary children also benefited from the SMG. The SMG had enabled many vulnerable mothers to care for their children and it contributed to the survival of extremely vulnerable woman-headed (mainly single-adult) households.

Beneficiaries reported that their quality of life had seriously deteriorated and that they were cutting back on life essentials such as food. They also experienced problems in covering other main household expenses such as rent, electricity and clothing. In those cases where the SMG was the only source of income, households were on the brink of total collapse.

Alternatives to the SMG

The following sources of income were identified by the government as some of the alternatives to make up for the loss in income as a result of the phase out of the SMG: caregivers could find employment in the open labour market, they could engage in some activity in the small, medium or micro enterprise (SMME) sector, they could apply for private maintenance, they could be referred to DSW programmes/projects or public works programmes and/or they could qualify for a CSG or another state grant. The next paragraphs explore the viability of these options for recipients.

Participation in the labour market: The majority of beneficiaries were at some stage involved in the job market even before the cut. Thus it would appear that the SMG did not necessarily act as a disincentive to find work. However, it seems that a significant number of those who acquired a job before the second reduction in the grant have lost it since. At the time of the study a significant percentage of beneficiaries were participating in the job market, either doing paid work or looking for a job. Due to a combination of factors, including the poor performance of the economy, their age, educational level and child care responsibilities of beneficiaries, the few who did manage to acquire a job found employment in mainly low-paid casual jobs. In the majority of cases SMME (small, medium and micro enterprises) activities produce only survivalist incomes, that is if they last at all. For the beneficiaries the only reliable source of income remained the SMG. Thus the SMG also played an important role in the covering of risk associated with a fluctuating market economy.

Developmental social welfare initiatives: Hardly any beneficiaries were referred to or participated in public works programmes or DSW programmes/projects. These alternatives are also limited in their scope and long-term feasibility due to scale, type of project, markets, temporary status, capacity in the Department of Social Development and lack of co-operation with other departments and the private sector. There was also a general lack of knowledge and expertise regarding the implementation of DSW programmes among welfare staff, as well as in other state departments. As it were, and in the majority of cases still is, there was nothing that welfare staff could divert SMG (and CSG) beneficiaries to.

Private maintenance: A large portion of SMG beneficiaries received the SMG precisely because the fathers of their children are deceased. The few who were receiving private maintenance received only a relatively low amount and it was sometimes too expensive and emotionally taxing for women to try to secure income from this source. Private maintenance, even for the minority of beneficiaries to whom it was available, was also of a low level and not necessarily secure due to the nature of the fathers' employment status.

Other grants: The majority of beneficiary children were seven years or older and did not qualify for the new CSG. There was however, in a significant percentage of SMG beneficiary households, children of non-beneficiaries who qualified but who had not (yet) applied for the CSG. The main reason for not applying was related to ignorance. The few beneficiaries who considered applying for another state grant would rather opt for the Disability Grant. It is the only substantial form of state relief to the non-aged needy and it puts considerable pressure on state surgeons as 'they know that they are the last port of call' (Ardington and Lund, 1995, p. 574).

Consequences for child care patterns

Some households will most probably change in form due to the phase-out of the SMG. The single adult household is the most vulnerable and will most probably cease to exist as children and their beneficiary caregivers are forced by economic reality to join other households and form or become part of multigenerational households. The majority of beneficiaries were, however, already members of multigenerational households. Women represented the majority, if not all of the adults in most of these households. In many of these households the Old Age Grant would be the only consistent source of income. In many instances households tended to group together around the Old Age Grant as single caregiver households became part of or formed a multi-generational household with caregivers moving in with their mothers who received an OAG.

Some women also entered into relationships with men just to secure some form of livelihood for their children. In some cases the only option to survive economically was for children to start working.

7. Current system of social assistance for children in South Africa

There are currently three state grants for children and their caregivers, namely the Child Support Grant (CSG), Foster Child Grant (FCG) and Care Dependency Grant (CDG). In terms of the number of beneficiaries the CSG is the main grant, while the FCG and CDG represent five per cent and three per cent of all family and child grants respectively (see Table 3.3.1).

Child Support Grant

With the termination of the SMG during April 2001, the CSG became the main grant for children and their caregivers. As indicated above, the CSG is paid to poor primary caregivers for up to six children below the age of seven and amounts to ZAR110 per month. Just more than a million children were registered for the grant at the beginning of May 2001 compared to the SMG with 326,774 child beneficiaries and 225,941 parent beneficiaries in 1999. In line with the Department of Social Development's policy of developmental social welfare (DSW) adult beneficiaries of the CSG were initially required to participate in development programmes and to have immunisation records of the children. These regulations were scrapped as many caregivers did not have the immunisation records and there were hardly any development projects to refer beneficiaries to. The requirements of the means test for the CSG were also changed to include only the personal income of the primary caregiver and not household income. This, together with a greater awareness of the grant, contributed to a huge increase in the application rate.

The relatively low level of the grant was rationalised in terms of budget constraints and the hope placed on income-generating activities as well as other projects linked to DSW. The scrapping of the regulation that CSG beneficiaries are required to participate in development programmes is however in total contradiction with the aims of DSW. Hardly any CSG beneficiaries participate in or benefit from DSW programmes, largely because in the majority of communities these programmes are not functioning (yet) (Datadesk & CASE, 2000). There is also doubt about the ability of the public sector, even in combination with the private sector, to implement development projects on the required scale.

From our research it seems that the CSG is reaching poor households since in one out of five beneficiary households the CSG is the only source of income. In spite of its low level, it also contributes significantly to the standard of living in households where it is not the only source of income. Nearly all primary caregivers are women and close to 90 per cent are the biological mothers of the children receiving the grant. The majority non-mother caregivers are grandmothers and the few other caregivers are other close relatives. Almost three-quarters of beneficiary mothers are single parents. Fifty per cent are 30 years or younger and 81 per cent 40 years or younger. (Datadesk & CASE, 2000, pp. 24-27).

Foster Child Grant

Foster Child Grants (FCGs) are paid to registered foster parents of children who have been placed in their care after a certain court procedure in the children's court. The FCG plays an important role in keeping children who cannot be cared for by their biological parents in a nurturing family environment. The process of fostering children is complicated, takes a long time and is costly. Many foster parents are close relatives of the child but no exact statistics are available. The FCG is not means tested and amounts to about ZAR410 per child per month. Proportionally more coloured and Indian than African children are in foster care partly because of discrimination under apartheid, but also because many Africans live in under-serviced rural areas and are not so familiar with the social assistance system as the other groups.

The approach of social workers to foster care applications seems crucial in the success of applications. Poor households hardly ever adopt these children because of the lack of subsidy available for this option. Foster parents have repeat foster placements, resulting in insecurity for the child and foster parents. Although foster care is supposed to be a temporary arrangement, in the majority of cases children are not united with their biological parents. Because of economic reasons, it is also not to the benefit of many of the impoverished households to allow foster children to be united with their parents.

Care Dependency Grant

The Care Dependency Grant (CDG) is awarded to caregivers of children whose physical and intellectual impairment is so profound that they require full time care. The motivation for the grant is to enable disabled children to be cared for by their parents within their own homes. Home care is much less expensive to the state than institutional care. The amount of the grant is ZAR570 per month. This is a relatively new grant only implemented since 1996. There is a lack of clear definition between non-disabling or chronic illnesses and those that lead to disablement. Eligibility criteria of the CDG such as that children should require permanent home care or 24 hour care exclude children with HIV/AIDS and other chronic illnesses.

Discussion

Research indicates that all social assistance grants in South Africa share some important functions. It is widely shared within households, it contributes to the care of children in a household environment, it provides some form of food security, it contributes capital to micro enterprises and/or it contributes to education costs. Compared to other alternatives the delivery of grants is also easier and cheaper and the larger part of the allocation reaches the intended beneficiary (Lund Committee, 1996, p. 9). In absence of a comprehensive system of social insurance, social assistance grants have the unintended consequence of providing some protection to households against the contingencies of a dynamic market economy.

There are two underlying principles inherent to all existing grants available to children and their caregivers in South Africa. First, there is the recognition that in general children are best cared for in a family/household environment and second that a grant will hopefully curb the flow of children to more expensive options like institutional care. However, the current system of grants for children is fragmented and does not provide for all vulnerable groups. With the termination of the SMG, there is no coverage of poor children seven years or older who are not disabled or in foster care. Neither are children suffering from HIV/AIDS or other chronic illnesses covered, while street children and children-headed households are unable to access grants.

A general child grant for all children will be more equitable than the vast difference between the CSG and FCG and CDG. It will also contribute to lower administration costs and cater for the growing number of AIDS orphans more efficiently if it is connected to community care (a DSW programme). It also remains a question whether the current FCG and CDG systems will survive the pressure of the estimated large number of AIDS orphans and children living with AIDS, if they succeed in getting onto the system. However, it will probably not be easy finding foster parents for future abandoned babies with HIV, even if they can get a FCG.

Under the paradigm of developmental social welfare, the ideal is to lower spending on social assistance and to shift financing to social welfare services, including development projects. The target group of the DSW programme includes primary caregivers of children who receive the CSG, former SMG beneficiaries and any needy or poor person. Research indicates that the DSW programme is especially weak on setting concrete targets for restructuring and delivery (Datadesk and CASE, 2000). For example by April 2000 over ZAR240 million of funds for the alleviation of poverty were not spent (Department of Social Development, 2001c). While development projects struggle to get off the ground and the benefits of these initiatives do not reach caregivers on a scale large enough, it should be recognised that cash grants remain the most successful state initiative to alleviate the plight of poor children. However, state pensions and grants should not be viewed as alternatives to these broader programmes, but should be viewed as complementary. Concentrating on grant provision and the role of social assistance can easily detract from the fact that other government departments also (have to) play a crucial role in efforts to establish a safety net for children and their caregivers. There are important contributions from departments like health, education and housing. The social assistance system should be seen as complementary to these efforts, specifically targeting those who cannot support themselves. In the facilitation of DSW, insufficient linkages and coordination between government departments and other partners, e.g. from the NGO, CBO and private business sectors are areas of concern. Central government coordination is necessary for successful intersectoral collaboration between these sectors in order to create development on a scale that is required.

There is increasing pressure on the government from NGOs, organised labour and human rights groups for the expansion of child grants to include all children. Some economists indicate that this expansion 'could be accommodated with little fiscal discomfort' (Van der Berg, 1997, p. 28). During this year, the minister of Social Development appointed the Committee of Inquiry into a Comprehensive Social Security System to generate proposals for an improved and a better structured social security system for South Africa. An important task of the committee is to review the existing system of social grants also within new realities created by the HIV/AIDS pandemic. The committee also investigates a basic income grant for all South Africans, a proposal made by the minister of Social Development in early 2000. It should however also be recognised that an income grant would not necessarily address the challenge of creating more jobs. Economic growth with an increase in employment is required to eventually balance the South African social security needs with the fiscal resources of the economy.

8. Conclusion

Although fragmented and not comprehensive, the system of social assistance in South Africa is making a valuable contribution to the social security of poor children, the elderly and the disabled. While the economy is not delivering, development projects are not in full operation yet and social insurance covers only a small minority of our labour force, cash assistance does what these programmes should be doing - it alleviates the plight of the poor. Social security measures like these will be most efficient if they are accompanied by an integrated poverty alleviation programme.

If child grants are improved, community care enhanced with the private sector and NGOs as important partners, and central government focuses on job creation and the curbing of the HIV/AIDS pandemic, we would begin to close the gaps in the safety net for children in a systematic and comprehensive way.

Notes

1   This paper is largely based on research undertaken for the South African Department of Social Development. It is published as Vorster, J., Rossouw, H. and Muller, G. 2000. *Phasing out the State Maintenance Grant within the context of Developmental Social Welfare.* Separate references to this study will not be made in the text.

2   Available information on HIV/AIDS trends from the Department of Social Development is based mainly on short-term estimates of the period 2000 to 2009. These estimates originate mainly from the ASSA600 model of the Actuarial Society of South Africa (Dorrington, 1999). This model was calibrated on the basis of annual antenatal clinic HIV prevalence figures.

3   This included reducing the budget deficit, keeping inflation down, creating tax incentives, phasing out exchange control regulations, introducing greater labour market flexibility and speeding up privatisation (Marais, 1999, pp. 161-62).

4   There are two forms of social insurance: the state run Unemployment Insurance Fund paying benefits to contributors for a limited time in the event of unemployment, illness and/or maternity. An employer financed employment injury insurance scheme (COIDA) is paid to contributors who became disabled as a result of injuries and diseases sustained at work.

5   Fiscal constraints prevented the increase of black benefits to white levels. Thus pension equalisation occurred through increasing black benefits and slashing real pensions for the white population. During 1980 white pensions replaced more than 30 per cent of the average wage, compared to 15.5 per cent when pension parity was achieved during 1993 (Van der Berg, 1997, p. 10).

6   The SMG was divided into a monthly parent allowance of ZAR430 and a child allowance of ZAR135 per child for a maximum of two children, while the CSG is only ZAR110 per month with a limit of six children per individual caregiver.

References

ACESS (2001) 'Social Security for Children in South Africa: First Call for Children'. Submission to the Committee of Inquiry into a Comprehensive Social Security System. Alliance for Children's Entitlement to Social Security (ACESS), Cape Town.

Ardington, E. and Lund, F. (1995) *Pensions and Development: How the Social Security System can Complement Programmes of Reconstruction and Development*, Occasional Paper 61, Development of Bank of Southern Africa, Midrand.

Case, A. and Deaton, A. (1996) *Large Cash Transfers to the Elderly in South Africa*, Discussion Paper 176, Research Programme in Development Studies, Princeton University, Princeton.

Constitution of the Republic of South Africa Act 108 of 1996.

Datadesk and CASE (2000) *Social Security for Children: An Investigation into the Child Support Grant and the State Maintenance Grant*, Department of Welfare, Pretoria.

Department of Welfare (1997) *White Paper for Social Welfare*.

Department of Welfare (1998) *Child Support Grant Programme Description*.

Department of Welfare (1999) *Annual Report 1998/1999*.

Department of Welfare (2000) *Draft Annual Report 1999/2000*.

Department of Social Development (2000) *The State of South Africa's Population Report*.

Department of Social Development (2001a) *Fact Sheet No. 4: Social Assistance (Pensions)*.

Department of Social Development (2001b) *Payment Extraction Report for Pay Period May 2001*.

Department of Social Development (2001c) *Fact Sheet No. 1: Poverty Relief Programme*.

Dorrington, R. (1999) *ASSA600 (Programme)*, Actuarial Society of South Africa, Cape Town.

Kruger, J. (1998) 'From Single Parents to Poor Children: Refocusing South Africa's Transfers to Poor Households with Children'. Paper delivered at ISSA 2nd International Research Conference on Social Security, Jerusalem, January 25-28.

Lund, F. (1993) 'State Social Benefits in South Africa', *International Social Security Review*, vol. 46, no. 1, pp. 5-23.

Lund, F. (1998) 'Social Welfare and Social Security'. Draft paper prepared for the Conference on the Politics of Economic Reform, Cape Town, January.

Lund Committee on Child and Family Support (1996) *Report of the Lund Committee on Child and Family Support*, Department of Welfare, Pretoria.

Marais, H. (1999) *South Africa: Limits to Change: The Political Economy of Transformation*, Zed Books & University of Cape Town Press, London and Cape Town.

May, J. (ed) (2000) *Poverty and Inequality in South Africa: Meeting the Challenge*, David Philip Publishers, Cape Town.

May, J., Woolard, I. and Klasen, S. (2000) 'The Nature and Measurement of Poverty and Inequality', in May, J. (ed), *Poverty and Inequality in South Africa: Meeting the Challenge*, David Philip Publishers, Cape Town.

Nattrass, N. and Seekings, J. (1996) 'The Challenge Ahead: Unemployment and Inequality in South Africa', *South African Labour Bulletin*, vol. 20, no. 1, pp. 66-72.

Poverty and Inequality Report (1998) *Poverty and Inequality in South Africa*. Report prepared for the Office of the Executive Deputy President and the Inter-Ministerial Committee for Poverty and Inequality Praxis Publishing, Durban.

RDP (1994) *Reconstruction and Development Programme White Paper*, Government Printers, Pretoria.

Robinson, S. and Sadan, M. (1999) *Where Poverty Hits Hardest: Children and the Budget in South Africa*, Idasa, Cape Town.

UNAIDS (2000) *AIDS in Africa*, United Nations, New York.

UNICEF (1999) *State of the World's Children Report*, United Nations, New York.

Van der Berg, S. (1994) *Issues in South African Social Security*. Background paper prepared for the World Bank, University of Stellenbosch, Stellenbosch, mimeo.

Van der Berg, S. (1997) *South Africa After Apartheid: A Welfare State in the Making?* Paper to the International Conference on Socio-Economics, Montreal, 5-7 July.

Vorster, J., Rossouw, H. and Muller, G. (2000) *Phasing out the State Maintenance Grant within the Context of Developmental Social Welfare*, Datadesk, University of Stellenbosch, Stellenbosch.

3.4 Is it possible to satisfy people who encounter the system of social services?

Steen Bengtsson and Nina Middelboe

Although we have social rights and a civic policy providing help in nearly every situation where people are without private means - plus subsidies in cases where they have the means but where society has nevertheless chosen to accept responsibility - social benefits are not something disbursed automatically. To claim one's benefits one usually has to encounter the system face to face in order to claim these rights. What happens when people meet the system is important: The result of the encounter will be influenced by the applicant's qualifications.

In the present study we asked parents with disabled children which aspects of the system of social services functioned well and which less well. The replies led us to the conclusion that parents with disabled children are often unaware of their social rights and the relevant benefits. They also lack an elementary knowledge of how to cope with child disability and of the conditions that enable families with a disabled child to function adequately. This knowledge is important for their ability to use social services and secure something like 'normal' conditions for the family. The purpose of this project has been to obtain knowledge that can be used by the social administration in developing services that will meet the parents' needs.

Compensation for disability

In most countries, a disabled child is a heavy economic burden on the family. Even in countries like Britain and the United States families with disabled children are poor because they must pay for most of their needs themselves and they are reported to have classic poverty problems (Middleton, 1988). In other places like Germany and Scandinavia, legislation entitles this group to compensation for the extra expenses. This alleviates the poverty problem, but is it sufficient as a general solution to the problems of this group? Is it possible to provide solutions that establish the framework for a family life comparable in quality to the family life of most other people? If there are problems, an immediate reaction could be to demand more benefits and to initiate new services. But do they solve the problems, or will they lead to an infinite circle of problems and demands?

Indeed, we must believe that we can solve the problems with the economic means available today if we want to retain our faith in social services. The content and quality of these services then become an important focus of interest. Quality must be seen in relation to the user's situation rather than in relation to professional standards alone. The way social services function in relation to the user's needs is largely a question of expectations and lifestyle. How does the public provision for social services relate to the concrete situation? The encounter between the applicant for assistance and the social authorities may be the clue to producing satisfactory solutions. The more dependency on social services, the more this encounter determines the final outcome of the effort.

The word 'compensation' has to be understood literally in the Danish context. The law stipulates that all extra expenses should be reimbursed, not only for the necessary treatment, care, and equipment, but for everything that is a precondition for living a normal family life. This includes a 100 per cent reimbursement of wages the parents would have earned during the hours they spend taking their child to the doctor's office or the like. Often one of the parents is compensated for a reduction in the weekly wage, in some cases even for the entire wage. This includes expenses for paid assistants accompanying the family on holidays. It is a principle of compensation which in a very literal sense of the word is a consequence of the social model principle pervading Danish social legislation.

The social model

The social model of disability emphasises the relationship between the individual and the environment, as opposed to the medical model which emphasises the individual's physical defects (Oliver and Colin, 1998). The obvious way to solve a disability problem is to remove the environmental barrier so that disabled people have the same options as others, for example, by making all buildings accessible and all forms of education available to the disabled. Since 1976, the social model has been a main principle of Danish social legislation, not only in the disability area, but generally (Bengtsson, 2000, 2001). In Britain and the United States, the social model of disability has developed in a very radical direction due to deficiencies in the social security system (Low, 2001). However, it is not obvious how to implement the radical model without the unintended side-effect of discriminating against disabled people.

Acceptance of the full consequences of the social model of disability would mean totally forbidding the use of the medical model and hence the impossibility of assigning people according to disability. This implies disallowance of social benefits whenever disability is a condition for the right to receive them. Such an approach is clearly unrealistic from a Scandinavian viewpoint if we want to keep the provisions for disabled people that exist in this part of the world (as well as Germany, the Netherlands, and a number of other European countries). How could we provide for all people with disabilities if it is not possible to retain a type of pension to which these people are entitled? And how could we compensate for disability if we could not - in one way or another - divide people into those with disabilities and those without? Social legislation on disability covering all disabled people and not just the 'winners' simply has to divide people into such categories in order to decide who is entitled to a certain benefit.

People, therefore, must learn the hard way how the system works, even if this raises the question of human dignity. However, the social model can be used to argue that social services are not reducible to single-case decisions. The effort with respect to parents of disabled children involves removing barriers not faced by others, thus compensating for the disability. Taking our study on parents with disabled children as our point of departure, we shall argue that this effort must be both a collective one with respect to the group as a whole and an individual one with respect to each of the families. The rights of the individual are, in fact, of limited value. Few results would be achieved by sticking pedantically to the rights embodied in the law. As one of the municipalities participating in the study expressed it: 'This legislation gives the user very few concrete rights, but it makes many things possible'.

This does not mean that the user is without individual rights. Even if she or he in situation x has no clear entitlement to benefit y or provision z, appeals committees and the courts may, nevertheless, take the case and decide or judge whether a reasonable effort has been made. Høilund (2000) expresses this by saying that natural law and political law must be combined - natural law stressing that the objective is attained, political law requiring that formal rules are complied with. The rights angle on social policy must be observed, but it becomes fruitless if it is reduced to a mechanical measuring out of political rights - a tendency sometimes seen in circles fighting to maintain a social standard within particular areas.

The concept of 'encounter' between the user and public authorities

In recent decades, social services have developed in a direction where the user's encounter with the social authorities now looms larger in the overall picture - or one could say that service plays an increasing part. The 1970s social reform turned the municipal social office into a service centre where people could present themselves and receive help in case of need without having to feel ashamed about it. In the 1980s the trend was 'quid pro quo' and activation, a trend seen as a reaction to the liberality of the foregoing period, but which could just as well be interpreted as a continuation of the same trend: No longer is social assistance just an amount you get; services providing for integration are now included as well (Bengtsson, 1999).

'Disabled children' used to be regarded as a low status area for social workers. In one of the municipalities included in our study the caseworker told us that they were called 'wee-wee children' when the department was established. This was because the other social workers felt that the only problem was to figure out how much the parents of those children should receive to cover the extra expense of having a disabled child at home. Much has changed in the past decade: Legislation is much more comprehensive and nearly a score of specialised knowledge centres now guide the municipalities and counties in their work. But, with the increased number of provisions and with increased awareness of administrative procedures, there is a tendency for research to become influenced by concepts derived from everyday practice.

The encounter between the disabled user and the system as perceived by that user is the theme of a Swedish white paper, 'reception of persons with disabilities' ('Bemötande av personer med funktionshinder'), which has been the most important inspiration for our project. Lindquist (1999, p. 21) defines 'reception' or 'encounter' (the Swedish term 'bemötande' lies somewhere in between) in a number of ways that supplement each other: It is a relationship that has to do with the way individuals relate to each other, but the overall view of society as expressed in laws and regulations is also important. 'Reception' has to do with the general attitude of care personnel, with information, communication, interaction, user influence and quality of care.[1]

A recent Swedish project has investigated the encounter between parents with disabled children and the rehabilitation staff (Socialstyrelsen, 1998). It concluded that parents find it essential that they obtain information on disability, the routines and organization of social services, the various bodies involved, and economic and social rights. Many parents lack information and what information they have is obtained mainly from other parents. Professionals, too, consider information important, but they find it difficult to judge how much is needed and how much is actually understood by the parents - who stress that professionals are also human. None of the parents feel that caseworkers involve themselves 'too much'. However, professionals say that a certain distance should be kept, that a too close contact may place a strain on the family.

Our contribution

A basic aim of our research project (Bengtsson and Middelboe, 2001) has been to establish why there seems to be a rather high degree of dissatisfaction with services whose expenses have doubled in fixed value during the past decade. With this in mind we should try to understand the user's situation and needs in the most direct way, not determined by the instruments and methods that the system uses to remedy them. Our theoretical premise is the dual character of the social authority organization. The authority - in this case the municipality - is not merely the necessary practical means of meeting the user's needs, it is also part of the power system.

Against that background, the authority creates its own social reality, its own organizational 'world'. In this world, the user is easily reduced to the status of a client cut out to fit the pigeonholes of the system, such as Roine Johansson (1992) has shown, based on Lipsky (1980). That is a prerequisite if the organization is to function at all. In order, however, to deliver on one's promise of social services it is equally necessary that the effort from the user's viewpoint should not assume the appearance of an 'authority machine', but be determined solely by the user's situation and needs. A further motivation for the methods chosen was a desire to achieve results that are easily applied in practice. An official organization will often try to protect itself against the user's real world, whereas a close rapport with that world possesses a peculiar force of its own.

To obtain information on how parents with disabled children experience their encounter with the social authorities, parents in 11 municipalities of differing size throughout the country were asked to complete a so-called opinion sheet. The sheets were mailed to all parents whose children had disabilities beyond minor ones like bed-wetting. Replies were received from

229

parents of 415 disabled children, or 35 per cent of the sample - which we consider a satisfactory result in view of the fact that we asked them to use their own words and we did not send any reminder. The questionnaire consisted mainly of a single open question:

In which respects do you find that the social effort on the part of the public sector has functioned well in relation to your child, and in which respect do you find it has functioned less well?

This type of questionnaire turned out to be ideal for our project. Many parents wrote long and rather subtle answers, reflecting on both positive and negative aspects of the public effort and the possibilities of improving it.

To obtain a picture of the situation as a parent experiences it, we used a method where, uninfluenced by the system or any abstract ideas, they could express themselves freely about their situation and about how well the casework had succeeded. In the opinion sheet questionnaires, respondents did not answer questions formulated by others, but just stated their own opinion. These sheets, therefore, reflect more accurately the situation as it is experienced, thus improving the likelihood of reaching conclusions that identify the parents' most pressing problems. At the same time, it becomes more difficult for the municipality to predict and control the results and create a buffer zone between the investigation and its implementation, such as the concept of decoupling implies.

The opinion sheet questionnaire was used in three ways: First, the parents' responses were read in anonymous form by the municipal caseworker and social workers. The purpose of this was to penetrate the defence mechanisms that every organization builds up, and initiate reform measures in the municipality. Second, we constructed a quantitative questionnaire with 50 questions, which became a part of the second phase of the project. Third, we analysed the opinion sheets qualitatively in the above-mentioned report, the results of which are presented below.

Results of the qualitative investigation

What do the many accounts tell us about the situation of parents with disabled children? Have we solved the problems simply through the generous level of compensation provided by law? Yes, in some respects we have; most parents are satisfied and nobody is poor.[2] Yet, problems do remain - problems often expressed in terms of needs but which we believe cannot be solved by an even more generous system. It is far more important that social service departments improve their understanding of these parents. Above all, the responses show that parents are puzzled and that many lack an elementary knowledge of how to organise the everyday life of a family with children. We consider this an important finding which should lead to changes both in the existing legislation and in the practice of social authorities in handling families with disabled children.

A prevalent idea in the 'system' is what we have termed the 'shock theory'. This theory claims that having a child with a disability entails an experience of loss: One is traumatised and lives through a period of grief - and may even need crisis therapy. Most of the responses, however, suggest a cognitive interpretation of the process: The parents may well have experienced a trauma, but they *are* at a loss too. They simply lack the knowledge and experience necessary to envision a future like other parents.

As some parents express it: Everything is different when you have a disabled child. Each new phase of life presents its own problems: when the child starts in kindergarten, when it begins school, when it reaches adolescence, when it grows up and leaves home. Whereas other parents are in many ways prepared for the different situations, having seen other families tackle them, parents with disabled children can be fairly certain that each new situation brings unexpected problems in their wake. They simply lack the experience and knowledge that we normally base our lives on.

The shock theory is teaching material well suited to social workers. It describes the process of coping, expected of most people, as a series of stages which social workers should take into consideration when communicating with parents. This is a method to obviate problems of communication, which is good in itself. The social model, as we interpret it, emphasises that we should not merely wrap the parents in a cocoon but also enable them to learn to cope with their situation. To assist them in their reorientation, parents with disabled children should have an opportunity for some of the same learning experiences with their children as have other parents. It should be stressed that the former's reaction and need of obtaining knowledge of everyday life are normal behaviour patterns, and it is risky to consider them in too psychotherapeutic terms.

The caseworker's many roles

The municipal caseworker's job is to provide parents with all relevant information and, if the problems are complex, of establishing contact with the county and nationwide counselling system. However, in view of the lack of information described above, the present approach appears totally inadequate. People cannot simply be informed about 'everything'. It is not just factual information that people lack, but equally the sort of information which could be called experience and which always constitutes the basis for understanding the more formalised information. The proper basis can only be acquired partly by observing the behaviour of other children with the same disability and partly by talking to other parents in a similar situation - an option quite a few parents would like.

However, the caseworker's position complicates the matter of informing the parents. The caseworker has to combine a number of roles - a difficult balancing act: On the one hand, a professional role implicit in the title 'social counsellor' and, on the other, a bureaucratic role as a member of the municipal organization implicit in the title 'caseworker' (both names being used in Danish to designate the same function). In the professional role of 'social counsellor', the caseworker is responsible for giving the parents information, advice and support. Many parents feel that this has worked well and that the supportive role has meant a great deal to them.

On the other hand, there is the bureaucratic role of 'caseworker', involving loyalty to the municipal system and municipal policies. With local politicians having decided on a budget for the different spending areas, caseworkers have a certain responsibility for staying within that budget. Parents are well aware of this. Some of them say so directly and others more indirectly that they suspect caseworkers of concealing information to save on expenses.

Cooperation between caseworker and user is thus constrained by the fact that the former has to combine different roles. His or her credibility suffers in cases where it is not justified. Casework, therefore, must not be based on a one-sided flow of information directed at the user. For this reason, we propose that legislation and daily practice should aim to give parents the information they need in as many different ways as possible. This would include leaflets about social security benefits and a book on provisions for children with disabilities. In fact, a special 'Social ABC'[3] exists in this area (Simonsen and Damsø, 1998). The majority of parents want to know more about others facing the same situation.

This model of cooperation corresponds to the social model of disability because it is based on the supposition that the parents themselves want to solve the problems if only they are provided with the means to do so. Parents have to solve the problems in their own minds, that is, foster ideas about the kind of family life they want against the background of their particular situation. Enabling parents to do so is a form of preventive work in relation to the problems that families with disabled children may face and thus a vital task for the social services department. Only when the parents themselves have solved their problems mentally does it make some sense to begin thinking about which social services would be relevant.

Some of our findings point in the opposite direction, namely, that the social authorities occasionally immobilise parents, thus preventing them from solving their problems. This is a further reason for a substantial amount of the dissatisfaction registered, which may be an unintended consequence of some of the control procedures instituted with the aim of limiting expenses. Thus, most allotments have to be renewed every year or half-year, a procedure which may cause parents some anxiety, especially if organised in such a way as to create uncertainty.

A mother described how she was told only one week in advance that she had been awarded 'lost wages' (that is, compensation for wages lost by minding her child at home) for the next six months. In other cases, parents give up because of the time it takes for applications to be processed. One way to create maximum frustration is to ensure that applications have to be forwarded to another municipal department. Under those circumstances the caseworker, too, feels a sense of powerlessness vis-à-vis the 'system'.

Conclusion

Our research has shown that even large amounts of compensation for families with disabled children do not necessarily result in a smooth process of adaptation to existing conditions. Nor does it necessarily offer a better possibility of guaranteeing families a life comparable to what most other families enjoy. A municipality which sets its sights too high in relation to the financial means available, only to impose devastating control techniques, could easily do more harm than good by using the - after all rather considerable - resources on hand. The centralised policy of defining the rights to be applied by local authorities may likewise be an unhappy construction.

Nevertheless, expenditures of this magnitude must be subject to effective control. How then do we know whether the control mechanisms have the unintended effect of undermining service aims, rendering the parents dependent, and whether they clientise rather than assist the users? One way of finding out is to get feedback from the users, for instance through the kind of opinion sheets utilised in our study.

The parents of disabled children are involved in a conflict of interests with other users represented by the municipal employees. Parents and caseworkers are in a sense fighting for the same resources. But this fight must not become their sole concern. The social model aims to remove the obstacles preventing families from living on terms similar to other people. This presupposes cooperation between caseworker and family. Achieving such cooperation despite the conflict of interests - a fact of life - requires good communication and a high level of awareness on both sides. The methods used in the present study, as well as other methods seeking to increase user influence, are well suited to bringing about this form of communication and cooperation. It is therefore recommended that such methods be developed further and made an integral part of municipal social services.

Steen Bengtsson, Assistant Professor of Sociology at the University of Roskilde, has specialised in social policy since 1981. In 1986 he joined the Danish National Institute of Social Research in Copenhagen. 1991-92 he was social policy consultant to the Danish Council of Organizations of Disabled People, DCODP (De Samvirkende Invalideorganisationer, DSI), the national umbrella organization of organizations of disabled people.

Nina Middelboe received her degree in public administration from the University of Roskilde in 2001. At the Danish National Institute of Social Research she worked on the project on parents with disabled children and is now affiliated with the University of Southern Denmark in Odense.

Notes

1   According to Lindquist the good encounter is characterised by attention, thoughtfulness, empathy and equality. The starting point should be what the person - the user - recounts. The professional social worker must forget her/his role as expert and just listen and show respect for what the persons says. Social workers should empathise, that is, understand feelings during the interview and convey this understanding not just orally but also in all dealings with the user. They must have sufficient time for that. Explaining the rules when necessary is, of course, an aspect of the good encounter, but this does not entail embracing them as one's exclusive point of view and defending them at all costs.
2   The group of parents seems rather polarised: One-third of the replies contained only positive remarks, while one fifth contained only negative remarks. Some parents mention the failure of different municipal offices to coordinate activities, or their need to coordinate the effort themselves. Others mention they had to wait a long time for a diagnosis and that the 'system' frequently required this diagnosis as a prerequisite for offering assistance - in defiance of the law. Some cases seem to have reached complete deadlock. We hear about wiping-the-floor techniques such as 'Do you realise how much money you get?' and examples of families at odds with professionals in both the municipality and county as well as prolonged tugs-of-war and trials ending with families being finally granted their rights.

3   The Social ABC is a general handbook on social rights, sold in all bookshops and widely consulted by users of all types of social services. However, parents with disabled children are not generally familiar with the book we mention (Simonsen and Damsø, 1998) that specially treats social rights of disabled children.

References

Bengtsson, S. (1999) *Social Service til Alle (Social Service for All)*, SFI rapport 99:1, København.

Bengtsson, S. (2000, 2001) 'A Truly European Type of Disability Struggle. Disability Policy in Denmark and the EU in the Nineties', *European Journal of Social Security*, vol. 2, no. 4, 2000. This article is also included in the anthology: Van Oorschot and Hvinden (eds): *Disability Policies in European Countries*, Kluwer Law International, The Hague.

Bengtsson, S. og Middelboe, N. (2001) *Der er ikke nogen der kommer og fortæller, hvad man har krav på – forældre til børn med handicap møder det sociale system ('Nobody comes and tells you what you are entitled to')*, SFI rapport 01:1, København.

Høilund, P. (2000) *Socialretsfilosofi. Retslære for socialt arbejde (Social rights philosophy. Law for social work*, Socialpædagogisk Bibliotek, København.

Johansson, R. (1992) *Vid byråkratins gränser. Om handlingsfrihetens organisatoriska begränsningar i klientrelaterat arbete (At the frontiers of bureaucracy. On the organisational limits for the freedom of action in client related work)*, Arkiv, Lund.

Lindquist, B. (1999) *Nio väger att utveckla bemötandet av personer med funktionshinder (Nine ways to develop the reception of persons with disabilities)*, SOU, Stockholm.

Lipsky, M. (1980) *Street Level Bureaucracy. Dilemmas of the Individual in Public Services*, Russel Sage Foundation, New York.

Low, C. (2001) 'Have Disability Rights Gone Too Far?', *Disability World*, no. 7, March-April.

Middleton, L. (1998) 'Services for Disabled Children. Integrating the Perspective of Social Workers', *Child and Family Social Work*, vol. 3 pp. 239-46.

Oliver, M. and Barnes, C. (1998) *Disabled People and Social Policy. From Exclusion to Inclusion*, Longman, London.

Simonsen and Damsø (1998) *Handicappede børns sociale rettigheder (Social rights of children with disabilities)*, Frydenlund, København.

Socialstyrelsen (1998) *Hur får vi det vi behöver? Föräldrar - och habiliterare - berätter om möten, strukturer og förutsätningar inom barn-og ungdomshabiliteringen (How do we get what we need? Parents and social workers recount about encounters, structures and presupposition in rehabilitation of children and young people)*, Socialstyrelsen 1998: 2, Stockholm.

3.5 Costs and benefits of child care services in Switzerland - empirical results for Zurich

Karin Müller Kucera and Tobias Bauer[1]

In Zurich, the Department of Social Services plays an active role in pre-school child care by supervising quality and monitoring supply and demand for child care services. Although, the supply has nearly doubled from 1,150 to 2,200 places in the last ten years, a recent survey (Sozialdepartement, 1999) shows that there remains a significant excess demand for child care facilities. In 2000, the Department of Social Services was interested to know, what kind of quantitative and qualitative benefits return from investments in child care centres. Consequently, the Department mandated a study on the economic costs and benefits of child care.

The study undertaken by the authors (Müller Kucera and Bauer, 2001) includes 102 child care centres with a total of 2,200 places where an average of 3,500 children has been cared for in 1999. Most of them are run by private organizations receiving public subsidies to cover costs of children whose parents cannot afford to pay the full fee. The total of 3,500 children equals 17 per cent of all children under seven years in Zurich and can be split into two groups: (1) children whose parents receive some subsidies to finance the costs of child care (1,826 children) and (2) children whose parents cover the full costs by themselves (1,674 children). Overall, the city of Zurich spends about 17.8 million Swiss Francs for child care in 1999. This accounts for about 0.3 per cent of the total annual budget of 5.6 billion Swiss Francs. The rest of the total child care budget of 39.1 million Swiss Francs is mainly financed by parents (20.2 million Swiss Francs) and to some extent by firms that buy child care opportunities for their employees (1.1 million Swiss Francs) in 1999.

Applying cost-benefit analysis to child care

Previous research on impacts of early child care intervention has been mainly focusing on social, pedagogical, and psychological aspects relating to the development of children attending child care (for example, National Institute of Child Health and Human Development, 2000; Richardson and Marx, 1989; Andersson, 1992; Osborn und Milbank, 1987). However, only a few existing studies have included an economic perspective taking costs and benefits of early childhood intervention into account. In principle, Cost-Benefit Analysis can be applied to all public decisions that have implications on the use of resources. In analogy to a private investment decision - private costs and benefits are replaced by a comparison of social costs and benefits (Brent 1997, p. 3). An example of a Cost-Benefit Analysis applied to child care is the High/Scope Perry Preschool Project (Barnett, 1996; Schweinhart *et al.*, 1993) where long-term insights have been gained by a longitudinal study that compared former child care attendants to a control group of non-attendants for over 27 years. Participating families came mostly from socially disadvantaged backgrounds. The main observed results show that program participants have achieved in average better school results, have had fewer criminal incidences and have been socially and economically better integrated. The cost-benefit-ratio is 1:6, applying a discount rate of five per cent. Other projects based their calculations not on longitudinal observations but assumed a given increase in child care facilities and investigated the resulting costs and benefits using aggregated macro data. The empirical findings of Cleveland and Krashinsky (1998) show for example for Canada a cost-benefit-ratio of 1:2. The variation in results of these studies can be explained by the different types of data used as well as by the different groups of actors that have been included in the survey.

Method and limitations

The present study is the first one that evaluates and quantifies costs and benefits for child care centres in Switzerland. It is based entirely on individual household data. We identify costs and benefits by investigating the impacts on all actor groups that are affected by child care. In doing so, we assume the following hypothetical framework: we identify the current costs and benefits by investigating the impact on all actors, if existing private and public child care centres would be abolished in Zurich. In other words, we identify benefits by calculating opportunity costs, if the current child care centres disappeared. This is a strong simplification. For judging the benefit of child care investments it would be more appropriate to calculate the marginal effect of an additional investment. Unfortunately, the available data does not allow such a marginal analysis.

In respect to parents, we are only able to quantify economic benefits of parents who currently bring their children to day-care centres. It is well understood that childbearing and childrearing creates many more positive benefits that are left out of this analysis. It is important to note that we are not trying to compare and evaluate the benefits of day-care centre versus family based child care, but to investigate the opportunity costs of parents that actually rely on day-care.

First, we identify all involved groups of actors that are being affected. Second, we specify the costs and benefits for each group, and finally costs and benefits are being aggregated and evaluated. However, given that people have multiple social roles (for example, parents and the same time tax payers), the separation among those groups may not always be clear cut. This might result in some double counting when aggregating the group results. We refrained from the complex adjustment of such double counts. Therefore, the aggregated benefit effects lead to a net benefit which is slightly too high. This effect is compensated by the fact that the considerable effects of intangible benefits cannot be quantified because of lacking market prices or missing knowledge about shadow prices. We are including the intangible benefits in the form of qualitative arguments in order to summarise as much evidence as possible relating to child care services.

Concerning the question if child care does pay off the fiscal balance is of special significance. In the fiscal balance all cost and benefit effects for taxpayers are aggregated. Thus, the amount of tax revenue generated by investing one tax Franc into child care facilities can be calculated.

Costs and benefits that occur in the future, have to be discounted to their present value to make them compatible to the current costs and benefits. Therefore, we discount all future benefits to the year of reference (1999), using an interest rate of five per cent.

Cost-benefit results for Zurich

First, we provide an overview over all groups of actors that are being further investigated for this Cost-Benefit Analysis. We identify those actors that account for the overall effects to the society. Second, we list resulting costs and categorise benefits such as direct (i.e. relate to the intended main effects of the project), indirect (i.e. relate to not directly intended effects of the

239

project) and intangible benefits (i.e. effects that cannot be quantified) (Brümmerhoff, 1990). Figure 3.5.1 summarises potential costs and benefits for all actors such as children in child care centres, parents of those children, tax payers and firms in Zurich. The effects for the taxpayers can also be named as fiscal costs and benefits.

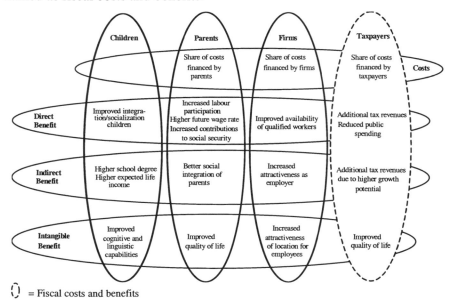

Figure 3.5.1   Costs and benefits of child care for all groups of actors

Finally, overall costs and benefits are being aggregated by different types - some are quantitative, others are qualitative. The results of the analysis are summarised in Table 3.5.1. We have identified on the one side total costs of about 39.1 million Swiss Francs for the year 1999. On the other side we quantified total direct benefit of 140.4 to 163.9 million Swiss Francs for the same period of time. Above that, all involved groups of actors benefit from various indirect and intangible benefits. Consequently, the total of benefits are likely to be even above the sum of the total direct benefits that could be quantified in this study.

As can be seen in Table 3.5.1, the quantified benefits result mainly for parents and taxpayers. We discuss these two important parts of the Cost-Benefit-Analysis in more detail below.

Table 3.5.1 Total costs and benefits of child care services in Zurich (million Swiss Francs, 1999)

Actor Groups	Costs	Benefits Direct	Indirect	Intangible
Tax payers	Subsidies of the city of Zurich: 17.8 M CHF.	Additional taxes by child care employees: 6.0 M CHF. Additional taxes from immediate income effect of parents: 7.3 M CHF. Additional taxes from annuity of long-term income effect of parents: 8.0 M to 10.9 M CHF. Reduced public expenditures on social aid: 6.5 M CHF. Reduced public expenditures on contributions to families with small children: 0.8 M CHF. Additional tax revenues of former child care attendees. Less public expenditures due to lower school repetition rates of students. Less public expenditures related to criminal incidences.	Benefits of future growth potential	Improved quality of life due to supply of child care facilities
Children attending child care		Improved academic achievements in school. Better social integration.	Higher academic degree and potential live income	Improved cognitive capabilities and language skills Improved social competence
Parents whose children attend child care	Costs covered by parents: 20.2 M CHF	Immediate income effect of parents: 44.1 M CHF. Additional contributions to social security from immediate income effect: 9.8 M CHF. Annuity from long-term income effect of parents: 48.2 M to 65.4 M CHF. Additional contributions to social security from annuity of long-term income effect: 9.7 M to 13.1 M CHF.	Reduced social isolation Improved integration of immigrated families	Improved quality of live due to supply of child care centres
Firms	Costs covered by third parties: 1.1 M CHF	Better availability of qualified labour force.	Improved competitiveness Improved attractiveness of employer	Improved attractiveness of location due to better availability of qualified workers
Total	39.1 M CHF	140.4 M to 163.9 M CHF	+	+

Notes: + = identified qualitative benefits; Benefits have been calculated based on the number of children attending child care on March 31, 1999 (i.e. 3,500) for the year 1999 to eliminate seasonal volatility.

Benefits for parents (mothers)

We were able to identify two main effects of child care that create benefits to parents: First, child care provides an immediate opportunity to (re)enter the workforce or to increase labour participation while children are still in their pre-school age. Second, by avoiding the complete exit of the work force during child bearing and child rearing years, parents improve their long-term opportunities on the labour market. On the one hand, continuous work experience allows to maintain the productive capacity such as qualifications and job skills (i.e. human capital), on the other hand parents avoid the difficult step to restart their professional career and remain socially integrated in a firm environment which is also an important factor for being able to benefit from career chances (e.g. job tenure has a significant influence on promotions).

In Switzerland, the sexual division of labour is still following a very traditional pattern. It is nearly exclusively mothers who reduce labour force participation after their children are being born and who carry out the increase of unpaid work in the household. Consequently, when we are discussing costs and benefits for parents in the following, we are in fact addressing largely mothers.

Short-term effects for parents

The methodological framework to identify the immediate effect of child care supply is to compare the income of households that currently benefit of child care with similar types of households that do not use child care at all. As mentioned before, this concept does not take into account possible utility gains resulting for parents staying at home with their children. In other words, benefits of child care are being quantified by calculating the possible loss of household income that would occur if current supply of child care was being abolished from one day to another.

Empirically we look at weekly hours worked of households using child care and compare it with the hours worked of equivalent households not using child care. The data for households with child care are taken from the anonym database of parents who accommodate children in child care centres in Zurich in 1999 (data provided by the Department of Social Services of the city of Zurich). The second set of data on households not using child care is taken from the representative Swiss Labour Force Survey (Schweizerische Arbeitskräfteerhebung SAKE) for the sample of Zurich. Differences in weekly hours worked and resulting income disparities are

242

being calculated for five different household types: single-headed household with one child (SH1), single-headed household with two or more children (SH2+), couple household with one child (CH1), couple household with two children (CH2) and couple household with three ore more children (CH3+). The additional weekly working hours worked of households with child care vary between seven (CH2) and 17 (SH1) hours (see Table 3.5.2).

Table 3.5.2   Average weekly working hours of households 'with' and 'without' child care

Type of Household	Average weekly working hours per household 'without' child care	Average weekly working hours per household 'with' child care	Additional weekly work hours of households 'with' child care
SH 1	18	35	17
SH 2	17	31	14
CH 1	52	63	11
CH2	53	60	7
CH 3+	47	58	11

Source: Weekly working hours for households 'without' child care are from the Swiss Labour Force Survey 1997-1999 (SAKE97-99) for the sample of Zurich. Weekly working hours for households 'with' child care are from the database of anonymous contribution agreements of parents with child care centres in Zurich that has been provided by the Department of Social Services on behalf of this study.

Note: Contribution agreements have to be signed between parents and the child care centre for each child who is attending child care. The agreement contains information on hours worked and salary upon which cost contribution of parents is defined.

Using the income data from the anonym database of parents we calculate overall annual opportunity costs of a total of 54 million Swiss Francs for the total of 3,500 households that accommodate children in public and private child care centres in 1999. Total opportunity effects contain the loss of net salary (44 million Swiss Francs) and the loss of contributions to Social Security (10 million Swiss Francs) that are equally contributed by employees and employers.

In addition to the immediate difference in household income, there result long-term opportunity costs for parents (mothers) from keeping away from the labour market during the child bearing and rearing years. The temporary exit of the labour force diminishes future career opportunities and salary expectations relative to continuous labour force participation. There are several reasons that may explain future differences in professional status and salary: the break in professional activities leads to a depreciation of individual productive capacity such as qualifications and job skills (i.e. depreciation of human capital), therefore re-entering the labour market at the same professional level as before the exit (for example, same professional responsibilities) is difficult to achieve and the re-entry salary is likely to be lower and to remain below the previously earned income. Beyond those pure productivity effects that can be attributed to a loss of unused capabilities there comes also a wide range of factors into play that also have a significantly diminishing effect on future career opportunities such as absence of internal and external professional networks. In the following, we quantify the long-term opportunity costs that result from the absence from the labour market during the family phase by simulating professional careers of women.

Again, we base the empirical analysis on the data of the Swiss Labour Force Survey (SAKE). The simulation is based on three regression models which explain the following four dependent variables: (1) probability of labour participation, (2) probability to achieve a position of a supervisor, and (3) potential salary. The regression results are presented in Müller Kucera and Bauer (2001), the background of the analysis is shown in more detail in Bauer (1998 and 2000). Based on these three regression equations, we set up a simulation model for all household types. In doing so, the estimated coefficients have been used to simulate professional female biographies assuming marriage and birth of children that are representative of Swiss women. Furthermore, we assume a medium level of professional education. In analogy to the calculation of the immediate short-term income effect of child care, we compare the two situations 'with' and 'without' use of child care applying the following four analytical steps:

First, we simulate for each type of household the working hours and income biography for the situation 'without' child care.

Second, the situation 'with' child care is simulated for two scenarios, i.e. (1) children attending child care for three years as well as (2) children attending child care for six years. In doing so, the working hours are raised by the respective number of working hours given in Table 3.5.2 for the two scenarios of using three or six years of child care. We assume - after children exit child care - that working hours of parents remain at least on the previous level (i.e. simulated work hours 'with' child care) until working hours of the model 'without' child care reach the level of 'with' child care (thereby taking into consideration that parents who previously participated in the labour market are unlikely to exit or reduce their participation after their children reached school age). Furthermore, as a consequence of the higher accumulated working experience, the potential wage raises in the scenario 'with' child care compared to the scenario 'without' child care - also in the years after using child care until retirement age. This last effect shows the long-term impact of child care on mother's life income.

Figure 3.5.2 shows an example of a simulated biography for a mother with two children. Area A indicates the short-term benefit during the use of child care services. Area B reflects the long-term benefit after children's exit of child care centres.

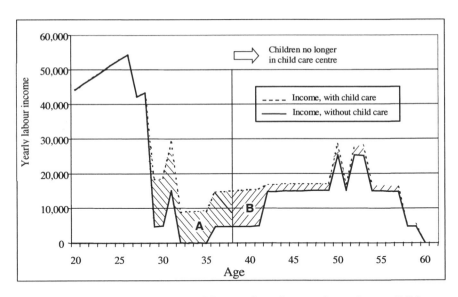

Figure 3.5.2   Stylised income biography of a mother of two children 'with' and 'without' child care services

Third, since results have been simulated on a household-level, we multiply the difference between 'with' and 'without' child care for the years after using child care by the respective number of household types to get the total long-term opportunity costs that would be caused, if child care services that existed in 1999 would be abolished.

Fourth, the last step is to calculate the annuity of the long-term opportunity costs that can be compared to the other costs and benefits on an annual basis. Given the scenario with six years of child care, the annuity of long-term opportunity costs amounts to 48 million Swiss Francs while the annuity for three years of child care is 65 million Swiss Francs.

Benefits for tax payers

There are two main benefits for tax payers: first, additional tax income due to additional income of parents and employees in child care centres. Second, reduced public spending due to better social and economic integration of families with children.

Additional tax income

We have previously argued that parents who actually use child care services work an additional seven to 17 weekly hours compared to similar households that do not request child care. Given this difference in hours worked we were able to calculate the resulting additional income. Now, we run the tax simulation model on this additional income of parents. However, since we base our calculation on actual data, we cannot calculate the potential additional tax revenues caused by higher education and potentially better paying jobs of former child care attendants in the future.

The tax simulation model incorporates tax laws of the city of Zurich, the canton of Zurich and the federal government since taxes are paid to all three public authorities in Switzerland. The applied simulation model is documented in further detail in Bauer and Streuli (2000). First, we calculate the marginal tax income caused by the additional annual income that is being earned by those 3,500 households that have used child care services in Zurich in 1999. The total additional tax revenues resulting from the immediate extra income are 7.3 million Swiss Francs. With respect to the previously identified short-term additional annual income of 44.1 million Swiss Francs this is equivalent to a marginal tax rate of 16.7 per cent.

Second, since additional tax revenues also result from the long-term additional income of parents, we apply the determined marginal tax rate of 16.7 per cent to the calculated annuity of long-term additional income of 48.2 million Swiss Francs ('6 years child care attendance'), respectively

246

65.4 million Swiss Francs ('3 years child care attendance'). Consequently, the total additional tax revenues (immediate and long-term effect) caused by parents are estimated to be between 15.4 million Swiss Francs (lower boundary) and 18.2 million Swiss Francs (upper boundary).

In addition to the supplementary tax revenues of parents, employees in child care centres pay taxes too. We also include these tax revenues into the Cost-Benefit-Analysis, since they have a cost reducing effect. In other words, they represent a benefit for tax payers, since some of the public expenditures are being paid back via tax revenues. Hence, we apply the previously run tax simulation model to the income of people employed with child care centres. The anonymous income data of child care employees has been provided by the Department of Social Services of the City of Zurich. The total marginal tax revenues from employees in child care centres amount to a total of 4.3 million Swiss Francs in 1999 representing another benefit to tax payers.

Reduced public expenditures

In addition to tax revenues, tax payers benefit from reduced public expenditures such as fewer payments for social aid, smaller expenses to finance school for repeating students and fewer costs caused by criminal incidences. Unlike other studies that were able to include savings on school and crime expenditures based on longitudinal observations (for example, Barnett, 1996), we only include savings on expenditures for social aid. The city of Zurich provides two kinds of social support to families in need: (1) 'Contribution to Families with Small Children' ('Kleinkinderbeiträge') and (2) general social aid for people living below the poverty line, according to the guidelines of the 'Swiss Conference of Social Aid' (Schweizerische Konferenz für Sozialhilfe 'SKOS'). Again, we calculate the benefits resulting from reduced public expenditures by comparing the two situations 'with' and 'without' child care. By reducing the weekly work hours we identify for each household: (1) whether the household becomes newly eligible for 'Contributions to Small Children' and (2), whether the reduced income is below the poverty line and furthermore to which amount. Aggregating the two categories of social aid over all households indicates the additional public expenditures that could be claimed by households if child care centres would be abolished. Or, the other way around, assuming that all eligible households claimed their justified amount, the city of Zurich would have to spend consequently an additional amount of about 7.3 million Swiss Francs on social aid expenditures and contributions to families with small children. In other words, currently this amount of public expenditures is saved and tax payers benefit due to existing child care.

Summary and conclusions

Investing in child care is paying off. Based on the results summarised in Table 3.5.1, we calculate an annual cost-benefit-ratio of 1:3.5 (lower boundary), respectively 1:4. In other words, each Swiss Franc spent on child care returns (at least) between 3.5 to 4 Swiss Francs to the overall society. This result ranges in the middle of the previously cited cost-benefit-studies that have been carried out in the US and Canada (Cleveland and Krashinsky, 1998; Barnett, 1996). As already mentioned, the meaningfulness of the cost benefit ratio is reduced by possible double counts of benefit effects.

The fact that child care facilities are paying off economically is also proved by the fiscal balance. The result remains positive also from a narrower fiscal perspective focusing on public authorities only. The public cost share of 18 million Swiss Francs is set off by at least 29 million Swiss Francs of additional tax revenues and reduced public spending on social aid. However, the balance for the city of Zurich is slightly negative since it finances the total of public subsidies of 18 million Swiss Francs while about half of the fiscal benefit (14 million Swiss Francs) is generated on the cantonal and federal level.

In the city of Zurich as well as in the whole country, the results of the study lead to considerable discussions. Unlike many other OECD countries, Switzerland's attentiveness to early child care policy remained at a low level in recent decades. The need for affordable and reliable child care provision to promote equal opportunities for women and men in the labour market has been largely unacknowledged. Despite increasing female labour force participation, balancing work and family life continues to be a private challenge to mothers juggling employment and household demands. It is only very recently that the scarcity of qualified workers led the Swiss employer's organisation to stress the importance of child care facilities to recruit and retain female workers (Schweizerischer Arbeitgeberverband, 2001). As a consequence, it is not surprising that only about two per cent of all children between 0 and 6 years have access to a day-care centre in Switzerland, while their peers in other European countries benefit from a significantly higher coverage rates (for example, Italy: 6 per cent for 1 to 3 year-olds and 60 per cent to 70 per cent for 3 to 6 year-olds; Belgium: 11

per cent for 1 to 3 year-olds and almost 100 per cent coverage for 3 to 5 year-olds, Sweden: 64 per cent for 1 to 6 year-olds) (EKF, 1992; OECD, 2001a).

In this situation, the reaction to the study was positive on a large political scale. On Federal Governmental level, in summer 2001 the parliament agreed on spending 100 million Swiss Francs during the next 10 years for setting up new child care facilities.

To what extent are the results for Switzerland also relevant for other European countries? As mentioned before, child care coverage in Switzerland is very modest compared to other countries in Europe. Consequently, due to the law of diminishing marginal utility, the benefits may be higher in Switzerland than in other European countries providing a better child care endowment. However, it becomes evident for Switzerland and also for other countries that child care contributes significantly to the overall social integration and economic security of parents.

Our Cost-Benefit Analysis shows for example that a significant number of households would have fallen below the poverty line if child care was abolished. This suggests, that numerous households depend on two incomes. Still, even two incomes do not prevent many of them from living as 'working poor'. Above that, given that more than 40 per cent of all couples get divorced in Switzerland, it is crucial - especially for women - to keep participating in the labour market. The resulting advantages are manifold: (1) higher future salaries due to maintenance of productive capital (for example, human capital, on-the-job skills etc.) and integration in professional networks, (2) higher contributions to social security and savings, (3) less dependency on public support (for example, social aid) during productive age as well as during retirement age. In conclusion, we consider the improvements of social and economic security of parents as one of the most important benefits of child care. Besides being a significant benefit to parents that allows especially mothers to combine family life and labour force participation child care also contributes to the society as a whole since more households can ensure their own savings and provide their economic and social security.

Acknowledgement

We acknowledge funding received from the Department of Social Services in Zurich to carry out this research.

Note

1   Karin Müller Kucera, Service de Recherche en Education (SRED), Quai du Rhône 12,
    CH-1205 Geneva, Switzerland, phone +41 22 327 57 11, fax + 41 22 327 57 18,
    homepage: www. http://agora.unige.ch/sred, e-mail: karin.muller-kucera@etat.ge.ch.
    Tobias Bauer, Bureau for Studies in Labour and Social Policy, Eigerplatz 8, CH-3007
    Bern, Switzerland, phone +41 31 372 44 55, fax +41 31 372 33 55, homepage:
    www.buerobass.ch, e-mail: tobias.bauer@buerobass.ch.

References

Andersson, B.E. (1992) 'Les Implications Des Modes De Garde Sur Le Développement
    Cognitif Et Socio-Émotionnel Des Écoliers Suédois', in B. Pierrehumbert (ed), *L'accueil
    du jeune enfant* (ESF éditeur, Paris), pp.181-92.
Barnett, S.W. (1996) *Lives in the Balance. Age-27 Benefit-Cost Analysis of the High/Scope
    Perry Preschool Program*, High/Scope Educational Research Foundation, Ypsilanti,
    Michigan.
Bauer, T. (1998) 'The Impact of Family Structure on Time Use and Potential Wage in
    Switzerland', *International Journal of Manpower*, vol. 19, no. 7, pp. 507-19.
Bauer, T. (2000) 'Die Familienfalle. Wie und warum sich die Familiensituation für Frauen
    und Männer unterschiedlich auf die Erwerbsbiographie auswirkt - eine ökonomische
    Analyse', Chur und Zürich, Rüegger.
Bauer, T., Streuli, E. (2000) Modelle des Ausgleichs von Lasten und Leistungen der
    Familie. Im Auftrag der Eidgenössischen Koordinationskommission für Familienfragen
    (EKFF), Büro für arbeits- und sozialpolitische Studien (BASS), EDMZ, Bern.
Brent, R.J. (1997) *Applied Cost-Benefit Analysis*, Edward Elgar, Cheltenham under Lyme.
Brümmerhoff, D. (1990) Finanzwissenschaft, München und Wien, Oldenbourg Verlag.
Cleveland, G. and Krashinsky, M. (1998) 'The Benefits and Costs of Good Child Care. The
    Economic Rationale for Public Investment in Young Children', *Policy Study*, University
    of Toronto at Scarborough, Scarborough.
Eidgenössische Kommission für Frauenfragen (1992) Familienexterne Kinderbetreuung -
    Teil 1 und Teil 2, EDMZ, Bern.
Müller Kucera K. and Bauer, T. (2001) Volkswirtschaftlicher Nutzen von
    Kindertagesstätten, Hrsg. Sozialdepartement der Stadt Zürich, Edition Sozialpolitik Nr. 5,
    Zürich (a short version is available on http://www.buerobass.ch/pdf/kindertagesst.pdf).
National Institute of Child Health and Human Development, Early Child Care Research
    Network (2000) Summary of Results of the NICHD Study of Early Child Care, January,
    http://www.nih.gov/news/pr/jan00/nichd-07.htm.
OECD (2001a) *Starting Strong: Early Childhood Education and Care*, OECD Publications,
    Paris.
OECD (2001b) Balancing Work And Family Life: Helping Parents Into Paid Employment,
    in OECD (ed), *OECD Employment Outlook*, OECD Publications, Paris, pp. 129-66.
Osborn, A.F. and Milbank, J.E. (1987) The Effects of Early Education: A Report from the
    Child Health and Education Study, Clarendon Press, New York.
Richardson, G. and Marx, E. (1989) A Welcome for Every Child: How France Achieves
    Quality in Child Care: Practical Ideas for the United States, French-American Foundation,
    New York.

Schweinhart, L.J., Barnes, H.V. and Weikart, D.P. (1993) Significant Benefits: The High/Scope Perry Preschool Study Through Age 27, High/Scope Educational Research Foundation, Ypsilanti, Michigan.

Schweizerischer Arbeitgeberverband (2001) Familienpolitische Plattform des Schweizerischen Arbeitgeberverbandes, Arbeitgeberverband, Zürich.

Sozialdepartement der Stadt Zürich (1999) Bedarf an Betreuungsplätzen in der familienergänzenden Tagesbetreuung in der Stadt Zürich, Stab Bedarfsplanung und Controlling, Zürich.